The Ganamey ❤ Sawaya Family Cookbook

ALICE'S KITCHEN

My Grandmother Dalal & Mother Alice's

TRADITIONAL LEBANESE COOKING

◆

Linda Dalal Sawaya

◆

RECIPES OF DALAL HAGE GANAMEY
ALICE GANAMEY SAWAYA
ELIAS GEORGE SAWAYA & LINDA DALAL SAWAYA

 NEW EDITION ◆ REVISED & EXPANDED

The Ganamey ❤ Sawaya Lebanese Family Cookbook

ALICE'S KITCHEN

MY GRANDMOTHER DALAL & MOTHER ALICE'S TRADITIONAL LEBANESE COOKING

4th edition 2005. Published by Linda Sawaya Design ◆ Portland, Oregon
Text, illustrations, photographs copyright © 2005 Linda Dalal Sawaya
Cover design and illustration copyright © 2005 Linda Dalal Sawaya

Writing, illustration, food styling, photography, recipe testing, design, and production by Linda Dalal Sawaya
Recipes, food styling, editing and overall assistance, love and support by Alice Ganamey Sawaya

Excerpts from the first edition appeared in *Aramco World* magazine, January/February 1997

Cover: Alice Ganamey and her mother, Dalal Hage Ganamey, Detroit, 1926
Inside front cover (from top left): Alice Ganamey & Elias Sawaya, Detroit, 1934; Alice & Al; Aunt Adele Ganamey, her mother, Sitt Nazira Samrah, *Sitto* Dalal Ganamey; Alice at 92; *Jiddo* Anton Ganamey, 1939; Linda with books, 1953; Shirley, Lorraine, & Joyce, 1941; Alice, Carl Lawyer, & Lorraine, 1954
Inside back cover (from top left): Lorraine, Alice, Joyce, Elias, Shirley, & *Sitto* Dalal; Uncle Edmond Ganamey, Linda, *Sitto* Dalal, Vivian, Elias; Dad's mother *Sitto* Sharife Sawaya

ISBN 978-0-9660492-2-0
Library of Congress Control Number: 2005902458

A PORTION OF THE PROCEEDS FROM SALES OF **ALICE'S KITCHEN** WILL BENEFIT THE CHILDREN OF LEBANON.

FOR INFORMATION, ADDITIONAL BOOKS, OR COMMENTS:

linda@lindasawaya.com
www.lindasawaya.com

LINDA SAWAYA DESIGN ◆ PO BOX 91192 ◆ PORTLAND, OREGON 97291

◆

To my mother, Alice, on her 95th birthday
and her mother, Dalal
and her mother, Sharife
and to all the mothers before them
and to all the children after them

and

To my father, Elias Jerius Samia Sawaya,
whose tomato salad was made with love

In commemoration of
the 110th anniversary of his birth
1895–2005

For my sister Lorraine
in spirit and love
Lorraine Jean Sawaya Brown (1936–2003)

And to Lebanon, our motherland, to heal

❤

1970s Doumna

*Work is love made visible . . . For if you bake bread with indifference,
you bake a bitter bread that feeds but half man's hunger.*

Khalil Gibran

One who has patience, attains what one desires.

Dr. Anton Ganamey

If you're going to do something, do it with love—from your heart.

Dalal Hage Ganamey

Moderation in all things, including moderation.

Elias Jerius Sawaya

Dear, if you make it with love, it will be delicious.

Alice Ganamey Sawaya

ABOUT THE FOURTH EDITION

More than 20 years ago, the idea to record our family recipes in a cookbook enthusiastically began and took root. My epicurean Mama, Alice, created beautiful food; I photographed it, recorded the recipes on index cards, and then moved to Portland. Countless long-distance calls asking, "Mom, how do you make . . . ?" transpired over the years. Her responses were scribbled on anything handy. The box full of handwritten notes was typed into my computer in 1990. A year later, the smeared recipes on snippets of paper were added, editing continued, deadlines came and went.

Finally, in December 1992, a few copies of the first edition, essentially a tiny draft, were printed and shared with my family and friends for Christmas. More recipe gathering, testing, questions to Mother, more stories shared, recipes clarified, and inconsistencies eliminated, such as the ten different ways I spelled *hommus* or *mjaddrah* (which continues to evolve!). These transliterated Arabic words in *italics* are my interpretation of our family's Doumani *jabaliye* (mountain) pronunciation of them.

In 1994, *Aramco World* magazine miraculously expressed interest in publishing an excerpt from my little book! In early 1997, Alice and I became *Aramco World* cover girls! with eight pages from **Alice's Kitchen**, we went all over the world. Their fine publication and excellent editorial guidance helped launch the second edition, which sold out quickly. Amazing letters and postcards came from people sharing their own family stories and photos, bringing tears to our eyes, joy to our hearts. It is so deeply touching to read "Dear cousin" from someone I've never met because of our cherished shared past and the connection felt through recipes and story. The third edition was printed in fall 1997 with a few revisions, and it too sold out. The beautiful love-filled letters I have continued to receive have shown me how extensive my family really is, reaching, through food as the thread that brings us together, far beyond my biological family. It has been a phenomenal blessing to me, and a well-deserved tribute to my mother and my grandmother Dalal, who were known as the best Lebanese cooks in L.A.!

At long last, now comes the fourth edition of **Alice's Kitchen**, with Alice 95 years old this May, *still* in the kitchen (thank God!) as I write this, making *mammouls* for visiting granddaughters to take home. She continues to do amazing things—like cooking lunch recently for 25 church friends with an elaborate Lebanese menu! And she continues to be creative and productive, making the most of every moment on the earth, and being an inspiration and role model for her family and friends.

This fourth edition is bigger, with 40 more pages, a larger format, new recipes, clarifications on earlier recipes, more stories, and many new photographs. My gratitude for the many blessings that this book has brought in the process of creating it over the

course of so many years—a deep and beloved connection with my mother Alice, as the most precious gift. A sense of connection with our ancestors and our traditions. A greater learning about Lebanese food, our sustenance on this planet, and how it has evolved over generations. A deep love and appreciation of our Lebanese culture: its people, geography, fruits, foods, creativity, music, joy, and the expansiveness of its heart, as well as its human frailties. And especially a rich connection with my world family: all the readers of this book!

The third edition of **Alice's Kitchen** was done with the generous help of my dear friends, Lee Ann Ward, for proofreading and editing, and Josephine Raad Chism, for her gracious and generous efforts to improve my Arabic transliteration, as she did again for the fourth edition, along with dear Father Joe Bitar of Detroit and Aseel Nasir Dyck!

This new, revised fourth edition has come about through the friendship and blessings of so many dear hearts in my life, without whom this publication would not have been possible. With joy and gratitude, I have the presence, love, and support in my life of the angels: Jacquie La Plante, Rima and Haitham Akkary, Father Joseph Naoum Bitar, Fadwa Abeid, Virginia and Bill Barber, Pam Brown and Wayne Potter, Deborah Buchanan and Scott Teitsworth, Josephine and Ralph Chism, Gloria Tuma, Aseel and Steve Dyck, James and Vicki Peck, Judy Ros, Judy Lamb, and Karen Kemper.

I am deeply grateful to Patti Morris and Martin White, for their generous proof-reading of the text, technical support, book wizardry, and encouragement; Aseel Nasir Dyck for her attention to detail and meticulous indexing; editors Ellen Lockwood for her cosmic support and Jill Kelly for her grace; Joel Horwitz, Carol Van Zuylen, Ancil Nance, and Kobe Kemple for their Mac wizardry; Katie Radditz, Dennis Stovall, Jim Hanna, Adnan Haddad, Violeta Noriega, Alixa Naff, Paula Wolfert, and Naomi Shihab Nye, for their friendship, nurturing, and support of **Alice's Kitchen** in various ways, as did so many others. Thanks to my Dad, family photographers, and friends whose photographs accompany mine in these pages.

Our dear family and friends in Lebanon, who welcomed us with loving, open arms and bountiful, abundant tables will never be forgotten: George, Nassif, and Elias Sawaya and their families; Najla Sawaya, and all the Sawayas; Noula and Nina al Bacha, Tony Ganamey, Eli Ayrouth, Adele Fishfish, Chaffic and Rose al Bacha; and the Ganameys, Hages, Haddads, Shaheens, Schwairys, Maloufs, Hashems, Samras, and so many more! We returned, our hearts overflowing with love and precious memories.

Words cannot express my unending gratitude to my mother, Alice, without whom this book would never be and whose wisdom, love, and support I cherish. And to my ancestors and family, especially my sisters Shirley, Lorraine, Joyce, and Vivian, whose loving presence contributed to who I am and to this book.

Your comments and feedback in response to **Alice's Kitchen** are welcomed. *Shukran!*

Welcome to **Alice's Kitchen**! *Ahlan wa Sahlan, Tfaddalou,* and *Sahteyn!*

ALICE'S KITCHEN

TABLE OF CONTENTS

INTRODUCTION ◆ 3

ABOUT THE RECIPES ◆ 21

MEZZA ◆ APPETIZERS ◆ 25

HALEEB, LABAN, OU SAMNE ◆ CHEESE, YOGURT, & BUTTER ◆ 33

SALSAAT ◆ SAUCES ◆ 41

SHOURBAT ◆ SOUPS ◆ 45

SALATAT ◆ SALADS ◆ 57

GHANAM ◆ LAMB ◆ 73

DJEJ ◆ CHICKEN ◆ 115

SAMAK ◆ FISH ◆ 125

AKL SIYEME ◆ VEGETARIAN ENTRÉES ◆ 131

KHUDRA, HBUB, OU FASSOULIA ◆ VEGETABLES, BEANS, & GRAINS ◆ 157

KHUBZ ◆ BREADS ◆ 177

HILOU ◆ SWEETS ◆ 187

MURABBA ◆ PRESERVES ◆ 211

MASHROUBAT ◆ BEVERAGES ◆ 219

BHARAT, BUQUL, OU RAWAYEH ◆ HERBS, SPICES, & FRAGRANT WATERS ◆ 223

FINDING INGREDIENTS & TOOLS ◆ 230

GLOSSARY, TOOLS, & MISCELLANEA ◆ 231

INDEX ◆ 237

Photos

Alice & Dalal Ganamey in America (1926)   i
Alice & Linda Sawaya departing for Lebanon (1998)   ii
Douma women & children at a picnic (c. 1915)   iii
Sawaya wedding party, Detroit (1934)   iv
Alice & Linda at booksigning (1998)   v
Alice photo booth, Detroit (c. 1928)   2
Douma souk with Alice, Dalal, Uncle Edmond (c. 1920)   3
Our Lady of Redemption Ladies' Society, Detroit (c. 1937)   3
Alice tossing bread dough (1995)   4
Marie Talalai's tannour oven Douma (1998)   5
Elias, Alice, & Linda Sawaya (1950)   5
Sawaya family patio dinner, Los Angeles (1955)   6
Linda with eligible cousin, Cedars of Lebanon (1971)   8
Douma Fountain, l. to r. Najib Eid, Yusef Samia, Michel
   Shammas, Hanna Yazbek (c. 1900)   11
Dalal Hage Ganamey & Dr. Anton Ganamey (1939)   13
Alice, Sitto, Aunt Selma, Cousin Yvonne, Detroit (1928)   14
Wedding of Alice & Elias Sawaya, Detroit (1934)   15
Father Gerasimos Sawaya (c. 1920)   15
Sawaya brothers: Uncle Nassim, Dad, Uncle Mike (1950)   15
Dr. Nick Khoury & Dad, Los Angeles (1961)   16
Sawaya family, Los Angeles (1947)   16
Alice with her beaded floral arrangement (1997)   17
Alice with her five daughters (1990)   17
Joyce, Shirley, Vivian, Lorraine, & Linda (1947)   17
Alice & Linda in Tannourine, Lebanon (1998)   18
Alice gazing out window of her birth home, Douma (1998)   18
George Sawaya & Alice, Raoche, Beirut (1998)   19
Alice admiring olives, Douma (1998)   19
Alice in front of her uncle's store, Douma (1998)   19
Alice in Zahle riverside restaurant, Lebanon (1998)   20
Alice in her California kitchen (2001)   20
Ancient olive tree, Douma (1996)   27
Alice & Dalal Ganamey, California (1929)   33
Sadie Hashem & Sitto Sharife Sawaya, Calexico (1918)   35
Joyce, Lorraine, Shirley by Mamie Khoury/Detroit (1940)   38
Lorraine, Joyce, Shirley (1990)   39
Sawaya family (1950)   45
Abouna Tuma, Um Mariam, & Linda at monastery
   Mari Hanna, Kfar Hilda, Lebanon (1996)   46
Sitt Amine Hadeed Hanna, Portland (1989)   50
N'oula al Bacha & Alice, Douma (1998)   53
Uncle Edmond, Linda, Alice, Dad, & Sitto, LA (1964)   54
Shabab: Uncle Nassim, Uncle Mike, Fr. Sawaya (c. 1920)   59
Mom & Dad (1949, 1934)   64, 65

Alice, grandchildren, & great-grandchildren (1999)   66
Alice, Edmond, & Adib, Douma (1913)   68
Sawaya family in Pantell wedding, L.A. (c. 1951)   71
George Shaheen, butcher, Douma (1996)   73
Alice & best friend, Adele Nakle Shamis (1995)   81
Uncle Edmond Ganamey, Adele Samrah Ganamey,
   & Albert Samrah, Los Angeles (1974)   82
Dinner party, L.A. (c. 1960) l. to r. sitting: Sitto, Marie
   Schwary, Alma George, Bishop, Eva Rizk, Wedad Frenn,
   Auntie Mabel Ganamey, Kay Adamo; standing: Joe
   George, Helen Sawaya, Millie George, Eli Antaky,
   Father Bardawil, Mary Antaky, Lulu Sphier   84
Sitto's mother Sharife Ganamey, her brother Isshac l'Hage, his
   daughter Saidy Hage, & Gabriel Ganamey (c.1910)   95
Alice & Sayyidna Bishop Nicholas Samna (2000)   100
Sitto (r.) & friends collecting pine nuts, Douma (c. 1910)   103
Alice and her five daughters (1990)   105
Faddoulis & moms: Soham, Josephine, Virginia, Gloria,
   Alice, Linda, & Elaina, Portland (1996)   107
Auntie Kamilie, Alice, Hanne Mitchell, Sitto (1929)   113
Mom, Marylou George, & Alma George, L.A. (c. 1955)   115
Jiddo, Alice, Sitto, Edmond, Lorraine, Joyce, Shirley (c. 1942)   119
Marylou, Joe, & Ernie George, Dad (c. 1955)   125
Alice in her garden with ceramic duck (2001)   128
Uncle Tom Ganamey & Dad, California (c.1923)   130
Sawaya girls: Joyce, Lorraine, Linda, Shirley, Vivian (1947)   136
Gloria Malouf, Nina & Noula al Bacha, Douma (1996)   140
Linda, Dad, & Vivian (c. 1950)   147
Fr. Athanasius Hage & Saidy Frances (center), L.A. (1960)   150
Uncle Halim, Mom, Auntie Kamilie, Uncle Edmond,
   Sitto, & Uncle Adib, Los Angeles (c. 1929)   157
Lorraine & Mom, Palm Desert (2003)   158
Uncle Adib & Auntie Rose, Los Angeles (c. 1950)   164
Uncle Adib Ganamey, Detroit (1932)   165
George Ponza, Joyce, cousin Mary Ponza, & Mom (2002)   166
Mom & Lorraine, Palm Desert (1990)   168
Mom dancing, listening to walkman, Beirut (1998)   169
Adele & George Shamis, Mom & Dad, Miami (c. 1960)   172
Sitto Sharife Sawaya, Los Angeles (c. 1925)   176
Marie Talalai making tilme bi zaatar, Douma (1998)   178
Father Joseph Naoum Bitar, Detroit (2005)   184
Fr. Sawaya, Dad, St. Anne's Melkite Church, L.A. (1916)   194
Alice's grandchildren: Karen, Cheri, Laurie, L.A. (c. 1963)   197
Sitto Mariam Ganamey, Jiddo's mother, Douma (c. 1900)   204
Alice picking oranges, Los Angeles (c. 1929)   206
Dad & Uncle Halim Ganamey, Los Angeles (1929)   210
Washington D.C. (c. 1940): John & Emily, Sheahin, Sitto,
   Aunt Selma, Nora & Adele Sheahin, Uncle Edmond,
   Yvonne & George Aued & children   214
Carl, Mom, Dad, Adele Shamis, Philip, Effie Simon (1956)   217
Cousin Tony Ganamey, Tannourine, Lebanon (1998)   219
Ibree' communal Lebanese water pitcher, hand-painted   222
Mahlab   223, 227
Miski, sumac, & sahlab   228
Mom, Portland (1996)   229
Linda & Alice in Alice's Kitchen (1998)   248

INTRODUCTION

Many, many generations ago, mothers began passing on to daughters the ways of preparing wonderful food that have made the Lebanese famous throughout the world. Each generation made their own improvements and additions to the traditions, creating a marvelous, diverse, and healthy cuisine where one encounters mountain traditions, coastal traditions, village traditions, urban, religious and seasonal traditions. Within each of these, variations occur from place to place and family to family.

In the late 1800s, when my grandmother, Dalal Hage Ganamey, whom we always called *Sitto*, was sent as a child to the convent school in her Lebanese mountain village of Douma, she was taken not into the classroom to study but into the kitchen to cook. As a result, she didn't learn to read or write—instead, she became an incredible cook.

Alice, my mother, learned the ways of her mother, Dalal, first in Douma and then in Detroit, where the family immigrated in 1926. In 1934, Mother married my father Elias, who was living in southern California, thus continuing her westward migration, leaving her Detroit Arab-American community and her parents behind.

Five years later, *Sitto* and *Jiddo*, my grandfather, joined them in Los Angeles. By the time I was a child, Mother and *Sitto* had become renowned for their great cooking. And I had the great fortune, as the youngest of five daughters, of being their assistant. Thus began my apprenticeship in our Lebanese kitchen. My primary role as dish-dryer and table-setter expanded after I begged to roll

grape leaves and cabbage rolls—*waraq 'inab* and *malfouf*; stuff our special light-green summer squash, *kousa*; and pinch *mamouls,* Easter cookies. Most of all, I longed to twirl the bread dough high in the air and toss it from arm to arm like Mother did. Despite my pleading, handling those huge rounds of dough was *not* a possibility. Mama refused to risk its inevitable fall to the floor from the arms of her ten-year old. Despite this setback, years later I decided to teach myself. At last, I have mastered a much smaller loaf of bread than the mammoth twenty-inch rounds that Mother twirled so effortlessly. Tiny, eight-inch rounds nevertheless thrill me as I spin them into the air—they store easily in the freezer and are quickly reheated, enriching our meals with hot bread and great memories. The stacks of fresh *khubz marqouq* wrapped in slightly dampened towels, steaming from Mama's oven, and the incomparable smell of bread as it bakes, go straight to the essence of my being. A dab of butter and a drizzle of honey on bread hot from the oven is like paradise. This is why I, too, must bake bread.

In our house, there was always an abundance of food. There had to be enough—for our large family and for visitors, who were always welcomed at our table. At dinner, seconds were essential. If you refused, even after the customary three-times offering, Mother still slipped another helping onto your plate. It wasn't because she didn't want leftovers—we *loved* leftovers—it was because of *Sitto's* and Mother's tradition of generosity and their genuine desire to satisfy everyone. Sharing food was the greatest gift one could give, and that was how our family lived.

Over the years, our family ate traditional Lebanese mountain village cuisine modified by Mother and *Sitto* according to what was available in Los Angeles grocery and import stores in the 1950s. Whole lambs were not found in supermarkets. Mother and *Sitto* painstakingly cut legs of lamb into appropriate components for various dishes, carefully removing most of the fat. In Douma, this had been done by the town butcher, who would take requests from village families for the cuts they wanted and then butcher the lamb or goat several times a week, delivering the fresh cuts of meat to each home.

There, in the old country of the early 1900s, *Sitto* didn't bake her own bread; she didn't have an oven—no one but the village baker did. Her own kneaded bread dough was carried to the baker, *khubbazze*, who was my Aunt Adele's mother, *Sitt Nazira Tannous Abi Samrah*, to form and bake the loaves in a wood-fired oven, the *tannour*. The traditional payment for *Sitt* Nazira was a portion of the baked

bread. After Mother married, she was determined to learn the difficult technique of making those huge, paper thin loaves for our family, for there was no village baker in Los Angeles.

The adaptations that Mother and *Sitto* made for the Western world made sense. Our stove in Los Angeles had four burners and two ovens, instead of the typical one-burner charcoal stoves or open fires, *haroun*, of the village that led to a whole tradition of one-pot meals in early Lebanon. Certain spices and herbs were impossible to come by in California. Friends shared with friends the precious contents of a parcel from the old country containing *zaatar* or *mahlab* or special vegetable seeds to plant from the village.

We kept a small kitchen garden in our sunny California backyard, and dared to raise chickens for a while until loud phone calls from our otherwise quiet, affluent neighbors came in, complaining of the rooster's early morning serenades. *Ba'dounis, na'na', baqle, kousa abyad,* and *waraq 'inab, limoun, akkidinne,* and *teen* graced our table—these seasonal harvests that were essential to our meals, many of which were unknown and otherwise unavailable here. When I came home from school one day, I discovered *Sitto* chasing one of our chickens around the backyard. I was not prepared for what my eyes were about to see. Wielding a knife, she managed to capture and actually chop the head off of the poor creature, who, for what seemed like a very long time, continued running around in circles without his head. Sure enough, stuffed chicken was the special dinner that night. And as sure as that chicken ran in circles without his head, I could not eat it.

I remember one difficulty growing up Lebanese in the 1950s in Los Angeles—going to school and taking *hommus, mjaddrah,* or *laban* for lunch was just too strange. My sister Vivian and I, after endless teasing, begged Mother to buy bologna, American cheese, or peanut butter and jelly for sandwiches. Only at home did we devour *hommus* and everything Lebanese. Occasionally we asked Mother to cook hamburgers or spaghetti for dinner and although she accommodated us, somehow, even to these, she added parsley!

Having a garden and eating foods in season is our inherited ancestral tradition of living gently on the earth, using its resources respectfully, and preparing and sharing food with love. Food, of course, is a central part of Lebanese culture.

Our family dinners were a lively gathering time, full of talk and laughter. Everyone was present—rarely did we eat dinner at our friends' houses. More often than not, we brought school friends and neighbors home to eat our "strange" but delicious food. To us, their food was just as unfamiliar. At the dinner table, my father was overwhelmed by the energy of five daughters, yet despite his deep longing for a son, he radiated happiness in our midst.

I remember rich moments in the kitchen after school with Mother and *Sitto*. Because Lebanese food is labor-intensive, sometimes they began preparing dinner right after breakfast. When we arrived home from school, they were *still* cooking, and I was finally allowed to roll, wrap, stuff, or pinch whatever was in progress. Meal preparation often began days ahead: laboriously cutting the leg of lamb just right; making cheese; curing olives or stirring kettles of preserves to be stored for use in the days or weeks to come.

Bread baking was a festive occasion in my eyes, watching Mom toss the dough into the air and gracefully twirl it over her arms. Eventually, she let me slide the loaves off huge wooden boards that she had specially made into our old gas Wedgewood stove in the basement. Now I know these are called peels, and they're readily available for purchase thanks to home pizza-baking trends.

Dad had his specialties in the kitchen: his fabulous tomato salad, yogurt, banana splits, hot fudge sundaes, and "maple syrup"—sugar, water and maple flavoring! He would come home with lugs of California fruits or huge bags of French rolls fresh from a bakery. Over the years he planted ten fig trees alongside the grapevines, apricot, avocado, orange, and lemon trees in our garden and tended them as Mother tended her five daughters.

◆

MY FIRST TRIP TO LEBANON

In 1971, a three-month visit to Lebanon transformed my life. It also provided the beginning of this cookbook, perhaps just as much as my ancestry, my childhood, and every evening meal did. The trip catalyzed my identity with my roots and showed me the fragility of our culture once transplanted to another continent.

6

ALICE'S KITCHEN
IF YOU MAKE IT WITH LOVE, IT WILL BE DELICIOUS!

Many Lebanese-Americans in the process of assimilating into American culture lost connection with Middle Eastern culture. Being in Lebanon delineated my duality as both an American and a Lebanese Arab, and not merely one or the other.

Flying into Beirut, I felt like I was coming home. The land of Lebanon looked so much like the Southern California landscape at that time, and even more, the experience of being surrounded by an entire country of people who looked like me, spoke our language, and ate our foods, was transformative. For once, I belonged. In Lebanon, the cultural source of my family's generosity and hospitality reiterated itself in every encounter, in every greeting kissed on both cheeks, in every invitation to *ghada*, a meal. This generosity has been an integral part of Middle Eastern life as long as memory.

The roots of Mother's artistry were visible on every dish, garnished and embellished with sprigs of parsley or mint, pine nuts, pomegranate seeds, or paprika. In presentation, I saw an art form; in sharing, a ritual of pleasure and friendship. Food brings together family, friends, and strangers; it is a medium for laughter and stories. It is no less powerful outside the home, where street markets, vendors, cafés, and restaurants all celebrate life. When I walked Beirut's streets, saw Lebanon's orchards, and delighted in its food and language, recognized its music and dance from our *mahrajans*—the huge outdoor festivals and Lebanese parties of my childhood in Los Angeles—I felt that I had come home. Lebanon in 1971 was lovely.

Lovely, and yet, this Paradise found of Lebanon was mortally fragile. No one could have believed that a war was imminent that was to last almost twenty years and irrevocably transform Lebanon. If one did not pay attention to the many Palestinian refugees camped in the empty lots and open spaces of Beirut and its suburbs, it was a heavenly place.

Yet I saw those refugees camped throughout Beirut and in the countryside, along the beautiful pine tree (*snobar*) lined road from the airport that the Israelis later bombed and burned all the way to the Burj and the port. They could not be ig-

nored in their camps under trees that would be the pride of any urban capital and in cardboard shelters where there were no trees. It was wintertime in Beirut, and the pressure of 100,000 refugees built up over too many years stressed the people and their infrastructure to a breaking point. I felt the tension building, yet had no foresight into the depth and scope of the tragedy about to haunt this incredibly lovely land—a land whose peoples were to be shattered and scattered for years. Greed and denial, war and divisiveness, occupation and repression, daily tragedy and violence visited a land where ease, generosity and hospitality had been an integral part of community life for centuries.

At that time, for me to be traveling alone to Lebanon was disconcerting for my relatives since women, young or old, did not typically travel alone. In those days, even going alone to downtown Beirut was unthinkable for some Lebanese women. What I was doing was considered outrageous to my relatives; yet they comforted themselves in the thought that I was sent there to find a husband, until I told them that was not why I was there. In disbelief, they nevertheless introduced me to what seemed to be *every* available young man in Lebanon. Oh how American I felt then! Indeed, I was young, the first generation born in America, a feminist, and a Lebanese. I returned to the States transformed by greater awareness and intrigue with my cultural heritage and the political crisis that was unfolding. And as much as I felt I had found home in Lebanon as a Lebanese, I also found how American I am. My journey congealed the mix of values within me that is a combination of old and new, Middle Eastern and Western, Lebanese and American, which manifested in my life through cooking, art, and gardening. And Lebanon *was* a sensory feast—of the visual, auditory, and culinary realms.

One of the most wonderful meals I remember was at an outdoor restaurant in Chtoura, a little town overlooking the Bekaa Valley on the way to the ruins at Baalbaak. We ate Lebanese appetizers— *mezza,* consisting of at least fifty tiny oval plates filled with delicacies from small grilled birds to *fistuq,* and Lebanese classics from *hommus* and *baba ghannouj* to *tabbouli.* We sat in the sunshine gazing at the expansive, tranquil farmland that provided this abundance. From that moment I understood that *mezza* is the heart of

ALICE'S KITCHEN
IF YOU MAKE IT WITH LOVE, IT WILL BE DELICIOUS!

Lebanese cuisine, just as lamb and rice are its backbone, *laban*, olives and bread its fragrant spirit, garlic and onions its soul, and mint and salads its breath.

The food of Lebanon evolved over the centuries: a little meat and lots of fresh vegetables, grains, herbs and seasonings aromatically combined. Even meatless Lebanese dishes are protein-rich. Lentils and rice in the one-pot dish, *mjaddrah*, are one example; *hommus bi tahini*, puréed garbanzo beans with a sauce made from ground sesame seeds, eaten with wheat bread, is another. Our vegetarian cuisine evolved as a major part of the diet where Christian practices such as Lent (*siyem*), economic circumstances, and the scarcity of meat created a need for meatless protein sources.

Traditional Lebanese cuisine uses relatively small amounts of meat, almost always lamb and chicken. When meat is eaten, every part of the lamb is utilized, even the head—there are recipes that use virtually every part of the animal. On my trip to Lebanon I ate wonderful little omelettes—until I found out that they were filled with *cerveau*, brains. I also ate a bite of a *baydaat ghanem* sandwich—lamb's testicles—of course without knowing what it was until too late. My squeamishness was the only problem, and both were difficult to swallow once I found out what I was eating. At home, my sisters and I refused to even taste *ghamme* (tripe) or tongue (*lisannat*), while Mother, Dad, *Sitto,* and Uncle Edmond relished them as the absolute delicacies they were in their eyes—a reminder of home.

Poor people have traditionally had less access to meat. In our village when my parents were growing up, meat was eaten only once or twice a week, with chicken dinner the Sunday feast. In America, beef production (and perhaps lamb) is accomplished by means of excessive use of grains that are suitable themselves for consumption. Methane produced by cattle is said to be seriously harming the ozone layer. In Lebanon, sheep are strictly grazing animals and do not eat grain that humans could eat. These facts make the Lebanese diet both less expensive and more healthful than diets heavy in beef. A few cubes of lamb on a *shish kebab* is typically the most meat an average person would eat. Lamb combined with bulgur in *kibbe,* for example, successfully extends the quantity, adding flavor, protein, and additional nutrition.

Lebanese food, a model of the healthy Mediterranean diet, is fast being integrated into the American diet, just as pizza, stir-fried dishes, tacos, and crêpes have been in the past. *Tabbouli, hommus,* and *falafel* appear regularly in newspaper recipe columns, and they are available in health food stores, supermarkets, and delis. Pocket bread, olive oil, and yogurt are in vogue. And with olive oil as its main fat source, Lebanese cuisine can be quite low in cholesterol. Our cuisine is based on eating

what's in season—lots of legumes, grains, and vegetables with spices, aromas, and flavors that are fresh, fragrant, and relatively low in cost, providing high quality nutrition with protein-rich sustenance. And although some of our recipes are labor intensive, many are healthy *and* very simple to prepare. But health is only part of the appeal. There is a spiritual component as well. Lebanese tradition uses resources carefully, prepares what is in season locally and, above all, shares. Mother continues to speak of the most important ingredient when she says,

DEAR, IF YOU MAKE IT WITH LOVE,

IT WILL BE DELICIOUS.

LIFE IN DOUMA

Douma, a small beautiful village high in the mountains of north Lebanon, was the birthplace of my mother, Alice Ganamey, in 1910, and of my father, Elias Sawaya, in 1895. Terraced olive trees, apple orchards, *arishes*—arbors abundant with grapes, conform to the steep mountainous land overlooking the Mediterranean Sea, three thousand feet below. To the north, across the valley (*wadi*), a notable geologic formation juts out and up from the earth, paralleling Douma and creating a background to the village so, as one turns the bend from the mountain road above, a most breathtaking view fills the eyes and warms the heart. The same geologic formation can be seen from the north as a mirror-image looking across the Qadisha Valley from artist and writer

Khalil Gibran's village of Bcharre. Douma appears on Lebanese tourism posters as a classic picturesque village.

Red tile roofs on hand-cut stone houses line the hill town above the valley. Kitchen gardens with parsley, *baqle*, mint, onions, and chard nestle beside homes. Douma was a cultural and commercial center at the turn of the century. Mama proudly recounts, "We had a paved street from cobblestones—the *souk*. It was the best town in 10 miles! With a good store selling fabrics that came from France." In fact, very few towns in Lebanon had cobblestone streets such as Douma. Brass, copper, and stainless steel utensils were made by the Douma *haddad*, blacksmith. Douma was called *Douma il Haddeed*—Douma, the iron town, because of the iron mines nearby. Fine furniture was carved by local woodworkers. Plays were performed in Douma, as well as in Beirut and Tripoli, and traveling entertainers came through town. A photographer lived in Douma and took formal portraits of Mother and her brothers and cousins when they were children, and other families as well.

A restaurant in the center of Douma's *souk* owned by Isshac l'Hage, Mom's great-uncle, and *Sitto* Sharife's brother, was famous for the best *hommus* around; people came from neighboring towns of *Tartaj* and *Bchaale* to eat there. Mama recalls that food was served in wooden dishes on little tables, and guests dined seated on cushions on the wooden floor.

My grandmother, *Sitto* Dalal, an exceptional cook and mother, survived 14 years, from 1912 to 1926, of single parenting, World War I, and food rationing while raising her three young children. Knitting, embroidery, sewing, and crochet came easily to her, and she followed the custom of making fine lingerie. Her daughter and granddaughters learned these crafts and the art of food. *Sitto* taught us about recycling and conservation of energy as did Mom and Dad. As I rinse rice in the kitchen sink, I remember watching *Sitto* pick up every grain that may have fallen out of the strainer, letting nothing go to waste. She collected rubber bands and rinsed out the new plastic bags of the 1950s. To Mother's dismay, I still do this.

In 1917, there was a tremendous earthquake in Lebanon that Alice remembers well; she was playing at her neighbor's when it happened. Mama tells the story of Dr. Salim Beik Bashir, who was visiting her family hillside home with its high balcony overlooking their garden and the *wadi*, valley, below Douma. When the tremor began, it was so forceful and Dr. Bashir was so terrified, he ran out to the wrought iron balcony and was about to jump from the more-than-two-story height. *Sitto* and her visiting women friends shouted at him to stop, which he did. Eventually the tremor came to a halt; both he and the handcarved stone building with the red tile roof survived.

And Mama, too, lived through this historical earthquake as well as a swarm of locusts, the First World War, hunger, and other difficulties. She remembers going to the spring, *ein*, to get water in the evening and visiting with friends as they stood in line for the water. In the dry season, the springs flowed slowly, so there was time for much talk. She'd carry water in a *jarra* from the springs at the top of the village, *ein al fou'a*, from the one in the middle that dried up long ago, or from the spring below, *ein at'tahta,* which is surrounded by terraced olive trees.

Mother remembers feeding mulberry leaves to silkworms that were being commercially raised in a neighbor's home. Um Rashid rented sections of racks in a special room to village women so they could raise their own silkworms. *Sitto* rented a section to keep silkworms, and Mama collected mulberry tree leaves to feed them. The worms started as tiny eggs, like seeds (*bizr*), and then hatched into larvae and began to grow, eating lots of mulberry leaves, which Mother cut into shreds they could eat. The worms continued to grow and grow to several inches long. Then they climbed the tumbleweeds placed alongside the racks and each magically spun a silk cocoon. *Sitto* made exquisite applique art pieces with silk cocoons, paid Um Rashid with some, and sold others to silk factories in Batroun or Trablos—a thriving Lebanese cottage industry beneficial to many.

Mama learned French along with her native Arabic in the village school. Her father, Dr. Anton Ganamey, our *Jiddo*, a remarkable person, fluent in eight languages, founded the first pharmacy in Douma with his brother Halim. *Jiddo's* name is etched into a marble stone that was perhaps the beam across his pharmacy door. This stone sits beside an ancient Roman sarcophagus in the center of Douma bearing the inscription, *"Farmashiyeh Anton Ganamey"*—Pharmacy of Anton Ganamey.

12

ALICE'S KITCHEN
IF YOU MAKE IT WITH LOVE, IT WILL BE DELICIOUS!

Journey to America

After a brief migration to Mexico and Uncle Adib's birth in 1908, *Sitto* Dalal and *Jiddo* Anton returned to Lebanon where my mother, Alice, was born in 1910. In 1912, *Jiddo* departed for the United States unaware of the fact that *Sitto* had just become pregnant with their third child, Uncle Edmond, who was born in 1913. *Jiddo* wanted, along with many others who desired to leave behind the hardships of Lebanon, to find the opportunity that America promised. His plan was to practice medicine in the U.S., but since he was a multi-lingual doctor, he was detained in Marseilles for six months, treating American-bound immigrants who had trachoma, a then-common eye disease that prevented their departure until they'd healed.

Finally, *Jiddo* made it to the U.S. and settled in the great Arab-American community of Detroit. World War I began; immigration quotas for "Syrians", as all people from Lebanon, Syria, and Palestine were then labeled, prohibited *Sitto* and their children from coming—the start of an enduring legacy of anti-Arab sentiments harbored in the U.S. At least those of us growing up in the 1950s had the Danny Thomas TV Show for a positive self-image!

Fourteen long years later, in 1926, *Jiddo* was able to send for my *Sitto* and her nearly grown children: Adib, Alice, and Edmond. Arriving at Ellis Island in July, they were met by Father Joe Bitar's father, Yusef al Bitar, my *Jiddo's* dear friend, who took them to the long-awaited reunion in Detroit, where *Jiddo* had established his medical practice. In May of 1926, Yusef al Bitar and his wife named their newborn son Naoum, after my grandfather's and their friend, Naoum Mokarzel, an Arab-American media pioneer and the publisher of **Al-Hoda**, New York's Arabic language newspaper founded in 1898. When Yusef died, Naoum was only seven months old, and he was then baptised as Joseph Naoum al Bitar, to carry on his father's name. Thus, he came under my grandfather's wing and was raised and educated by my dear *Jiddo*. Joseph Naoum al Bitar grew up to become Father Joe Bitar and remains a dear family friend to this day, living in Detroit.

Alice was 16 and did not speak English when they arrived in America; to her embarrassment, she was placed in a class with first-graders! She soon became adept with the new language and culture and began to feel at home in Detroit. *Sitto* Dalal assisted her husband, Anton, with patients since his practice was in their home. Before she learned English, her greeting to patients was "Doctor *bil yensoon*" (the doctor is in the anise!), which sounded like the phrase *Jiddo* had asked her to say "The doctor will be in soon."

Dr. Ganamey, an avid reader and lover of books with interests from medicine to metaphysics and art, was a philanthropist and a forward-thinking doctor. In 1928, according to Mother, my grandfather was recognized in an article in Detroit's *Free Press* for saving a stillborn infant's life by injecting adrenaline into its heart. Mother recalls his recommendation of artificial insemination to a couple who were having difficulty conceiving a child. He used acronyms well before his time to facilitate remembering expressions or information, and numerology. His personal journal is a mosaic of art, anatomy, acronyms, numerology, and words of wisdom in many languages, from *Ripley's Believe It or Not* and *Reader's Digest* to quotes from beloved Lebanese artist/writer Khalil Gibran.

Jiddo moved his family to California in 1928 to open a clinic. There in L.A. in that fateful year, Alice met a man from her village of Douma whom she would marry in 1934, Elias Jerius (George) Samia Sawaya. Established in California were Elias, his mother, Sharife, his brother, Michael, and his uncle, Father Gerasimos Sawaya, who in 1908 founded the first Melkite Eastern Catholic church in Los Angeles. The big economic crash of 1929 compelled *Jiddo* to return to Detroit with his family after only one year in California, but Elias and Alice had met. He was smitten and travelled to Detroit in pursuit.

In 1934 the marriage took place and Alice moved to Los Angeles with her new husband. The following year, *Sitto* came to help for six months after the birth of their first daughter. Three years later *Jiddo* came to Los Angeles for eye surgery that, although unsuccessful, kept them in Los Angeles near their only daughter and her new husband. This was the birthplace of all five daughters: Shirley, Lorraine, Joyce, Vivian, and me, Linda. I am fortunate to have known *Jiddo*, who taught me to read

and write, and who passed on to me his love of books. He lived with us until he died, when I was five years old, in 1952.

My father, Elias, was born in Douma in 1895, the oldest of three sons of Sharife and Jerius Samia Sawaya. He attended boarding school in Tripoli and then returned to the village to teach children. In 1912, when he was 17, he immigrated to California to join his mother, Sharife, her sister, Nimnum, and her brother, Father Gerasimos Sawaya, who had arrived in 1908. My cousin, Mary, remembers Father Sawaya as a wonderful cook, making *kibbe* for big Sunday

dinners. Elias, also known as Ellis, and sometimes Al or Leo, joined his younger brother Mike, while their youngest brother, Nassim, remained in Douma a few years before joining his brothers in California arriving via Mexico! Another brother of my father's mother Sharife was Yusef Fares Sawaya, who was a merchant in Los Angeles.

Like many Lebanese, Elias and his brother Michael were entrepreneurial young merchants. In 1920, they had a pool hall and cigar shop in Yuma, Arizona. Uncle Mike loved cigars, hats, and fancy cars! Then Uncle Mike got married and moved back to L.A. They then began working with their uncle, Yusef Fares, in Los Angeles, after which they opened a wholesale dry goods store in the early 1920s. Sawaya Brothers Dry Goods was established on Los Angeles Street in the heart of downtown L.A.'s garment district, at 645 S. Los Angeles Street, around the corner from Cole's Famous French Dip Sandwiches, where the sandwiches were memorable and the dill pickles the crunchiest. The Sawaya Brothers store stayed in business until the mid-1950s, when my father's health necessitated its sale. But I remember the long and narrow building facing east, with high ceilings and wooden floors, amber light coming through the storefront windows. There were shelves along both

walls with a ladder that slid along a track, allowing us to climb to the top shelves. Especially memorable to me (besides the pickles at Cole's) was the giant lettering that stretched from the front to the back, painted in black on a white background, way up high on the side of the brick building, which read in all capitals SAWAYA BROTHERS. Now, that was something—we must have been famous!

One of many things I inherited from my dear generous father is his entrepreneurial spirit and the idea that running one's own business is possible, which has manifested in the career choices my sisters and I have made. Dad was also a prolific amateur photographer, taking lots of still photos as well as movies. His creative inclinations came to me in my love of photography at an early age, while his love of his garden and planting fig and fruit trees became a joyful tradition I continue. Mom's passion for gardening and her green thumb were an early influence for me as well, as I fondly remember an early outing to a nursery where she let me choose flowers, which I still remember—flaming red *celosia!*—to transplant into the garden. Planting and harvesting carrots and strawberries was exciting while picking parsley and mint was a frequent almost-daily ritual.

During many rich years of marriage to her husband, Elias, and raising five daughters, cooking Lebanese food for us every day, Mother still found time to continue her creativity and handwork with knitting, embroidery, needlepoint, beading, and rug hooking, just to name a few!

Our dear *Sitto* Dalal lived with us until she passed away in 1970 at the age of 84. After *Jiddo* died in 1952, I was blessed to share a bed with her and remember how we slept like spoons—my arm lightly circling around her belly after saying our nighttime prayers together.

In 1972, shortly after my return from Lebanon, my beloved father, Elias, passed away. He and Mother were planning to visit me in Lebanon in 1971; it would have

16

ALICE'S KITCHEN
IF YOU MAKE IT WITH LOVE, IT WILL BE DELICIOUS!

been their first trip to their home-land since their immigration decades earlier. I waited three months in Beirut, working as a designer. Tragically, Dad became ill, I rushed home, and he died several months later, God rest his soul, *allah yirhamu*. His memory remains vivid in our lives, and he was dearly loved by many.

THE ELIAS SAWAYA DINNER PARTY

THE ELIAS SAWAYA DINNER PARTY

Mrs.Dalal Ganamey,Mr.& Mrs.Elias Sawaya & daughters & Mr.& Mrs.Edmond Ganamey.

Mother gradually created a new life for herself without her husband. Her passion as an appreciator and collector of fine china and porcelain dolls led her to study ceramics and china painting. Now, thirty-three years later, at 95, Alice maintains an enthusiasm and infectious vitality that defy age. Her art has flourished over the years, and she continues to innovate and create: porcelain earrings and pendants with fused glass, porcelain desk accessories, figurines, draped dolls, and beaded floral arrangements. Alice does gold wire work on jewelry with the dexterity of a person half her age!

Food presentation is one of Mother's art forms and is central to our culinary tradition. Using beautiful serving dishes, adding color and texture for garnish, is an integral part of the art of Lebanese cooking—the beautifully presented gift of food.

Mom's passion for learning, creating, and sharing with others is an inspiration to those she meets—young and old. And she remains at the center of the family nurturing and nourished by the love for and from her daughters, grandchildren, great-grandchildren, and friends, showing us well how to age with grace and her big, generous, and loving heart.

Mama and I return to Beirut and Douma, 1998

Finally my lifelong dream of going to Lebanon with my mother came to fruition in October of 1998. She was 88 years old and, thank God, well enough to make the long trip, 72 years after she left at the age of 16. We had an amazing journey, which was primed by my solo trip in 1996 where I re-established contact with our family and friends that I had met 25 years before in 1971. Beirut was unrecognizable to me from the devastation of war. Douma, our mountain village in the north of Lebanon, was thankfully untouched and remarkably unchanged from my mother's time there.

We were welcomed with open arms and so much love and, of course, fabulous meals. All who met Mother were amazed at her skill and fluency with Arabic, as she hadn't been to her native land in 72 years. Additionally, they were amazed by her youthfulness and her creativity and vitality—she brought gifts of her handcrafted jewelry. Alice was delighted with the convenience and comfort of the modern hotel in Douma—since at the time she immigrated, there was neither indoor plumbing nor electricity in the village! But the cobblestone streets that distinguished it in its prime endure to this day.

Mama was surprised that people remembered her and knew more about her than she expected. Most of her peers were deceased, but their children and grandchildren knew of her and my father as well—the oral tradition and stories living on through generations. We found the very house she was born in, now in the care of my cousin, Tony Ganamey, and were blessed to have a meal there prepared by his sister. Mama stood on the balcony in her home, pictured on page 12, where the story of how Dr. Bashir wanted to jump from that balcony is told, and Mama retold it with enthusiasm and detail.

Cousin George Sawaya drove us from the Beirut seashore of the Mediterranean to Douma with our first stop at the compelling overlook of the picturesque village

as you round the high mountain bend after a very windy journey from sea level. Next essential stop for Mom was 'Ein il Fou'a (the upper spring), where villagers still come to fill their now plastic containers with the spring waters of Lebanon, and Mom took her first taste of that natural mountain spring water in seven decades. We visited Ickfour and saw the tree where Mother remembered swinging as a girl—there was a group picnicking, kids swinging, and a woman playing the *derbake* (Arabic drum) with others dancing and clapping.

We visited the ancestors in the cemetery, the olive groves, monasteries, and churches. Apples, figs, grapes, *'unnab* (jujube), persimmons, and pomegranates were in season. Marie Talalai gave us a *tannour* bread baking experience that was truly memorable, sending us off with hot fresh baked loaves of *tilme* and *zaatar*!

Of our trip to Lebanon, Mother says,

It was so beautiful and a reminder of my life. I remembered every inch of Douma. We had a great time because I spoke the language with my family and friends, who didn't speak English. There were not many of the old friends I knew, but their children, who were very attentive, loving and caring. They gave us a wonderful reception and were kind and warm. Every-

one wanted to meet me; they knew a lot about me. It was wonderful to make this trip at my age and I thank God for enabling me to make this trip and see my hometown that I have always dreamed about. Seeing the home I was born and raised in gave me a beautiful feeling that it was still standing.

I found Douma as I remembered it, with a lot of improvement on the church buildings. I felt wonderful being there; it reminded me of my youth. Memories came flooding back. It gave me a chance to know Lebanon more. The destruction from the war was stressful to see. Luckily Douma didn't have any damage.

The food was excellent! It reminded me of the old times when we had a picnic. We visited the *karam* (orchard or vineyard) of my uncle where he had every kind of grapes planted. I had forgotten the big round ones called *'ein il ba'ara* (eye of the cow) until our trip when we enjoyed them again in Douma. My uncle slept outside in the vineyard to guard the orchard, the grapes were so prized!

I remember being interested in the silk worms that my grandmother raised and I liked learning about them, learning new things.

Well, some things don't change: Mama still loves to learn new things, and in her 90s, Mother is still just as enthusiastic as she has been all her life. She never stops finding ways to create—making jewelry, firing her ceramic and glass kilns, growing sumptuous orchids, and cooking lunch for twenty-five people!!! Here's the menu for the Agape luncheon she recently hosted:

Chicken and bulgur (*riz bi tfeen*), vegetarian cabbage rolls (*malfouf mihshi siyeme*), vegetable patties (*ijjet khudra*) "I made 80 and they ate them like mad!," *fattoush* salad, and *ghraybe* cookies.

Because of her love of family, tradition, great food, cooking with love and loving to cook, we have her, and those before her, to thank for these recipes. Even today, Mother cooks Sunday dinners "for the family and whoever can come."

Welcome to **Alice's Kitchen**!

20

ALICE'S KITCHEN
IF YOU MAKE IT WITH LOVE, IT WILL BE DELICIOUS!

ABOUT
THE
RECIPES

HONORING INTUITION

Mother's cooking is done intuitively. I have never seen her use a cookbook, though she is literate in four languages. As I recorded our family recipes, her intuitive style proved both a joy and a challenge. Mother would say "Add enough salt" and somehow I knew or learned just how much "enough" was. The fact that we could relate this way showed me how deep our communication had become, because "enough" could mean a dash or a tablespoon or a cup. The challenge then became to transform Mother's instructions into actual measurements. When Mom says, "Just put in a heapful teaspoon," I smile at her attempt to be specific in a Western way, and yet her charming use of language that is truly Middle Eastern.

Most of the recipes here are written as told to me and as cooked by my family and me. My goal has been to preserve the simple, more traditional versions of the recipes as they were made when I was growing up. Cooking evolves with each generation, and thus Mother's cooking has changed over the past 25 years, since I first recorded many of these recipes. In reading this book, one may notice that she and I continue our conversations about how to cook! I have incorporated some of her changes as well as my own, where appropriate. I have included new recipes, some that I have developed based on my trips to Lebanon, especially vegetarian recipes.

THE FOLLOWING PAGES
PERTAIN TO MOST OF THE RECIPES IN ALICE'S KITCHEN
PLEASE READ THEM AND THE INTRODUCTIONS TO EACH SECTION

◆ MEASUREMENTS OR HOW MUCH IS ENOUGH?
Our style of cooking is very forgiving, and although I have quantified the recipes,

if you do not have enough of what a recipe calls for, in most cases, it is not essential to be precise. Cooking is an art, and the more one cooks, the better one gets, as in any art form. And our individual touches, preferences, and differences make us all the more interesting. Mistakes are often our best creations and our greatest teachers, so explore, try variations and make these recipes your own. If your mother or *Sitto* or father or *Jiddo* used some spice that you love, and that we haven't used, please indulge yourselves!

◆ SERVING SIZE

Most of the recipes serve 4 to 6 people, unless indicated otherwise. If the recipe is served as an appetizer with other appetizers, it might serve 8 to 12. Cookies and sweets recipes have an approximate yield. In Lebanese tradition, it is important to have more than enough to offer guests, with food left over. This is a cultural custom, so when in doubt, make more than you think you need and share the abundance with family and friends with love.

◆ SALT

In many recipes, the amount of salt has been reduced for health's sake. It is up to each cook to do what is comfortable and further reduce salt, as desired. As Mother says "You can always add more." Our recipes suggest "taste and adjust," so start with a little and add more as needed. We both use sea salt in our cooking and olive curing. An alternative to salt for our traditional way of mashing garlic into a paste with salt is to use citric acid (see LEMON SUBSTITUTES).

◆ BOUILLON

Although Mother uses chicken or beef bouillon granules in some of her cooking, it's not included in the book since it adds salt and unnecessary chemicals, such as MSG. Mother describes how she uses bouillon on page 75.

◆ FAT AND OLIVE OIL

Some recipes specify clarified butter or olive oil; clarified butter (*samne*) is preferable with meats according to Mother, because of olive oil's flavor and tendency to burn easily. Olive oil is a good substitute, however, especially if there is concern about intake of saturated fat. Low in oleic acid, an undesirable fatty acid, and flavorful, organically grown olive oil is an excellent and healthy food choice. Cold-pressed, extra virgin olive oil is best for salads, and regular extra virgin oil is fine for cooking, since it's going to be heated. Light vegetable oils like corn, sunflower, or safflower are for frying, with either of the latter two for garlic mayonnaise.

◆ Flour and Rice—brown or white?

In bread baking, a combination of organic whole wheat flour and unbleached white flour is my preference. Mama adds wheat germ to white flour to increase its nutritional value. If wheat flour is a problem, try using spelt flour. Organic brown rice or brown basmati rice rather than the traditional white rice is primarily what I use, but occasionally, white basmati rice is what my mood calls for. Mother uses and recommends Mahatma Indian extra-long white rice. Pre-soaking rice, beans, and grains is an old, traditional technique with recently proven health benefits: this deactivates enzyme inhibitors making nutrients more available and digestable.

◆ Organic and Sustainable

Organic homegrown or store-bought vegetables and grains are preferred; they have more nutrition and fewer chemicals than commercially grown, manufactured foods. Mama still keeps a small vegetable garden along with her flowers, and I have nurtured a garden with fruits and vegetables for the past 25 years. A song I once heard on the radio whose lyrics were "two things you can't buy are love and homegrown tomatoes!" says it all! Amen! And in the old days, everything was organic!!!

◆ Arabic Ingredients and Words

Herbs, Spices, & Fragrant Waters (p. 223) has information on special ingredients. The **Alice's Kitchen** page on my website has resources on where to buy special ingredients (www.lindasawaya.com). Words in transliterated Arabic appear in *italics*, and most are translated. Words common to many Americans, such as *hommus*, are not translated. At the end of the book is a glossary with Arabic expressions, sample menus, and an extensive index with Arabic and English recipe names.

◆ Meat

Lamb, goat, and chicken are the primary meats of rural Lebanon, used sparingly as in other Asian cuisines. Beef is available in urban areas and can be used in place of lamb, although there is a taste difference and health concerns due to factory processes that have created Mad Cow disease. If you are carnivorous, buy your meat and fowl from local farms, with sustainable farming practices, growing free-ranging, non-steroid-injected animals, much preferable to commercially raised and processed products. Eggs from chickens raised outside are very different from eggs of factory chickens—if you have ever tasted farm fresh eggs, you know what I mean. And this is the old-country, humane, and compassionate way to raise animals. Ask your butcher as well. Before cooking lamb recipes, read about lamb pages 73–77.

◆ Lemon Substitutes—citric acid

Our recipes commonly use lemon juice but occasionally suggest that citric acid (made from citrus fruits) be used with or instead of lemon juice—both are used

as a preservative. Because lemon juice is not always available or in season, or it added too much liquid to a recipe (such as in spinach pies), citric acid or other tart seasonings are used. When making garlic paste, citric acid works well to mash garlic into a paste instead of salt, or with a little salt, to lessen the amount of salt. Lemon substitutes traditionally used in our cuisine are citric acid, sumac in *tabbouli* and *fattoush,* and sour green grapes (*hesroum*) mashed and strained for use in *hommus* and *baba ghannouj*—an old country technique worth trying, although I haven't. Some Lebanese use tart pomegrante juice instead of lemon in *fattoush* salad and other dishes—delicious and available in bottles at Middle Eastern stores. Here's an approximate measurement for substituting citric acid for lemon juice.

¼ TEASPOON CITRIC ACID EQUALS 2 TABLESPOONS OF LEMON JUICE

Processed lemon juice (in plastic lemons) and reconstituted lemon juice is not recommended. Fresh lemons (Eureka variety) are available most of the year, and are the best. Meyer lemons, which are more like oranges, would only be desirable in a few recipes, so when in doubt, use common lemons!

◆ CLEANLINESS

Mother and *Sitto* were justifiably conscientious about cleanliness. It is important to rinse vegetables and to pick over grains, rinse, and drain them. Clean chicken by rubbing with baking soda and salt and then rinsing well. Rinse fish in water before preparing. Another aspect of cleanliness in our cooking is the way we use our hands to make and form foods. Careful hand-washing prior to and through the process of meal preparation is essential to healthful and delicious meals. If you prefer to use spatulas, food processors or bread machines for kneading dough, these are options, as are food-handling gloves. We love using our hands to create.

◆ PRESENTATION AND ORGANIZATION

One of the most important things I learned from my mother about food is the art of presentation and importance of organization. Presenting the food in an artful way with garnishes on beautiful plates is a part of the gift of food. At 95, she's organized and energetic enough to cook for large groups of people, saying it's easy and what she loves to do!! Preparing in advance is one of her secrets as well as good menu planning and her desire to give with love.

◆

Sallem dayetkoom! is an expression of gratitude to the cook meaning "God bless your hands!" Enjoy and *sahteyn!* and much pleasure to you from our collective efforts in these recipes and the fruits of your time spent with love and joy in the kitchen creating them. *Yallah!* let's cook!

24

ALICE'S KITCHEN
IF YOU MAKE IT WITH LOVE, IT WILL BE DELICIOUS!

MEZZA

◆

APPETIZERS

Mezza—tiny plates of Lebanese traditional delicacies—are served as appetizers with beverages while dinner is simmering and as guests arrive. *Mezza* can be an entire meal—an array of finger foods, enticingly sliced vegetables and fresh herbs, or dips with snippets of bread festively set out. Here's a list of ideas; recipes for appetizers appear in various sections within the book. What lies in these few pages are suggestions for combining and serving them, and recipes for curing olives and making pickles. For *mezza*, anything goes. For beverage ideas, see that section. In Lebanon, fifty small plates with different items are not unusual for a *mezza* spread. And remember, presentation is as important as preparing the food: it is an art. So garnish with sprigs of parsley, mint, and thyme; slices of lemons; drizzles of olive oil; dashes of paprika; dots of pomegranate rubies; sprinkles of pine nuts . . . you get the idea! Make it beautiful!

But first, a story: A fabulous spread was laid out before us on a twenty-foot long table at our lunch (*ghada*) stop in the Lebanese mountains. Mother and I were invited on an amazing bus tour of Lebanese monasteries with the Greek Orthodox choir and pastor from the Douma church, Saide Nyah. The bus arrived at our hotel in Douma before dawn to pick us up. All was quiet, but for the birds, and people sipping their morning coffee, talking softly. By mid-morning, the bus was as far from quiet as could be. The choir singing, a drummer drumming, and all, including the bus driver, clapping to the music along windy mountain roads and congested Beirut traffic, in joyful song: at first church music and then folk songs! Even

Mother was clapping and singing, remembering songs from her childhood! A memorable trip, topped off by a spectacular Lebanese feast—a *mezza* extraordinaire, with a new, tasty red pepper and walnut dip that I've improvised on page 175.

•FRESH VEGETABLES AND SALADS

Platters of beautifully arranged and sliced or whole radishes, carrots, celery, romaine lettuce leaves, fresh endive, green onions, tomatoes, Armenian cucumbers (*miiti*), Middle Eastern cucumbers, sprigs of fresh mint and thyme, bell pepper, *tabbouli* salad, yogurt and cucumber salad (*laban ou khyar*), *fattoush* salad, fresh green fava beans (*ful akhdar*)

•DIPS AND COOKED VEGETABLES

Garbanzo bean dip (*hommus*), eggplant with tahini dip (*baba ghannouj*), eggplant dip (*batinjan mtabbal*), fava bean dip (*ful mdammas*), red bell pepper and walnut dip (*mhammara*), fried eggplant, squash fritters or vegetable patties, sautéed veggies (*khudra mahkluta*)

•FINGER FOOD ENTRÉES

Stuffed grape leaves (*warak 'inib*), raw lamb and bulgur (*kibbe nayye*), baked lamb and bulgur (*kibbe bil sineyeh*), lamb or vegetarian stuffed cabbage rolls (*malfouf mihshi*), *falafel* with tahini sauce, meat or spinach pies (*fatayir* or *sambousik*) with yogurt cheese (*labne*), vegetarian bulgur and pumpkin diamonds (*kibbet jlunt*)

•CHEESE

A variety of cheeses from homemade to processed such as *jibn baladi*, feta, kasseri or kashkaval (*'ashawan*), yogurt cheese (*labne bi zeit*), yogurt (*laban*)

•BREADS FOR SCOOPING AND DIPPING

Arabic bread (*khubz*) cut into small triangular pieces for scooping, Arabic herb breads (*tilme bi zaatar* and *tilme bi kishk*), pita chips, crackers

•NUTS AND PRESERVES

Pistachios (*fistuq*), roasted almonds, cashews, peanuts, Jordan almonds (*mlabbas*), pumpkin seeds, roasted garbanzo beans (*'aadami*), fig jam

•PICKLES AND OLIVES

Black and green olives (*zeitoun*), pickled vegetables (*makbous*), pickled turnips (*lifit*), pickled beets (*shmandar*), pickled peppers

Following are recipes for curing olives and making pickles.

26

ALICE'S KITCHEN
IF YOU MAKE IT WITH LOVE, IT WILL BE DELICIOUS!

Zeitoun ◆ Olives

Olives ripen from August through February, depending upon the variety, climate and elevation. Green olives are olives picked before ripening to black, still green and on the tree. For successful processing, these need to be opened by scoring each one with a knife or by the quicker method of pounding them with a mallet. On a trip to Lebanon in the fall, my cousin Eli served fantastic just-picked green olives cured only four days, with sprigs of fresh Lebanese thyme—*zaatar*.

When olives are deep, rich, and purple-black in color, they are ripe for picking and processing without scoring—the type I grew up eating in Los Angeles: *zeitoun makbous*. A big sheet was positioned under the tree in our front yard to collect the falling olives. Since we no longer have olive trees of our own, Mother and I have been picking black, ripe olives rather than ground-gathering them. Olives that are picked tend to be firmer and more pungent, without the wrinkles of older fruits that are beginning to dry out.

A great amount of salt is used in processing *zeitoun makbous* to draw out the bitterness that makes an olive picked from a tree inedible. The salt also functions as a preservative, along with lemon juice and citric acid in the brine. The longer that olives are stored in brine, the weaker their flavor becomes; keep this in mind when deciding at what point to put them into jars. Vinegar or lime is used in the brine

by some families, while we prefer lemon juice. If lemons weren't in season, Mom and *Sitto* would use vinegar. Experiment with your own variations!

An old country method of determining the correct salt content of the brine is to fill a jar with water and add salt to it. When the salt has thoroughly dissolved, place an uncracked raw egg in the jar. Continue to add salt slowly; the egg begins to rise to the top when the salt to water ratio is correct for preserving olives! About two tablespoons per pint is the ratio that floated the egg in the test I performed using sea salt. Boil the water first to remove chlorine and other impurities.

Zeitoun Marsous

GREEN OLIVES

◆

1 quart fresh green olives
¼–½ cup olive oil
2 tablespoons salt
water, boiled and cooled, to fill jar
½ cup lemon juice
1 teaspoon citric acid (optional)
a sprig of fresh oregano, savory, thyme, or Lebanese *zaatar*
1 sterilized glass or ceramic quart jar with lid

    1. In the late summer or fall before olives ripen, pick green olives and crush with a mallet or score each one with a knife.

    2. Sprinkle with enough salt to coat olives. Mix. Lay on several layers of clean, old, cotton sheets and spread out to dry in the sun, if possible, or indoors.

    3. Stir olives once a day for 4 to 10 days, adding a little more salt every day, as needed to keep a dusting of salt on the olives. Beginning the fourth day, taste an olive. If the taste pleases you—great, enjoy them. If they're bitter, continue the salting process several more days until they're no longer bitter and ready to pack in jars.

    4. Fill sterile jars with olives; then add fresh oregano, salt, lemon juice or citric acid, and water to 2" from top of jar. Add olive oil to cover the olives with at least a ½" layer of oil at the top. Shake the jar and store it in a cool, dark place or in the refrigerator. Enjoy, they're ready to eat!

Makes one quart.

28

ALICE'S KITCHEN
IF YOU MAKE IT WITH LOVE, IT WILL BE DELICIOUS!

Zeitoun Akhdar

GREEN OLIVES

◆

This recipe is a simpler method of curing green olives directly in the jar.

> 1 quart fresh green olives
> ¼–½ cup olive oil
> 2 tablespoons salt
> water, boiled and cooled
> ½ cup lemon juice
> 1 teaspoon citric acid (optional)
> fresh oregano or thyme sprigs
> 1 sterilized glass or ceramic quart jar with lid

1. Score olives with a small knife and pack into sterile jars. Coat with oil, add salt, and fill with water to several inches from the top.

2. Add lemon juice and citric acid; add more olive oil to cover the olives at least ½" at the top of the jar. Shake jar and allow to cure for a few weeks in a cool, dark place. Taste and when they're no longer bitter, they're ready to enjoy!

Makes one quart.

Zeitoun Makbous

BLACK OLIVES

◆

Deep, purple-black, shiny olives cured in the straightforward old-country style sat in a glass jar on our kitchen counter that would have seemed bare without them. What you'll need to make these memorable, flavorful olives: old, clean cotton sheets that you won't mind staining purple, and a big tray to spread olives on—a surface that won't be damaged by moisture or salt. In the damp Northwest where olives don't grow, I use large, flat woven baskets. But I remember deep enamel pots filled with olives sprinkled with salt that Mom and *Sitto* cured in our warm, dry Southern California kitchen. In such a desert-like climate, they can be cured in a deep pot, pouring off the water drawn out by the salt. *Mabrouk* to your success!

1 gallon olives
1 cup salt, approximate
1 cup olive oil
¼ cup lemon juice
⅛ cup citric acid
water
1 gallon sterilized glass jar with lid

1. When olives are ripened and dropping from the tree, collect them to cure. The best olives are picked from the tree—firm, black, and shiny.

2. Rinse well and place them in an enamel pot, adding water to cover them. Soak small olives for four days and large ones for one week, every day draining and rinsing them and adding fresh water.

3. On the last day, drain and rinse olives. Spread them out on several layers of cotton sheets on a drying tray. Sprinkle with salt, about three tablespoons or enough to coat them well and mix.

4. Place trays in the sun or a warm, dry place for four or more days, depending upon the size of the olives and pungency desired. Once a day, mix them

30

ALICE'S KITCHEN
IF YOU MAKE IT WITH LOVE, IT WILL BE DELICIOUS!

and add more salt, which draws out the water and bitterness, and prevents mold from forming.

5. On the fourth day, taste. If they taste good and are just slightly bitter, they are ready to preserve. Place them in sterile jars, add olive oil, and shake up the jar to coat them; add lemon juice and/or citric acid or vinegar, 3 tablespoons salt (to one gallon), and filtered water. Olives preserved this way will last over a year if there is a minimum of ½" of olive oil, which separates and rises to the top, forming an air barrier that keeps them from molding. Of course, they're much better when they're fresh; as they age, they become soft and less flavorful.

Makes one gallon.

Lifit

PICKLED TURNIPS

◆

In this earthy and time-honored Lebanese pickle recipe, white turnips take on the red of the beet and have a mysterious appearance through the dark beet brine in a jar. Their bright pink color adds a marvelous part of the spectrum and a zesty flavor to *mezza, falafel,* or any meal. Keep refrigerated and they'll last several months, like most pickles.

2½ pounds turnips
2 small beets
⅓ part boiled water
⅔ part white vinegar
3 tablespoons sea salt, divided in half
5 whole peppercorns
3 red chili peppers, fresh or dry
3 cloves garlic
1 quart sterilized glass jar with lid

1. Rinse and trim turnips. Cut into thick slices or wedges. Sprinkle with half of the salt and let stand for several hours to drain.
2. Slice raw beets. Pack beets, turnips, remaining salt, peppercorns, chili peppers, and garlic into a large sterile jar. Fill jar with water and vinegar in above proportions and seal tightly. Allow to pickle for a few weeks, but they can be eaten within a few days. Keep refrigerated once pickled.

Makes one quart.

Makabis

PICKLED VEGETABLES

◆

Pickling has long been used as a method of preserving vegetables for winter use. Try this combination of cauliflower florets, sliced carrots, and onions, with garlic cloves, hot peppers, and tiny Armenian cucumbers left intact. Serve with meals or as appetizers (*mezza*), and keep refrigerated once pickled.

> 3 pounds mixed sliced vegetables
> ¼ part boiled water
> ¾ part white vinegar
> 2 tablespoons sea salt
> 2 tablespoons sugar
> 5 whole peppercorns
> 3 whole chili peppers
> 4 whole garlic cloves

1. Rinse and trim vegetables into relatively even sizes.
2. Arrange assorted vegetables in large sterile jars with salt, sugar, garlic, peppers, and spices. Fill jars with water and vinegar in above proportions. Allow to pickle for three weeks, but you may taste them in a few days. Once vegetables are pickled, enjoy them while they're crunchy, as they soften with time.

Makes two quarts.

ALICE'S KITCHEN

IF YOU MAKE IT WITH LOVE, IT WILL BE DELICIOUS!

HALEEB

◆

CHEESE, YOGURT
& BUTTER

Homemade yogurt and cheese were staples of our household. Mother and *Sitto* kept the yogurt (*laban*) culture going without fail. As one batch was almost gone, a little of the culture was preciously saved and a new batch of yogurt begun. In Los Angeles in the 1950s, cow milk was what was available while in our Lebanese mountain village, the milk came from sheep or goat, which renders a very different product than cow milk. Sheep milk is richer than the thinner milk from goats. Goat milk, goat cheese, goat milk yogurt, and sheep milk cheese are again available—even locally made and sold at farmers' markets, with some supermarkets carrying them as a more digestable alternative to cow milk. If you use cow milk, check that it isn't treated with the Bovine Growth Hormone (rBGH). Whole milk is a richer, more fattening product than non-fat, 1%, or 2% milk.

Clarified butter (*samne*), similar to Indian *ghee*, was another staple in our refrigerator that is made with cow milk. Clarified butter does not burn as easily as regular butter or olive oil, so it is preferable for cooking, nor does it have the salt, as most of it is discarded in the clarifying process.

If you've never tried making homemade yogurt or cheese and you love to cook, you'll want to give these a try. When we say yogurt (*laban*), we never think of anything sweet and pink with fruit, as most Americans do. We think white, tart, and the more sour, the better! We don't think spoon: we think bread—thin pieces of Arabic bread folded into little scoops to deliver the yogurt. *Laban* is probably the first food of Middle Eastern babies after breast milk—nurturing and nourishing, with cultures that are more readily digestible than unfermented milk.

Jibn Baladi

ARABIC CHEESE

◆

Simply delicious and easy to make, this fresh homemade cheese was a staple at our breakfast, lunch, and dinner table, and an essential part of *mezza*, the Arabic name for a big spread of appetizers. It's a perfect complement to olives, both eaten wrapped in snippets of Arabic bread. Cheesecloth and a colander or a fine strainer are used in making *jibn*, which is a soft, unriped Neufchatel-type cheese. If you can find good goat milk, try using it instead of cow milk and taste the difference.

> 1 gallon milk, at room temperature
> 1 rennet tablet
> 1 tablespoon salt

1. Warm milk for about 5 minutes on medium heat in an enamel or stainless steel pot.

2. While milk is heating, place rennet tablet into a saucer and crush it into a powder. Blend it with a couple tablespoons of milk and stir it into warmed milk. Remove from heat. Cover and let mixture stand for two hours.

3. Reheat until it thickens and begins to separate and curdle. Continue to stir until the water—whey—begins to clear. Pour into a colander draped with cheesecloth or a fine strainer with a container underneath to collect the whey, which can be set aside and used for making a ricotta-style cheese, *'arishe,* whose recipe follows this one.

4. While curds are still warm, gently scoop out a handful and press together between your palms, squeezing out as much water as possible, at the same time shaping the curds into a flattened round of cheese. Or you can place a handful in cheesecloth draped over a strainer to drain, pressing out the liquid. When it begins to hold together, set into a glass bowl and sprinkle with a little salt. The salt will draw out more of the liquid. Continue forming remaining curds into 6 or more rounds of *jibn*.

5. Before storing in a glass container, drain off and discard excess liquid. This very light and simple cheese keeps for about a week refrigerated in a covered container but is most delicious when fresh.

Makes 6 small rounds
of cheese.

'Arishe

FRESH RICOTTA CHEESE

◆

Arishe, an easy-to-make ricotta-style cheese, is served fresh with a little salt or sweetened with a little sugar, and eaten with Arabic bread. Lebanese pastries such as our filo pastry cheesecake (*knafe bi jibn*) and Lebanese crêpes (*'atayif*) use *'arishe* sweetened with sugar and flavored with orange blossom water—heavenly to be sure. If you do not have time to make this, you can use ricotta cheese.

> whey remaining from making Arabic cheese (*jibn*)
> 1 quart milk
> ⅓ cup lemon juice
> salt or sugar to taste

1. In a deep pot, add milk and lemon juice to whey remaining from the gallon of milk used for making Arabic cheese (previous recipe) and bring to a boil over medium heat.

2. Milk will begin separating, curdling, and rising to the top. Use a slotted spoon to lift and strain curds from the liquid. Place curds in a glass container adding either salt or sugar, if desired. Best when it is absolutely fresh, *'arishe* may be stored in the refrigerator for a few days or made ahead for use in one of the desserts mentioned above. Find recipes for these in the Dessert section.

Makes one pint of cheese.

Labne

Yogurt cheese

◆

A tart excellent substitute for sour cream or cream cheese, *labne* is easily made from plain yogurt—either homemade or commercial—and tastes terrific eaten with Arabic bread. For appetizers (*mezza*), spread it out on a beautiful little plate, add a sprig of parsley, and drizzle with olive oil. It is a companion to *kibbe bil sineyeh*, rolled grape leaves (*waraq 'inab*), and is used in savory pastries. The water content of yogurt is drawn out by the addition of salt, creating a luscious, tart, thick, and creamy cheese. Mother has been making it recently without any salt at all, and it is satisfying either way. It needs to sit all day or overnight for the yogurt to drain in a cheese bag, which Mom makes out of cotton sheets. Instructions to make a reusable cheese bag are below. A large coffee filter works. *Labne* is available as kefir or yogurt cheese in natural food stores or as *labne* in Middle Eastern food stores, but it's so easy to make, why buy it? This recipe makes one cup of yogurt cheese.

> 1 quart yogurt (*laban*)
> ½–1 teaspoon salt (optional)
> cheese bag (*kees*) or coffee filter

1. Remove a little yogurt and reserve as starter for your next batch of yogurt. Mix salt into remaining yogurt.
2. Turn cheese bag inside out; thoroughly wet it, and then wring out. It's helpful to have a second set of hands here: hold the bag open and pour yogurt into it or into a coffee filter, if you're using that method. Tie bag at the top and hang it up over the sink or a bowl to drain overnight. Or let coffee filter drain over a bowl overnight.
3. Remove cheese from bag or filter by turning upside down. Drizzle with olive oil before serving and store in the refrigerator. A half gallon of yogurt makes about one quart of *labne*.

To make a cheese bag (*kees*):

Cut two pieces of thin, but finely woven, muslin or white cotton sheeting to make a rectangular bag, 8 x10 inches. Sew together at the bottom and sides, forming a bag with the opening at the top. At the top, sew a channel for a drawstring to close the bag and to use as a hanger. Make a drawstring by sewing one or using a piece of string or a shoelace and insert it into the channel. Wash bag after sewing and before filling with yogurt.

Alice's Kitchen

36
If you make it with Love, it will be Delicious!

Laban

Yogurt

◆

Laban is one of the most ancient foods in the Middle East. According to one account, milk held in sheepskin bags on camels in desert climates naturally fermented and was found to be delicious; thus, *laban* began to be intentionally made. Easier to digest than regular milk because of its acidophilus content, *laban* helps balance the intestinal flora.

My earliest memory of eating fresh *laban* was for breakfast with crisp Arabic bread, although Mama fed it to all her five daughters as their first food after breastfeeding. One of the mysterious, unmarked containers in the corner of the refrigerator invariably contained a precious amount of *laban* saved as starter, *roube,* for the next batch of yogurt. If you don't have starter, ask a friend, as some commercial yogurts are processed in such a way that they will not work; save some of your homemade batch for the next time.

A reader of an earlier edition of **Alice's Kitchen**, Craig Coté, wrote and asked about making *roube*—he remembered his grandmother making it. Mother's memory was jogged by Craig's question and sure enough, she recalled the old country way of making a starter! In the process of doing this book, her memories of the old country, from more than 70 years ago, keep flooding back. A piece of bread was placed in a saucer of milk and left on the kitchen counter to sour. In several days, the soured milk and bread were mashed together and added to the heated milk as the starter. Although I have not tried this yet, we thank Craig for writing and asking!

Because there are so many variables and making yogurt is such an alchemical process, read the suggestions following the recipe to help you make *laban* that successfully suits your taste.

> ½ gallon milk (sheep or goat milk was used in Douma)
> 1–2 tablespoons *roube* (yogurt culture for starter)

1. Simmer milk until it rises and becomes frothy, stirring frequently with a wooden spoon so it does not scorch. Bring it **almost** to a boil, being careful not to let it boil, and immediately remove from heat.
2. Cool until you can put your baby finger in and count to 10; this is *Sitto's* tried-and-true-method.
3. Meanwhile, blend starter (*roube*) in a saucer with a little milk, remov-

ing any lumps. Stir into the cooled milk, immediately pour mixture into a crock, and cover. *Sitto,* Mom, and Dad always made the sign of the cross over the *laban* to bless it and insure that it came out. Now's the time to bless it.

4. Place crock in a warm spot wrapped in a towel, and then a couple of layers of wool blankets or a down comforter, where it can remain warm and undisturbed for 8 to 12 hours while the bacterial action happens and the milk is converted into yogurt. Let it sit overnight if made in the evening or, if made in the morning, leave it all day. An amazing and ancient alchemy transforms the milk into *laban,* creating a more digestible form of milk (other than mother's breast milk!)

5. Refrigerate and remember to save a little of this batch as *roube,* starter, for the next batch.

Suggestions for successful *LABAN*

• Thickness can be controlled by how long milk is heated, whether you use whole or low fat milk, and how long you've let it set. The longer you heat it, the fatter the milk, and the longer it sets—all make for thicker yogurt.
• Sourness or tartness can be controlled by the temperature at the time the starter (*roube*) is added. The warmer the milk, the more sour. If *roube* has been refrigerated for one week or more, it will be more tart. If *roube* is fresher, the *laban* will be sweeter. The more *roube,* the more tart the yogurt will become.

If the yogurt doesn't set:

• The milk may not have been warm enough during incubation.
• The container may have been disturbed.
• The milk may not have been heated enough to kill certain bacteria that inhibit the "yoging"; conversely, if milk is too hot, it can kill the needed bacteria.
• The culture may not be good. Some commercial yogurts cannot be used for starter because of the way they are processed, destroying some of the bacteria necessary for fermentation.

Makes 2 quarts of yogurt.

38

ALICE'S KITCHEN
If you make it with Love, it will be Delicious!

Samne

CLARIFIED BUTTER

◆

In the old country *samne*, butter that is clarified, much like Indian *ghee*, is used for cooking. Salts, some water content, and impurities in the butter are removed in this process and it is less likely to burn. *Samne* that is refrigerated hardens and keeps for quite some time. It is melted for making *baklawa* or other pastries and in our delicious basic rice recipe, *riz mfalfal*. It is good to have some on hand in the refrigerator. And it's great mixed with a little olive oil for our fabulous Lebanese omelette, *'ijjeh*.

1 pound butter
¼ cup bulgur (*burghul*), optional

1. In a one-quart pot, melt butter over low to medium heat and add bulgur, which absorbs the sediment and makes it easier to pour off the clarified butter. Let simmer for 30 minutes to an hour without stirring, but watch it so it doesn't burn. I have been making this without the bulgur, and it comes out fine, so either way works.

2. A little residue at the top will turn light brown when it's done. Skim and discard this. Set aside butter and cool to lukewarm.

3. Strain clear liquid through a fine wire mesh strainer or cheesecloth draped over a strainer into a container, leaving sediment at bottom to discard. If you haven't used bulgur, just pour clear liquid off as much as possible, without allowing the cloudy sediment to pour.

4. Refrigerate and when the butter hardens, remove the hardened, clarified butter and discard the milky sediment if any remains. Store in a covered glass container in the refrigerator.

Makes 2 cups of clarified butter.

Fatte bi Hommus

GARBANZO BEAN *FATTE*

◆

F*atte* can be made in a variety of combinations. It is the old country way of making great use of broken pieces of dry Arabic bread (*fatte* means broken up). Our family uses this bread in our salad, *fattoush*, which has the same root as the word *fatte*. This version of *fatte*, served as a side dish, was introduced to me by my dear friend Rima, from Tripoli, where the dish is also called *tissaye* and is famous for its excellent cuisine referred to in Lebanon as "Tripoli-style." *Shukran*, Rima!

1½ loaves pita bread
2 cans garbanzo beans, drained
1 quart yogurt
3 cloves garlic
1 teaspoon salt
1 lime, juiced
¼ cup pine nuts
paprika and allspice for garnish
2 tablespoons olive or vegetable oil

1. Toast the pita bread until light brown in a toaster or the oven, and break it into pieces half the size of a regular tortilla chip.

2. Place beans in a pot with fresh water to cover; cook over medium heat until they are really tender and easy to squeeze between your fingers—about fifteen minutes. Drain water and set aside.

3. Meanwhile, mash the garlic with salt into a paste; mix in the lime juice. Add garlic paste to the yogurt and mix well.

4. Sauté the pine nuts in oil until very light brown.

5. Just before serving, spread the pita bread pieces evenly in a 9"x12" glass baking dish and distribute the garbanzo beans evenly over the pita pieces, reserving ¼ cup of the beans for garnishing.

6. Pour yogurt mix over the beans and gently shake the dish until it settles well in all corners, spreading evenly over beans, and covering them completely.

7. Garnish by sprinkling the pine nuts over the top. Make decorative use of the reserved garbanzo beans and sprinkle paprika and allspice to your liking over it all. And Rima, like my mother, says, "Serve it with love!"

Serves 4 to 6.

ALICE'S KITCHEN
IF YOU MAKE IT WITH LOVE, IT WILL BE DELICIOUS!

40

SALSAAT

◆

SAUCES

Delectable sauces are one of the secrets of making our dishes so fantastic. *Falafel,* for example, without the tahini sauce can be dry and bland. Likewise, broiled chicken without our fabulous Lebanese garlic mayonnaise is good but the extra zing of *toum ou zeit* makes it: wow, scrumptious! Our tartar (*taratour*) sauce adds tangy flavor to fresh fish. *Zaatar* is an amazing and unique Lebanese spice mixture that my mother, Alice, calls "brain food." Mixed with olive oil, it is often eaten for breakfast as a dip with Arabic bread—a zesty way to start the day. The sauce is baked on thick Arabic bread, called *tilme bi zaatar.* Read more about *zaatar* in the Herbs and Spices section beginning on page 223.

Our classic Lebanese salad dressing is made with the essential, tasty, and healthy ingredients garlic, lemon, and olive oil that is the heart of our cooking. This dressing can be used in many ways besides salads, such as a dip or dressing for artichokes, asparagus, broccoli, cauliflower, beets, beans, spinach, chard, cucumbers, summer squash, carrots, and other vegetables, or for marinating vegetables, chicken, or fish.

A wooden mortar and pestle is an essential and well-used tool in the Lebanese kitchen—especially for making our incomparable garlic paste, made by pounding minced garlic with salt. A garlic press does not yield the same results. If you're in a huge American hurry making these sauces, you can do the sauces and dressings in a food processor. They can be made ahead and kept for a week or so in the refrigerator, read to use. And remember, if you make it with love, it will be delicious!

Taratour

Tartar tahini sauce

◆

Arich and tasty sauce drizzled over fish, chicken, lamb, *falafel*, sautéed vegetables (*khudra makhluta*), or steamed chard stems. Without the parsley, this sauce is also the base for *hommus* and *baba ghannouj*. Two methods of making this are offered here: the traditional way by hand or in a food processor. This recipe makes 2 cups.

> 2–3 cloves garlic, chopped
> ½ teaspoon salt
> 1 cup tahini (sesame seed butter)
> ¼ cup warm water
> ⅓–½ cup lemon juice
> 2 tablespoons parsley, finely chopped (optional)

In a wooden mortar and pestle, mash garlic with salt into a smooth paste. Spoon tahini into a bowl, stir in warm water, which increases its volume. Slowly stir in lemon juice and garlic paste. Stir in the parsley; taste and adjust seasoning. Add water or lemon if it is too thick to pour.

Quick food processor method

Put all ingredients in processor bowl; pulse until smooth, adding parsley last.

Taratour ma Laban

Yogurt tahini sauce

◆

Our basic *taratour* or tahini sauce with yogurt in it. Follow the recipe above except replace water with ¼ cup of yogurt. This recipe makes 2 cups.

Toum ou Haamid

GARLIC LEMON SAUCE OR DRESSING

◆

Tangy and classically Lebanese, this is our most essential sauce, dressing, and marinade used with chicken, fish, steamed or sautéed vegetables, or potatoes, and is our basic salad (*salata*) dressing. It has tremendous health benefits such as liver cleansing. It can be done in a food processor, but it's best to mash the garlic and salt by hand, making a smooth paste. It can be mixed ahead and refrigerated for a week.

>   2–3 cloves garlic, chopped
>   1 teaspoon salt
>   ¼ cup olive oil
>   ¼ cup lemon juice or ½ teaspoon citric acid

In a wooden mortar and pestle, mash garlic with salt (or citric acid) into a smooth paste. Add lemon juice and olive oil. Taste and adjust flavor adding more garlic, salt, lemon or oil, to your taste. Makes ½ cup.

Laban ou Toum

YOGURT GARLIC SAUCE

◆

This yogurt-based sauce is used on various dishes including the exotic stuffed tripe (*ghamme*) and on simple dishes such as rice, potatoes, chicken, or lamb.

>   2–3 cloves garlic, chopped
>   ½ teaspoon salt
>   2 cups yogurt
>   ¼ cup white vinegar

In a wooden mortar and pestle, mash garlic with salt into a smooth paste. Stir in yogurt and vinegar. Taste and adjust seasoning. This sauce can be made in the food processor as well, being careful to make sure there are not chunks of garlic in the final sauce. It can be made in advance and refrigerated. Makes 2 cups.

Toum ou Zeit

GARLIC SAUCE OR MAYONNAISE

◆

This Lebanese version of the Spanish *aioli* or the Italian *agliolio*, garlic mayonnaise, is fabulous on grilled chicken or sautéed vegetables. Vegetable oil thickens more easily than olive oil, but a little olive oil may be added for flavor after the mixture emulsifies. Or try a very light olive oil for the whole recipe. The amount of garlic depends on the size, freshness, and pungency of the garlic, and varies with personal taste. If you're a garlic lover, use 20!

> 10–20 cloves garlic, peeled
> 1 cup vegetable oil such as sunflower or safflower
>   or ¾ cup vegetable oil plus ¼ cup olive oil
> ½ teaspoon salt
> 2 tablespoons lemon juice
> dash cayenne pepper

Put garlic, salt, cayenne pepper, and lemon juice in food processor or blender and purée until smooth. Very, very slowly—this is the secret—drizzle oil into mixture, continuing to blend. As this blends, it thickens, becoming a creamy mayonnaise irresistible for dipping. Keeps refrigerated for 2 weeks. Makes 2 cups.

Zaatar

ZAATAR WITH OLIVE OIL

◆

A Lebanese favorite for breakfast, the herb mixture *zaatar* (pp. 223–225) said to be a mind-opening food, because of its healthy ingredients. Purchased in Middle Eastern stores, it is mixed with oil and sesame seeds, then baked on Arabic bread (*tilme bi zaatar*) or simply served in a bowl for dipping with bread.

> ½ cup *zaatar* herb mixture
> ¼ cup olive oil (*zeit*)
> 1 tablespoon sesame seeds
> ½ tablespoon sumac (optional)

Mix ingredients together in a shallow bowl. Enjoy! Makes ¾ cup.

ALICE'S KITCHEN

IF YOU MAKE IT WITH LOVE, IT WILL BE DELICIOUS!

Steaming hot soup in back warm memories gathered around the stories of the day, the wintertime brings of our big family dinner table full of laughter, and often silliness. My father, at the head of the table, was surrounded by women—his five daughters, his loving wife, Alice, and her mother, *Sitto*, both of whom literally stood by to make sure we all had enough to eat before they sat down to join us. Occasionally my uncles, Adib and his wife, Aunt Rose, who lived in Tucson, Arizona, and Edmond and his wife, Aunt Adele, who lived nearby, would join us.

We enjoyed very hearty, protein-rich, winter soups that include in their ingredients lamb or chicken, lentils, split peas with rice, and a wonderful soup called *shourbat makhlouta* that has a tablespoon of every kind of bean or grain in your pantry. This is definitely a one-pot meal. And in the summer, we enjoyed lighter soups, such as Mother's classic lentil soup with one of our salads—*tabbouli, fattoush*, my Dad's fabulous tomato salad, or our basic, refreshing *salata*—homemade Arabic bread and *hommus*, yum.

When making soup, I often start with vegetable broth from steaming vegetables or boiling potatoes that I've saved as soup stock in the freezer. This makes the soup more flavorful and provides additional nutrients.

Each recipe serves 4 to 6 as a soup course, unless otherwise indicated. Increase the recipe if it's the main course, and if there are leftovers, all the better!

Shourbat Adas

LENTIL SOUP

◆

Mother's classic lentil soup, so delicious.

      6 cups water or vegetable stock
      1 cup lentils
      1 onion, chopped
      2 cloves garlic, minced
      1 tablespoon olive oil (optional)
      2 celery stalks, chopped
      2 potatoes, diced
      ½ teaspoon salt
      ¼ teaspoon black pepper
      dash cayenne pepper
      ⅓ cup lemon juice
      1–2 cups chopped spinach or chard leaves (optional)

1. Put water, lentils, onion, garlic, olive oil, celery, and potato in a large soup pot; cover and bring to a boil. Turn down heat and simmer for an hour.

2. Add salt, pepper, and cayenne; simmer until lentils are cooked, another 15 minutes. Add spinach or chard just the last 10 minutes so it retains its color and vitamins. Add lemon juice just before serving. Taste and adjust seasoning.

Serves 4 to 6.

ALICE'S KITCHEN
IF YOU MAKE IT WITH LOVE, IT WILL BE DELICIOUS!

Shourbat Adas ou Haamid

LEMONY LENTIL SOUP WITH CHARD

◆

Down the hill, nestled in the valley below Douma, the town of Kfar Hilda sits beautifully backgrounded by the distant blue Mediterranean Sea. On a recent trip to Douma, friends took me to visit Kfar Hilda's ancient Greek Orthodox monastery, Mari Hanna. There, we were graciously served a refreshing, freshly-made juice from a fruit called *tout*, mulberry, as guests of *Abouna* Touma and *Um* Mariam, who are restoring the monastery, which had been damaged by a wartime militia. The ancient monastery and garden were being transformed into a spiritual and temporal oasis that I was blessed to enter.

That month, a Romanian icon painter was painting his splendid vision on the chapel's six-foot-thick walls. A few days later I returned there, on foot from Douma, about five kilometers. *Um Mariam* invited me to stay for lunch that included this heavenly soup made without *zeit* (oil), as their monastic practice calls for one day a week of their vegetarian diet to be completely fat-free; boiled potatoes with the herb mixture *zaatar* sprinkled over them; Arabic bread; and their own superb fig jam. I shared a simply divine, memorable meal with the icon painter and a monk. Once home, I created this version to replicate it.

6 cups water or vegetable stock
¾ cup lentils, rinsed
1 onion, chopped
6 cloves garlic, minced
salt and black pepper
dash cayenne pepper
1–2 cups chopped chard
 or spinach leaves, rinsed, drained, and chopped
½ cup lemon juice

1. In a large covered soup pot, bring to a boil and then simmer together the water, lentils, onion, and garlic for 1 hour.
2. Add salt, pepper, and cayenne; continue simmering until lentils are cooked. Add lemon juice and greens. Cook briefly until greens are bright in color and tender. Taste and adjust seasoning. Serve hot.

Serves 4 to 6.

Shourbat Adas ou Rishta

Lentil and Noodle Soup

◆

Another wonderful lentil soup to be enjoyed in winter because of the hearty addition of homemade noodles. Of course, you can substitute 8 ounces of commercial noodles since this will take less time, or you can make the noodle dough ahead and refrigerate it. In the old country, when Alice was growing up, they made their own noodles, using basic bread dough or flour and water with a little salt, which is actually quite easy to do, fun, and tasty!

> 7 cups water or vegetable stock
> 1 cup lentils, rinsed
> 1 onion, finely chopped
> ⅓ cup olive oil
> 1 teaspoon salt
> ¼ teaspoon cayenne pepper
> ½ teaspoon ground cumin
> ¼ teaspoon sumac or 3 tablespoons lemon juice

HOMEMADE NOODLES

> 1 cup flour
> ½ cup water
> ½ teaspoon salt

1. Put water, lentils, onion, oil, salt, and pepper into a deep soup pot. Cover and bring to a boil.
2. Reduce heat and simmer for 1½ hours.
3. Meanwhile, make noodles by placing flour in a mixing bowl and mix in salt and water. Knead well, divide into two balls, dust with flour, and let stand about 15 minutes, or refrigerate until ready to roll out, just before the soup is ready.
4. On a clean, well-floured surface, roll dough out to ⅛" thick. Cut into strips ½"x2" long with a knife or pizza cutter and add to soup right away—timing it just 10 minutes before soup is done.
5. When lentil soup is almost done, stir in cumin and sumac. Then add noodles a few at a time and cook for 10 more minutes until noodles are done. Add lemon juice, taste, and correct seasoning. Serve and enjoy.

Serves 4 to 6.

Shourbat Bazella ou Riz

SPLIT PEA AND RICE SOUP

◆

Split pea soup is one of my favorites, and our family recipe with rice provides a protein-rich combination that is wonderful with or without the meat. If you use brown rice, it can be added at the same time as the peas, as it takes longer to cook than white rice. I have made this soup without puréeing it, just cooking it a little longer, and it's still excellent, so if you're short on time like so many of us are these days, you can skip that step. Mother's version includes the ham shank, white rice, and the puréeing.

 1 quart water or vegetable stock
 1 ham shank (optional)
 1 onion, finely chopped
 ⅛ cup olive oil
 ¼ teaspoon salt
 ¼ teaspoon black pepper
 1 cup dried split peas, rinsed
 ¼ cup rice, soaked and rinsed
 2 stalks celery with tops, chopped
 ¼ cup lemon juice

   1. In a deep soup pot, place water, peas, ham shank, onion, olive oil, salt, and pepper. Cover, bring to a boil, then reduce heat and simmer ½ hour.
   2. Add rice and celery. Continue to simmer another ½ hour, stirring once or twice and adding water if necessary.
   3. Lift ham bone from soup; remove ham from bone, cutting into small pieces, and set aside, discarding the bone.
   4. Press soup through a coarse sieve with a mallet or purée in a food processor. This step is optional if you don't have time.
   5. Return soup to the pot, adding ham pieces; let cook 10 more minutes. Add lemon juice at the last minute, taste and add seasoning as needed. Serve hot with pita chips or crackers.

Serves 4 to 6.

Shourbat Bazella

SPLIT PEA SOUP

◆

Sitt Aminé, my dear friend and mother of Jim Hanna, an exceptional cook from the village of Amar, Syria, just across the northern border of Lebanon, made this split pea soup, which I love. Probably it is her generous addition of garlic in this that differentiates it from Mom's great split pea soup. Also, it has no oil but is very tasty and not fattening! Try both of these recipes and see which you prefer.

If you choose to use brown rice, add it at the beginning, as it takes longer to cook. Sitt Aminé also shared with me her way of making spinach pies in a less labor-intensive way, which is included with our spinach pie recipe. Another specialty of hers was a fabulous *shanklish* cheese, called *'arishe* in Amar, that was amply seasoned with cayenne pepper, aged in a crock for several months, and then rolled in *zaatar* before serving—a strong pungent cheese that I acquired a serious addiction to!

> 4 cups water or vegetable stock
> 1 cup dried split peas, rinsed
> 1 onion, finely chopped
> ¼ teaspoon salt
> ¼ teaspoon black pepper
> 4–5 whole cloves garlic
> ¼ cup rice, soaked and rinsed
> 2 stalks celery with tops, chopped
> 2 tablespoons lemon juice (optional)

1. In a medium soup pot, place water, onion, peas, garlic, salt, and pepper. Cover, bring to a boil, then reduce heat and simmer ½ hour.

2. Add rice and celery. Continue to simmer ½ hour, stirring once or twice and adding water if necessary.

3. Add lemon juice at the last minute. Turn off heat, taste and add seasoning as needed. Serve hot with pita chips or crackers.

Serves 4.

ALICE'S KITCHEN
IF YOU MAKE IT WITH LOVE, IT WILL BE DELICIOUS!

Shourbat Djej ou Riz

CHICKEN AND RICE SOUP

◆

Nutritious and satisfying, this soup can be a meal unto itself, especially if you are not feeling well—as in the old adage of the healing properties of chicken soup. Mother made this classic Lebanese soup with either rice or clusters of vermicelli noodles broken up into small pieces and added to the broth. Add one of our Lebanese salads, or fresh cut vegetables, a little Arabic bread, pita chips, or crackers, and you have a perfect, light meal.

1 whole chicken
1 quart water
3 cinnamon sticks
5 black peppercorns
6 whole allspice kernels
½ cup rice or 2–3 vermicelli clusters
1 small can tomato sauce
½ teaspoon ground cinnamon
¼ teaspoon black pepper
½ cup chopped parsley
⅓ cup lemon juice

1. Rinse whole chicken with water; then rub it with salt and baking soda thoroughly before rinsing well again.

2. Place chicken in a large pot and cover with water. Add cinnamon sticks that you have broken in half, allspice, and black peppercorns. Cover and bring to a boil. Skim any residue from top; reduce heat and simmer 15 to 20 minutes.

3. Remove from heat; lift chicken from broth and set aside to cool. Strain broth and place in clean soup pot. Add rice or vermicelli, tomato sauce, cinnamon, and black pepper to the soup stock. Cover and bring to a boil, then simmer 10 minutes for vermicelli or 20 minutes until rice is done (45 minutes for brown rice).

4. Debone chicken and add to the soup with chopped parsley and lemon juice, cooking 5 more minutes to heat through. Taste and adjust seasoning. Serve hot with pita chips or crackers.

Serves 6 to 8.

Shourbat Khudra ma Djej

CHICKEN VEGETABLE SOUP

◆

Mother's chicken vegetable soup was a family favorite. The clear, flavorful broth combined with a variety of colorful vegetables makes a hearty yet light soup with nutrition in every bite. Very little chicken is used in this recipe—just enough to flavor the broth.

1 chicken back, neck, and wings
2 quarts water or vegetable stock
2 cinnamon sticks
5 peppercorns
1 onion, chopped
3 stalks celery, chopped
4 cups chopped mixed vegetables (fresh or frozen
    carrots, corn, string beans, peas, lima beans)
2 potatoes, diced
1 quart whole tomatoes, chopped
    or 1 small can tomato sauce
½ teaspoon salt
½ teaspoon black pepper
¼ teaspoon ground cinnamon
2 tablespoons lemon juice
½ cup parsley, chopped

1. Rub chicken parts with baking soda and salt. Rinse well and place in a large soup pot with water, cinnamon, and peppercorns. Cover and bring to a boil. Reduce heat and simmer for 15 minutes.

2. Remove from heat and strain broth into a clean pot. Set aside chicken. Add all vegetables, tomato, salt, pepper, and cinnamon. Cover and bring to a boil.

3. Reduce heat and simmer for an hour. Meanwhile, remove chicken from bones and discard them. Just before serving add chicken, lemon juice, and parsley to soup and heat through. Serve hot with pita chips or crackers.

Serves 6 to 8.

Shourbat Lahm ou Riz

Lamb meatball, tomato, and rice soup

◆

Although lamb and chicken were the primary meats in our Lebanese household, this soup was one that *Sitto* and Mother only made once in a while for special occasions. Definitely protein-rich and flavorful with lamb meatballs, this is a hearty and thick winter soup.

> ½ pound ground lamb
> ½ teaspoon cinnamon, divided
> ½ teaspoon salt, divided
> ½ teaspoon black pepper, divided
> 2 tablespoons clarified butter
> 6 cups water or vegetable stock
> ½ cup rice
> 1 small can tomato sauce
> dash cayenne
> ½ cup parsley, chopped

1. Mix lamb with half of the cinnamon, salt, and pepper. Roll into balls about the diameter of a quarter.

2. Heat clarified butter in a deep soup pot. Add lamb and gently brown, stirring frequently.

3. Add water, rice, salt, pepper, cinnamon, cayenne, and tomato sauce. Cover and bring to a boil. Lower heat and simmer until rice is cooked, about 20 minutes, 45 minutes for brown rice. Stir in chopped parsley; taste and adjust seasoning. Serve hot with Arabic bread, pita chips, or crackers.

Serves 4 to 6.

Shourbat Makhlouta

Mixed bean and grain soup

◆

Thick and porridge-like, this hearty soup is made with a combination of each kind of bean or grain on hand in your pantry. A *kamshe*—small handful—of grains and beans listed below or any others you have on hand, or that you would like to procure just for this soup, slowly cooks into a nutritious, protein-rich soup. The more variety, the richer it will be. Truly filling, and definitely a winter soup.

7 cups water or vegetable stock
1½ cups mixed beans and grains
    1 tablespoon of each: *'amah* (wheat berries),
    bulgur, lentils, brown rice, white rice, split peas,
    beans such as: black, fava, garbanzo, red, pink, white,
    or pinto; barley, whole dried corn
2 onions, chopped
2 cloves garlic, minced
⅛ cup olive oil
1½ teaspoons salt
½ teaspoon black pepper
⅛ teaspoon cayenne pepper
⅓ cup lemon juice (optional)

1. Rinse grains and beans. Place all ingredients in soup pot with water and bring to a boil.

2. Lower heat and simmer for 1½ to 3 hours, until grains are cooked, stirring frequently and adding water if needed.

3. Just before serving, add lemon juice; taste and adjust seasoning. Serve hot with Arabic bread or pita chips, cut fresh vegetables and olives.

Serves 4 to 6.

ALICE'S KITCHEN
IF YOU MAKE IT WITH LOVE, IT WILL BE DELICIOUS!

Shourbat Kibbet Heeli

Vegetarian Lentil *Kibbe* Soup

◆

Areal old-country, mountain village comfort food, this lentil-based soup has po-tato-bulgur fritters as dumplings—yum! A food processor, grinder, or food mill is useful in creating this old family recipe that is very healthy and filling. *Kibbe* is like a meatball with bulgur; in this case it's vegetarian and is fried. Tasty!

Lentil soup recipe (p. 46) without potatoes and olive oil

Kibbe balls

2 medium potatoes, boiled and peeled
¾ cup fine #0 bulgur (*burghul*), soaked and rinsed
½ teaspoon each salt and black pepper
½ teaspoon ground cumin
½ onion, quartered
½–1 cup flour
½ cup olive oil, for frying
¼ cup parsley, finely chopped for garnish

1. Make basic lentil soup recipe, omitting potatoes and oil.
2. While soup is cooking, grind above ingredients except for olive oil, parsley, and flour into a large bowl and mix well. If using a food processor, start with onions, then potatoes and purée. Transfer to a bowl, add bulgur and season-ings, mixing well. Add flour until the consistency is easily rolled into a small ball.
3. Heat oil in frying pan. Roll bulgur-potato mixture into small balls, and fry on each side until golden brown. Place on paper towels to drain.
4. When lentils in soup are tender, add *kibbe* balls to soup and cook for about 5 minutes more. Garnish with chopped parsley and serve.

Serves 4 to 6.

Shourbat Kishk

KISHK SOUP

◆

Kishk is a traditional Lebanese food made by villagers in the summer for winter use. Made of bulgur (*burghul*), combined with yogurt (*laban*), and then sun-dried, it is laboriously ground between the palms of the hand into a coarse flour called *kishk*. It can be purchased in Middle Eastern grocery stores.

This recipe is for a winter soup that can be made with potatoes instead of lamb as a vegetarian version, both using *kishk*. The flavor of *kishk* is tart because of the yogurt, making the soup interesting and full of protein. My favorite way to eat *kishk* is baked on Arabic bread (*tilme* p. 183).

>2 tablespoons clarified butter
>1 onion, finely chopped
>½ pound ground lamb
>   or 3 potatoes, peeled and diced
>1 cup *kishk*
>1 quart water or vegetable stock
>3 cloves garlic
>½ teaspoon salt
>1 tablespoon dried spearmint

1. Heat butter in a deep pot. Add onions and sauté until golden brown. Add lamb and brown for 10 minutes, stirring frequently.
2. Stir in *kishk* and cook for 2 more minutes. Gradually add water, stirring constantly to dissolve *kishk*, removing any lumps that form. Continue cooking for 15 minutes more.
3. Mash garlic into a paste with salt. Stir in dried spearmint and add to the *kishk*. Serve immediately.

Serves 4 to 6.

ALICE'S KITCHEN
IF YOU MAKE IT WITH LOVE, IT WILL BE DELICIOUS!

SALATAT

◆

SALADS

Lebanon, a fertile land in a temperate, Mediterranean climate, has a glorious array of vegetables and fruits—the size and quality cause the Lebanese to gloat. Remember, this is the land of milk and honey, grapes and figs, and the biggest potatoes I've ever seen! Lebanese mountain tomatoes are similar to the heirloom types that are coming back into popularity here in our farmers' markets. Middle Eastern cucumbers are small, crisp, and rarely bitter. Every summer, I plant several varieties to have a ready supply for snacks all day. And they're great for dipping into *hommus*!

Kitchen gardens are typical in the villages of Lebanon—my mother and *Sitto* carried this tradition to America, growing parsley, mint, tomatoes, cucumbers, radishes, carrots, and Lebanese squash—special Middle Eastern varieties that were not available here until recently.

Fresh seasonal vegetables are always on the table, from breakfast through supper, if not made into a salad. This is what makes our cuisine healthy and appealing.

Salads are an essential part of the Lebanese diet all year and there are many varieties of *salata*. Alice's *salata* and variations on it are excellent. Our most famous salad is *tabbouli*, but *fattoush* is quickly catching on. The recipes here are authentic, different from how *tabbouli* or *fattoush* in some American delis might look. Our *tabbouli* provides a superb way to consume a large amount of fresh, iron-rich parsley in a most delicious salad. Winter salads, including a light cabbage coleslaw and potato salad, and summer salads illustrate our love of healthy, raw, organic fresh vegetables. My father's tomato and garlic salad is fabulous, made with vine-ripened tomatoes. Be sure to try this in the summertime—you won't be disappointed!

Recipes serve 4 to 6 when served as a salad course, unless otherwise noted.

Tabbouli

LEBANESE PARSLEY, MINT, AND BULGUR SALAD

◆

Fresh whole romaine leaves became boats for *tabbouli* when I was little—tidy containers delivering the salad straight to my mouth. We picked up the lettuce filled with *tabbouli*, like the tacos we loved so much from our kindred Mexican culture. Mama tells me that in the old country, young tender grape leaves are used to scoop *tabbouli*, much as we use Arabic bread. In Lebanon, cabbage leaves are presented as *tabbouli* utensils. There are many possibilities to try before resorting to a fork!

Authentic Lebanese *tabbouli* has more parsley than any other ingredient. Either Italian flat-leaved parsley or curly parsley, finely chopped, accompanied by bulgur (*burghul*), mint, tomatoes, onion, lemon—providing so much tasty nutrition, especially iron, in every bite! *Tabbouli* even tastes great the next day, so if you happen to have any left, store it in the refrigerator to marinate.

For a winter version of *tabbouli*, when fresh garden parsley is not as available in our cold mountain village, the Lebanese make *safsouf*, a variation on *tabbouli* with much more *burghul* and only dried mint. See recipe for *safsouf*, following this. Often we see a bulgur-dominant version of *safsouf* called *tabbouli*. Here's the real thing!

¼ cup #0 or #1 bulgur, soaked and rinsed
    use the smallest grind bulgur available
¼ cup olive oil
½ teaspoon salt
¼ teaspoon cayenne pepper
½ cup lemon juice
4 tomatoes, finely chopped
2 bunches parsley, very finely chopped
1 bunch spearmint, finely chopped
1 bunch green onions
    or ½ cup yellow onion, finely chopped
1 bunch romaine lettuce, cabbage, or fresh grape leaves,
    for garnish and scooping

    1. Rinse bulgur in a strainer, drain, and place in bowl. If bulgur is coarse, soak it for 15 minutes in warm water first; then rinse and drain. Add olive oil, lemon juice, and seasonings to bulgur; set aside to marinate. Chop tomatoes into ½" cubes and layer over bulgur so the juices absorb into bulgur.

ALICE'S KITCHEN

IF YOU MAKE IT WITH LOVE, IT WILL BE DELICIOUS!

2. Mince onions, parsley, and mint; layer them over the tomatoes. If you're making this ahead, cover and chill until ready to mix.

3. Using clean hands, mix very well. Taste and add seasoning as necessary—we love our *tabbouli* lemony and tart. If it's dry, add more oil or lemon. Chill 15 to 30 minutes before serving.

4. Arrange lettuce or cabbage leaves around the perimeter of a bowl or platter. Toss *tabbouli* again and then place it in the center and serve.

Alternate method for mixing *Tabbouli*

An alternate way to mix *tabbouli* is to place the drained bulgur in a deep bowl, add seasonings, and layer on the tomatoes and other vegetables. Then about 15 minutes before serving, add olive oil and lemon juice. Toss well, chill, and serve.

Serves 4 to 6.

Safsouf

WINTER *TABBOULI* SALAD

◆

A winter version of *tabbouli*, *safsouf*, uses much more bulgur (*burghul*); yellow onions rather than green; dried spearmint rather than fresh; and includes garbanzo beans, which adds protein. Neither tomatoes nor parsley are used since they were not readily available in Douma winters. *Safsouf* is traditionally eaten for lunch with Arabic bread.

1 cup #0 or #1 bulgur, soaked and rinsed
½ cup dry garbanzo beans, soaked overnight
1 onion, finely chopped
½ cup whole dried spearmint leaves (loosely packed)
    or 2 tablespoons powdered spearmint
    or ½ cup fresh spearmint, finely chopped, if available

DRESSING

¼ cup olive oil
⅓ cup lemon juice
1 tablespoon sumac
½ teaspoon salt
⅛ teaspoon cayenne pepper

1. Cook dry garbanzo beans in 2 cups of water for 1 hour or until just tender, but not soft as for *hommus*.

2. Meanwhile, rinse and drain bulgur. If the bulgur is more coarse than the finest size (#0 or #1) available, soak it in water while the beans are cooking and then drain it. Chop onion and add to bulgur in a bowl along with salt, sumac, and cayenne.

3. Place drained chick peas on a clean, dry surface like a kitchen towel. Gently run the rolling pin over them to split them in two. Add them to the bulgur.

4. Rub the whole dried mint leaves between your palms over the bowl or add fresh or powdered mint. Mix well and stir in lemon and oil. Toss again; taste and adjust seasoning. Chill and serve.

Serves 4 to 6.

60

ALICE'S KITCHEN
IF YOU MAKE IT WITH LOVE, IT WILL BE DELICIOUS!

Fattoush

LEBANESE CRISP BREAD SALAD

◆

Another memorable traditional Lebanese salad much less known than *tabbouli*, yet equally fabulous, is *fattoush*. No doubt *fattoush* originated long ago, as did croutons, to use up dry, leftover bread by tossing it into *salata*. Mother heats broken pieces of *khubz marqouq*, Arabic bread, in the oven turned on low for 20 minutes and there it remains overnight to cool and crisp for *fattoush* or to store for later use. Bread toasts quickly in a hotter oven; keep your eye on it. Or use pita chips.

A savory variation in Mother's *fattoush*—marinating onions in sumac—comes via our friends, the Haddads, also from Douma. Their exquisite Lebanese restaurant, Al-Amir, introduced *fattoush* to Portland in 1988 and sumac in *fattoush* to me, which gives it a tart zest. From wonderful Al Anadalou restaurant in the Hamra district of Beirut, where I dined in 1996, comes the festive addition of fresh pomegranate rubies. My *trabalsiyyeh* friend Rima uses concentrated pomegranate juice in place of lemon juice—Tripoli-style—an example typical of regional variations. It gives a deep color and tartness to the salad, and is quite delicious. Sumac is used only with lemon juice, not pomegranate. Either way, *fattoush* is an excellent salad. Toss salad just a few minutes before serving, so the bread doesn't become soggy.

3–4 tomatoes, finely chopped
1 medium cucumber, quartered lengthwise and chopped
3 green onions, finely chopped
½ head romaine lettuce, chopped
1 cup parsley, finely chopped
½ cup fresh spearmint, finely chopped
    or 2 tablespoons dried spearmint
½ cup celery and celery tops, finely chopped
½ cup purslane (*baqle*) (optional)
½ cup sumac onions (optional, see following recipe)
2 loaves of crisp dried or toasted Arabic bread
¼ cup pomegranate seeds (optional, and festive!)

DRESSING

½ teaspoon salt
¼ teaspoon black pepper
dash cayenne pepper
¼ cup olive oil
⅓ cup lemon juice

ALICE'S KITCHEN
SALADS

1. Put chopped tomatoes, greens, cucumbers, and onions into a large bowl. Break Arabic bread into bite-sized pieces over these vegetables and add pomegranate seeds. If using dried spearmint, crush it between your palms over the top.

2. Drizzle oil slowly and evenly over the bread, then add salt, pepper and lemon juice. Toss and set aside for 5 minutes before serving so bread can marinate and soften slightly. Taste and adjust seasoning. Serve within 10 minutes so bread doesn't become soggy.

Serves 4 to 6.

Bassel ou Summaq

ONION WITH SUMAC MARINADE

◆

During the months when lemons are not in season, tart-tasting sumac may be used as a substitute. When combined with onions and allowed to marinate, the sumac transforms the raw onion, removing its sharpness and bite; the mixture adds a tartness to *tabbouli* or *fattoush,* replacing lemon juice with sumac's own unique red zesty flavor. Beyond adding it to salads, *bassle ou summaq* is an excellent garnish for other dishes such as *falafel, hommus,* or *lahm mishwi,* and is tasty simply eaten with bread.

½ Spanish onion, julienne-cut
2 tablespoons sumac

Toss sliced onion with several tablespoons of sumac in a small bowl and set aside several hours before using. That's it.

Makes ½ cup.

Salata

Real Lebanese salad

◆

S*alata* just means "salad." This is a classic, simple salad that one would find probably anywhere in Lebanon during the season of these vegetables. Served with lentils and rice (*mjaddrah*), shish kebab, most other entrées, soups, or just on its own, it is simply delicious.

Baqle (purslane) is considered by some as a garden weed; however, it is a zesty addition to our salads that is rich in omega-3 fatty acids, adding nutrition as well as a fresh, tart flavor and crisp texture to salad. Every summer, it just shows up in my garden in Portland and as it did in our Los Angeles garden, too, when I was growing up!

3 large salad tomatoes, chopped
2 cucumbers, thinly sliced
8 sprigs spearmint, finely chopped
6 sprigs parsley, finely chopped
3 sprigs purslane (*baqle*), stemmed (optional)
1 green onion, finely chopped

DRESSING

1 clove garlic
½ teaspoon salt
¼ cup lemon juice
2 tablespoons olive oil
dash black pepper

　　1. Peel and chop garlic. In a bowl, mash it into a paste with salt. Stir in lemon juice and olive oil.
　　2. Place chopped vegetables in a wide or deep bowl. Toss with dressing and add a little black pepper. Taste and adjust seasoning. Enjoy with black olives, feta cheese, and Arabic bread.

Serves 4.

Salatat Elias

MY FATHER'S TOMATO SALAD

◆

Days when my mother wasn't around were a special treat because my father, Elias, would make us lunch. His specialty was this tomato salad, which tasted best in the summer, when made with garden-ripened tomatoes. It is laden with garlic, so eat it with friends. The bite-sized chunks of tomato are scooped up with Arabic bread or French bread that absorbs some of the juice. Serve with feta cheese, olives, and cucumber strips for a perfect summer picnic. Thanks, dear Dad!

>   3 cloves garlic
>   ½ teaspoon salt
>   5 garden-ripened tomatoes
>   ⅛ cup olive oil
>   ½ bunch fresh spearmint, stemmed, finely chopped
>   3 rounds of Arabic bread

1. Peel and chop garlic. In a bowl, mash it into a paste with salt. We like using a wooden mortar and pestle. Cut tomatoes into bite-sized pieces and add them with their juice to the bowl.

2. Add olive oil and spearmint; toss. Marinate for at least 15 minutes, if possible. A half hour in the refrigerator is perfect. Taste with bread and add seasoning if necessary.

Serves 4.

Salatat Alice

ALICE'S SALAD

◆

Alice's *salata* is the one Mother makes most frequently and is more like salads in America because of the lettuce and celery, which are not as common in Lebanese salads. Serve with lentils and rice (*mjaddrah*), other dishes, or on its own—it's great.

½ bunch romaine lettuce, chopped
3 large salad tomatoes, chopped
2 cucumbers, thinly sliced
2 stalks celery with tops, chopped
2 green onions, chopped
8 sprigs spearmint, finely chopped
6 sprigs parsley, finely chopped
3 sprigs purslane (*baqle*), stemmed (optional)

DRESSING

2 cloves garlic
½ teaspoon salt
⅓ cup lemon juice
¼ cup olive oil
black pepper

1. Peel and chop garlic. In a bowl, mash it into a paste with salt. Stir in lemon juice and oil.
2. Place chopped vegetables in bowl. Toss with dressing and add a little black pepper. Taste and adjust seasoning, adding more lemon or garlic if desired.

Serves 4 to 6.

Laban ou Khyar

YOGURT AND CUCUMBER SALAD

◆

Cool and refreshing in the summer, this native Mediterranean salad with its Asian counterparts from Greek *tzatziki* to Indian *raita* is a perfect complement to spicy meals any time of the year, or very satisfying on its own. We always peeled the waxy store-bought cucumbers, but homegrown, fresh cucumbers just need to be rinsed and sliced.

> 2–3 cloves garlic
> ½ teaspoon salt
> 2–3 cucumbers, peeled or not, thinly sliced
> 1 pint plain yogurt (*laban*)
> 2 tablespoons dried spearmint leaves
> 1 teaspoon lemon juice

1. Peel and chop garlic. In a medium-sized bowl, mash it into a paste with salt. Add cucumbers, yogurt, and garlic. Mix well. Crush the mint into a powder between your palms over the mixture, removing any stems.

2. Add lemon juice; mix, taste, and adjust seasoning. Chill the salad briefly before serving.

Serves 4 to 6.

Salatat Batata

LEBANESE POTATO SALAD

◆

A perfect spring potato salad with fresh green mint, parsley, and lemon. Served warm, at room temperature, or chilled, our visually appealing salad complements fish, green vegetables, eggs, kebabs, or soups and is a delightful change from heavy, creamy potato salads.

4 medium potatoes, rinsed
½ cup parsley, finely chopped
⅓ cup spearmint, finely chopped
⅓ cup chopped green onions
½ teaspoon salt
¼ teaspoon black pepper
dash of cayenne pepper
⅛ cup olive oil
⅓ cup lemon juice

1. Boil whole potatoes until they are just tender, being careful not to over-cook—for about 20 to 30 minutes in water.

2. Lift them out of the water and set them aside to cool, reserving the cooking water for use as soup stock.

3. When potatoes are cool enough to handle, peel, dice and put them into a bowl. Add chopped greens, seasoning, olive oil and lemon juice, and mix well. Taste and adjust seasoning. Chill and serve, or serve warm or at room temperature—each of these options for serving temperature yields a different result! Cold would be good for a warm summer day. Warm would be great on a chilly day or night with a bowl of soup.

Serves 4 to 6.

Salatat Sbanikh

SPINACH SALAD

◆

Healthy year-round, this salad is tart and fresh. It makes a wonderful complement to our potato salads. In addition to salads, Mom and *Sitto* used vitamin-rich spinach many ways: steamed, sautéed, in spinach pies, and in soups.

> 1 bunch spinach, torn into bite-sized pieces
> 3 green onions, chopped
> 2 cloves garlic
> ¼ teaspoon salt
> ⅓ cup lemon juice
> ¼ cup olive oil
> ¼ teaspoon black pepper
> dash cayenne pepper
> ½ cup chopped walnuts (optional)

1. Rinse, drain, and tear or chop spinach into a salad bowl. Add green onions and walnuts.

2. Peel and chop garlic, place in a small bowl, and mash into a paste with salt. Stir in pepper, lemon juice, and oil.

3. Pour dressing over greens, toss, taste and adjust seasoning. Serve immediately.

Serves 4 to 6.

ALICE'S KITCHEN

IF YOU MAKE IT WITH LOVE, IT WILL BE DELICIOUS!

Salatat Malfouf

CABBAGE SALAD OR LEBANESE COLESLAW

◆

Crisp and tangy, unlike creamy coleslaw, this salad is light and keeps well for a couple of days refrigerated, even with dressing, because it marinates. Mother loves vegetables chopped very finely, and in this salad the cabbage is indeed shredded.

½ head large cabbage, shredded
½ bunch parsley, finely chopped
5 green onions, finely chopped
3 tablespoons dried spearmint, crushed

DRESSING

1 large clove garlic
¼ teaspoon salt
⅓ cup lemon juice
¼ cup olive oil

1. Peel and chop garlic. In a bowl, mash it into a paste with salt. Mix lemon and oil with garlic paste.

2. Toss greens together in a medium-sized bowl. Crush dried mint over the top between your palms, removing any stems. Pour dressing over greens and toss. Taste and adjust seasoning. Chill and serve.

Serves 4 to 6.

Salatat Baqle

PURSLANE SALAD

◆

Many cultures besides Arabic eat *baqle* and consider it more than a weed. Called purslane in English, *baqle* is an herb that is high in Vitamin C and an anti-oxidant omega-3 fatty acid, which is said to be beneficial in reducing the risk of heart disease and preventing cancer. It is free for the taking in gardens from Mexico, where the Spanish name is *verdolaga* and it is cooked in a stew with meat, to the Pacific Northwest. Its lemony flavor and crisp, succulent leaves make it a zesty and unusual addition to any salad. In this recipe, it is the main attraction.

1 large clove garlic
¼ teaspoon salt
¼ cup lemon juice
⅛ cup olive oil
1 cup purslane (*baqle*)
¼ cup parsley, finely chopped
¼ cup spearmint, finely chopped
2 tomatoes, finely chopped

1. Peel and chop garlic. In a bowl, mash it into a paste with salt. Mix lemon and oil with garlic paste.
2. Put chopped vegetables together in medium bowl. Pour dressing over, toss, taste and adjust seasoning. Chill and serve.

Serves 2 to 4.

Salatat Shmandar

Beet salad

◆

Earthy and colorful, beet salad is tasty, easy to make, nutritious, and complements many dishes.

3–4 whole beets
1 large clove garlic
¼ teaspoon salt
⅓ cup lemon juice
2 tablespoons olive oil
2 green onions

1. Steam beets in a little water until tender.
2. While they are steaming, peel and chop garlic. In a bowl, mash it into a paste with salt. Mix lemon and oil with garlic paste.
3. Chop green onions. When beets are done and cool enough to handle, slice them into wedges and place in a bowl. Toss with scallions and dressing. Serve warm or cold.

Serves 4.

Salatat Khyar

CUCUMBER SALAD

◆

Cucumbers are a favorite Middle Eastern vegetable: crunchy, crisp, cool, full of moisture, and an excellent natural diuretic. They are perfect snack food and so refreshing in many salads, including this one, especially in summer when they are in season.

Middle Eastern cucumbers include several varieties quite different from those in the West. Armenian cucumbers (*miiti*) are light green, crisp, and slightly sweet, with slightly fuzzy skin that doesn't need to be peeled; the dark green but thin-skinned Persian or Middle Eastern are another type: small, firm, very crisp, rarely bitter, and they don't need to be peeled. Mother purchases small pickling cucumbers, as they come the closest to the Middle Eastern types in regular supermarkets.

If you can find Middle Eastern varieties in local farmers' markets, try them, or better yet, find seeds in catalogs and grow your own. They are very prolific, and allow you to have the freshest quality and choice by picking them at just the right size, and you can grow them organically.

> 3–4 small cucumbers, Middle Eastern varieties if available
> 2 cloves garlic
> ½ teaspoon salt
> ⅓ cup lemon juice
> 2 tablespoons olive oil
> 2 green onions
> 2 tablespoons parsley, finely chopped
> 1 tablespoon spearmint, finely chopped

1. Slice cucumbers into little rounds, or quarters and put into a salad bowl.
2. Peel and chop garlic, placing it in a small bowl or use a wooden mortar and pestle, and mash it into a paste with salt. Add lemon and oil to garlic paste.
3. Chop green onions, parsley, and mint, putting them on top of cucumbers. Add garlic-lemon dressing and toss. Chill and serve.

Serves 4.

GHANAM

◆

LAMB

G*hanam*, sheep, have been grazing our ancestral land for centuries along with goats. The role of the shepherd is significant from Biblical times: pastoral mountain scenes, feasts of roast lamb, luxurious and sturdy lambswool clothing, and exquisite woven rugs—these all find their source in the venerable lamb.

Sheep milk makes excellent yogurt and cheese. The fat stored in the exceptionally large tails of Lebanese sheep was prized in cooking for its flavor and preservative qualities. In the old days, small amounts of lamb were coarsely ground, then slowly simmered with seasonings in the tail fat (*dehen*). When cooled, the lard-like mixture, *ourma*, as it was called, preserved the meat for winter use prior to the availability of electricity and refrigeration. This flavorful mixture of meat and fat, *ourma,* was added to other dishes, imparting a savory flavor, without using much meat. In the mountains and villages of the old country, lamb was the meat of choice. Goat meat (*'anzi*), leaner and less tender, was more affordable and was substituted for lamb in the same recipes. Goat milk was primarily used as a beverage, or for making cheese and *laban*.

Lamb, goat, and chicken are the primary meats of Lebanon, used sparingly as in other Asian cuisines. Urban, coastal Lebanese eat beef that is locally raised and much less expensive than the mountain sheep or goat meat.

Mother remembers just once that her grandmother raised their own lamb to have butchered. When she was growing up in the early part of the 1900s, lamb was butchered twice weekly in Douma. The butcher would spread the word through town and take orders from families. The fresh meat would then be delivered to their door! Nowadays in Douma, the butcher daily prepares fresh lamb and goat meat since electricity and refrigeration are available.

In Lebanon, meat is slaughtered in the Halal manner—similar to Kosher, which is more humane to the animal and is better for the consumer. This process renders a very different meat or beef, for example, from American beef in color, texture, and flavor, due to the freshness and the method of butchering.

Many dishes were developed to use the entire lamb—including brains, tripe, tongue, eyes, testicles, and feet. Kidney and liver are eaten raw; the famous raw Lebanese *kibbe nayye* uses parts of the leg.

When we were growing up in California, Mother and *Sitto* painstakingly cut legs of lamb purchased in supermarkets into appropriate cuts for the dishes they wished to prepare—so important to them was the careful removing of fat, described in the next pages, that causes the unappealing odor and flavor that westerners often associate with lamb. Purchasing pre-packaged ground lamb or mutton results in strong-tasting dishes with lamb flavor that is too pungent. To avoid this, purchase cuts of lamb and remove the fat yourself; then you can chop or mince it.

If you have a butcher you trust, have the butcher remove the fat and grind it for you. If you need only a small quantity, such as a cup or two of lamb: buy lean chops; remove any fat; cut into stew-sized pieces, chop finely, or mince. And buy sustainably grown lamb. If you do prepare your own lamb, allow plenty of time for this labor-intensive but worthwhile task. Often Mother and *Sitto* would cut the meat and freeze it, ready for later use. Smart.

WHERE'S THE BEEF?

An alternative to this labor-intensive lamb cutting is to use sustainably raised ground beef. We ate lamb, expensive as it was in L.A., because our village family preferred it to beef. In the '50s and '60s, we rarely ate beef. *Sitto* and Mother always prepared lamb. Now, Mother uses ground beef more frequently. Here are Alice's words on the subject:

> In Lebanon, we only used lamb meat and cleaned out all the bad fat, which gave the food the strong taste. That took lots of skill, time, patience, and preparation. The American people don't like lamb because of the taste of

the bad fat left in it. Here beef is more accessible than lamb, so people use more beef. Beef has more fat, which makes it taste good, but fat is bad for us and we have to cut down for health's sake. We need to learn to use beef in our cooking.

We are now finding shortcuts in cooking and dealing with meats that are good to eat without all the fat. People following the same recipe will have different tasting food because of, in part, the varying amounts of fat left in the meat. Steero chicken or beef granules are an excellent addition to meat, fowl, and soup dishes—about 1 teaspoon per recipe; also using it will cut down the amount of salt added. Use chicken with chicken dishes and beef with lamb or beef dishes.

This is what I have learned from my experience for using beef—I buy the leanest ground round—less than 15% fat for raw stuffing, such as in meat pies, grape leaves (*waraq 'inab*), stuffed squash (*kousa mihshi*), etc. For some stuffings, I use ground chuck, which has more flavor, and I sauté it lightly in a pan and then drain the excess fat. I then add chopped onions, Steero beef granules, lemon juice, and a little clarified butter and seasoning and continue to sauté until the onion is translucent. The flavor is good and there is much less fat.—Alice

LAMB CUTTING

Following are instructions for cutting lamb and removing "the bad fat," and the uses for major cuts of lamb. Our method results in deliciously seasoned, time-tested dishes. Mother and *Sitto* bought a leg of lamb, shoulder, or breast and cut it into various sizes for particular recipes. They would then freeze it flat in freezer bags so that it thawed quickly—convenient for later use.

TRIMMING FAT

There are two basic types of fat: one is moist and smooth, which is fine to keep in small amounts; the other type is dry, flaky, and chalky—this is to be completely cut away and discarded; it is the fat that is unpleasantly strong tasting.

◆ CUTTING LEG OF LAMB

APPROXIMATE YIELD:

3 TO 4 CUPS OF LAMB PER LEG
lean pieces best for *kibbe,* shish kebab (*lahm mishwi*), stuffing (*mihshi*)

    1. With a sharp meat knife, carefully remove meat from bone. Then cut away and discard veins, arteries, and muscles.
    2. Set aside large, lean pieces for *kibbe*; large pieces with a little moist fat are suitable for shish kebab, smaller pieces for stew or stuffing.

HOW TO CUT LEG OF LAMB FOR SHISH KEBAB (*LAHM MISHWI*)
Cut larger pieces into 2" cubes, leaving on a little moist fat. Set aside smaller pieces for stew or stuffing. Remove and discard gristle and fat that is dry, flaky, or chalky.

HOW TO CUT LEG OF LAMB FOR *KIBBE NAYYE*
Cut pieces into 2" cubes, removing all fat. Set aside smaller pieces for stuffing. Remove and discard gristle.

HOW TO CUT LEG OF LAMB FOR STEW AND STUFFING (*MIHSHI*)
Remove and discard all dry chalky fat and gristle. Cut pieces, leaving a little of the moist fat, into 1" cubes. Pieces smaller than 1" can be cut into ¼" to ½" pieces and set aside for stuffing.

◆ CUTTING BREAST OF LAMB

APPROXIMATE YIELD:

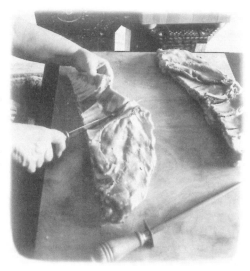

2 CUPS OF LAMB PER BREAST
flavorful, moist meat perfect for stuffing (*mihshi*) and bones for stew

    1. With a sharp meat knife, separate meat from bone, leaving a little meat on the bone for stews, or soups, or to place under grape leaves, cabbage rolls or stuffed squash (*kousa mihshi*).
    2. Section large riblets along cuts begun by butcher.

3. Cut off flange or flap on remaining end. Skin it, remove fat, and discard skin and fat. Remove and discard dry, chalky fat.

4. Cut in strips and then into ¼" pieces for stuffing.

◆ Shoulder

APPROXIMATE YIELD:

2 CUPS OF LAMB PER SHOULDER
used for shish kebab (*lahm mishwi*), stuffing (*mihshi*), or stew

Follow instructions for cutting leg of lamb on the previous page.

Mafroume or Mhamsa

SAUTÉED LAMB, ONIONS, AND PINE NUTS FOR STUFFING

◆

M*afroume* can be used for stuffing or just eaten with bread. I remember walking by the kitchen stove and not being able to resist scooping up a spicy bit, a *liqme*, with a piece of Arabic bread when it was done cooking. It is used as cooked stuffing for stuffed eggplant (*sheikh al mihshi*), shepherd's pie (*batata bil sineyeh*), and *kibbe bil sineyeh*. A layer of *mhamsa* can be served over a platter of *hommus* and eaten with Arabic bread in a dish called *hommus bi lahm*.

In our cooking there are two kinds of meat stuffing, one with raw lamb and the other with this sautéed lamb stuffing.

>1½ pounds lamb, cut very small or coarsely ground (p. 75)
>2 tablespoons clarified butter or olive oil
>1 large onion, finely chopped
>¼ cup pine nuts
>½ teaspoon salt
>¼ teaspoon pepper
>¼ teaspoon cayenne
>½ teaspoon cinnamon
>½ teaspoon ground allspice
>2 tablespoons lemon juice

1. Sauté lamb until well done in clarified butter with finely chopped onion, salt and whole pine nuts.

2. Season with black pepper, a dash of cayenne, cinnamon, allspice, and lemon juice just before cooking is complete. Serve with bread or use for stuffing.

Makes 3 cups stuffing.

Lahm Mishwi

SHISH KEBAB

◆

A classic Lebanese dish our family frequently enjoyed in our Los Angeles patio or at *mahrajans* (huge summer festivals with food, music, and dance) or at family picnics—this summer specialty was barbequed alongside a few hamburgers (with parsley) and served with Arabic bread and *tabbouli* or *salata* and french fries (*batata miqliyyi*). A cross-cultural feast! Mother and *Sitto* just used onions for the kebabs and this is how we love it; other families use additional vegetables such as tomato, bell pepper, or squash.

1½ pounds lamb, cut in 2-inch cubes (p. 75)
1 or 2 onions, cut into large pieces for skewering
¾ teaspoon salt
1 teaspoon black pepper
1 teaspoon cinnamon

5–7 metal or bamboo skewers (pre-soak bamboo in water)

1. Mix all of the above together in a bowl; cover and refrigerate for a couple of hours to marinate.

2. Place charcoal in barbeque and light it. While it is heating, place alternating pieces of lamb and onions on each skewer. Spear the onions through three layers and they will hold up and cook just right.

3. When coals are hot, barbeque for about 5–7 minutes on each side, being careful not to overcook, as meat can toughen.

4. Remove barbequed lamb from skewers by holding Arabic bread in your hand and sliding the *lahm mishwi* off. The bread soaks up some of the flavors of the meat—I remember everyone at the dinner table longed for that piece of bread with all the juices! The barbequed onions, wrapped with a little meat in the Arabic bread, made such tasty morsels!

Serves 4 to 6.

Kafta Mishwiye

GRILLED GROUND LAMB

◆

Lebanese cousin to hamburger, our well-seasoned *kafta* is wrapped around a skewer, elongated like a sausage; it is great grilled, served with bread and rice. If you prefer, bake it like a flattened meatloaf and pour garlic-lemon sauce over it for the last 5 minutes of baking.

> 1 pound ground lamb (read about lamb p. 73)
> 1 onion, minced
> ½ teaspoon each salt and black pepper
> ¼ teaspoon each allspice and cinnamon
> ½ cup parsley, finely chopped

To grill, broil, or barbeque

1. Mix the above ingredients thoroughly in a bowl. Roll and flatten into a patty and wrap each one around a skewer, shaping it with your hand to 4" long.

2. Grill over coals for about 4 minutes on each side until done. Remove from skewer by holding Arabic bread in your hand and sliding the *kafta* off.

To bake

1. Mix the above ingredients thoroughly in a bowl; spread into a 1-inch thick layer in a lightly oiled 8"x8" baking dish. Smooth layer with a wet hand.

2. Bake in a preheated oven at 400°F on the bottom oven rack for 15 minutes. Remove from oven and skim any fat residue that formed. With a sharp knife, cut *kafta* into 3-inch squares; return to oven for 10 minutes.

3. While it is baking, make garlic sauce; pour garlic sauce over meat the last 5 minutes of baking.

Garlic Lemon Marinade

> 1–2 cloves garlic
> ½ teaspoon salt
> ½ cup lemon juice

In a small bowl, mash garlic with salt; add lemon juice and pour over meat. Broil for 5 more minutes, until browned, and serve immediately.

Serves 4 to 6.

Kafta bil Sineyeh ou Bazella

LEBANESE MEATLOAF WITH PEAS AND TOMATO SAUCE

◆

A variation on the previous version of our well-seasoned *kafta* is baked topped with a tomato sauce and whole peas. Mother uses frozen peas, but garden fresh peas must have been what they used in the old country, and that would be perfect! Be sure to read the beginning of the chapter about lamb before making any of these lamb recipes.

1 pound ground lamb (read about lamb p. 73)
1 onion, minced
½ teaspoon salt
½ teaspoon black pepper
¼ teaspoon allspice
dash cinnamon
½ cup chopped parsley
1 package frozen peas, for top
1 small can tomato sauce, for top

1. Mix the above ingredients, except peas and tomato sauce, thoroughly in a bowl. Spread lamb mixture 1" thick into a lightly oiled baking dish. Dip your hand in cold water and smooth the surface.

2. Bake in a preheated oven at 400°F on the bottom oven rack for 15 minutes. Remove tray from oven and skim any residue that has formed. With a sharp knife, cut *kafta* into 3" squares.

3. Spread frozen peas evenly over the *kafta* and then the tomato sauce. Mom always rinsed the tomato can with a little water that she'd add to whatever she was making to not waste a bit of it! Return tray to oven, lower heat to 350°F, and bake an additional 15 minutes until done.

Serves 4 to 6.

Burghul Mfalfal

LAMB SHANKS WITH BULGUR

◆

One-pot meals were the practical solution to cooking on a one-burner stove in Lebanon's mountain villages. This recipe combines lamb with bulgur, stretching the protein of a small amount of meat with wheat to feed a large family. Serving this with yogurt (*laban*) adds more protein to the meal. The seasonings of cinnamon, allspice, salt, and pepper give the lamb its Lebanese signature.

2 pounds lamb shanks, rinsed
2 quarts water
3–4 whole cinnamon sticks
½ teaspoon salt
6 whole peppercorns
6 whole allspice kernels
1 cup #4 bulgur (*burghul*) rinsed
¼ cup clarified butter

1. Boil lamb shanks and bones with water, cinnamon sticks, salt, peppers, and allspice for about 30 minutes, until meat begins to loosen from the bone. Set aside to cool.

2. Place bulgur in a deep pot and brown for a few minutes, stirring constantly, before adding butter. Add clarified butter; stir and continue to brown.

3. Strain broth from lamb shanks and add 3 cups of the broth to *burghul*. Cover and steam for 15 minutes. Check and add more broth if needed.

4. Remove meat from lamb shanks, discarding gristle and fat. Add meat to *burghul*. Steam 10 more minutes. Turn off heat and let stand for 15 minutes before serving with yogurt, Arabic bread (*khubz*), or pita chips, and fresh cut vegetables.

Serves 4 to 6.

ALICE'S KITCHEN

IF YOU MAKE IT WITH LOVE, IT WILL BE DELICIOUS!

Kibbe Nayye

RAW MINCED LAMB AND BULGUR

◆

In the old days, lamb pieces were pounded by hand in a *jurn* to pulverize the meat into a paste, then combined with bulgur, onion, and seasoned with pepper and spices to create this legendary Lebanese raw lamb entrée, often referred to as the national dish of Lebanon. Mother had a fancy electric meat grinder she used to grind the meat with ice cubes in making the *kibbe* that she is famous for and that our family loved. Mama says, "the colder the meat, the better the *kibbe*."

My friend Josephine tells me a food processor will pulverize the meat so it will have some elasticity for binding with the rest of the ingredients; Mother still uses her meat grinder method. Typically serving it for special guests and celebrations, Mother garnishes it decoratively with long green scallions. *Kibbe nayye* is eaten by scooping up bite-sized portions with Arabic bread.

The leftovers are made into a dish that I have, since childhood, preferred to the raw *kibbe*, called *kibbe bil sineyeh,* the next recipe, which is baked and filled with pine nuts or made into little footballs (*kibbe 'raas*). There are vegetarian *kibbe* recipes in this book that are also excellent, using pumpkin, potato, onions, and bulgur.

> 1¼ cups #1 bulgur, soaked and rinsed
> 2 large onions, quartered
> 2 pounds lamb, cut into 2" chunks (pp. 75–76)
> 1 tablespoon black pepper
> 2 teaspoons salt
> 4 kernels whole allspice, freshly ground (¼ teaspoon)
> ¼ teaspoon cayenne pepper
> 1 tray of ice cubes

GARNISH

1 bunch of green onions for garnish, rinsed and trimmed

1. Rinse and drain bulgur. Squeeze excess moisture from bulgur with your hands and put into a large bowl. Grind onions into bowl over bulgur. Add seasonings, mix well, and set aside.

2. Grind meat—either use a meat grinder or have butcher grind it twice, fine like hamburger. To grind it yourself: Grind meat and several ice cubes through a meat grinder fitted with a coarse blade into a separate bowl. Then grind it a second time with a finer blade, using more ice to push the rest of the meat through.

3. Mix ground meat very thoroughly with bulgur and onion mixture. Now grind this mixture again with ice. If a butcher ground the meat for you, mix lamb and bulgur together with ice cubes, so the texture is smooth. In either instance, the mixture holds together best when cold and moist. Use more ice to achieve proper texture. Taste and adjust seasoning.

4. Serve raw *kibbe nayye* mounded on an oval platter garnished with whole green onions and Arabic bread. Smooth out the surface of the *kibbe* by dipping your hand in cold water and shaping the surface into an oval, domed shape. Mom then takes the back of a fork and presses a design into the surface, pokes a few scallions for garnish into the top with the tips sticking out and parades it onto the table, for this most famous and traditional dish.

Serves 6 to 8.

Kibbe bil Sineyeh

BAKED *KIBBE* WITH PINE NUTS

◆

Kibbe bil sineyeh transforms leftover raw *kibbe nayye* into an even more savory creation that is filled with pine nuts and baked, which I prefer to the raw lamb loved by most Lebanese. Traditionally eaten with tart yogurt cheese (*labne*) and Arabic bread, *kibbe bil sineyeh* can be served hot, warm, or cold, and the leftovers, should you have any, may be fried with scrambled eggs in *kibbe ou bayda*. The same basic recipe takes on a different shape in *kibbe 'raas*: football-shaped balls stuffed with the same filling and baked (page 114).

Kibbe bil sineyeh is a very traditional dish that can be baked in a round or rectangular tray. It is distinguished by the way it is cut just before baking into a very decorative and functional shape—a diamond, which can be dotted with a pine nut in the center of each piece.

> ¼ cup clarified butter, cold, divided
> 2½ cups *kibbe nayye* (see previous recipe)
> ½ cup #1 bulgur, soaked and rinsed
> a bowl of ice water for dipping your hands
> ½ cup pine nuts
> ⅓ cup olive oil

    1. Coat the inside of an 8"x13" tray, or a 12" round baking dish evenly with olive oil. Preheat oven to 400°F.
    2. Rinse and drain *burghul*; in a bowl, mix thoroughly into *kibbe nayye* with your hands.

3. Wet hands and form half of the *kibbe* into balls. Flatten each ball into a patty about ½" thick between your hands and place them on the bottom of the tray completely covering it. Smooth out surface with your hand dipped in ice water, blending the layer so there are no gaps.

4. Rinse and drain pine nuts, sprinkle evenly over surface, and pat down gently. Cut one-half of clarified butter into pieces and dot evenly over the pine nuts. Form remaining raw *kibbe* into balls and patties to cover the filling with another ½" thick layer. Smooth out the surface with your hand.

5. Cut a decorative pattern into the tray as follows: Cut into lengthwise strips 1½" wide, cutting all of the way through to the bottom of the tray. Make another series of parallel cuts at 45 degrees, also 1½" wide, creating diamond shapes. With the point of a knife, incise the center of each diamond all the way through to the bottom of the tray. Not only is this decorative, it allows for thorough cooking. Use the knife to cut around the edge of the tray to separate the *kibbe* from the pan.

6. Drizzle olive oil over the top and divide remaining clarified butter into teaspoon-sized chunks and evenly scatter over the top. Bake 30 minutes on lower oven rack until edges brown. Move to upper rack and continue baking until top browns. Remove from heat; sprinkle with a handful of water to moisten. Recut diamonds and serve.

Serves 4 to 6.

ALICE'S KITCHEN
IF YOU MAKE IT WITH LOVE, IT WILL BE DELICIOUS!

Sfeeha or Fatayir

SAVORY PASTRY OR MEAT PIES

◆

Another family favorite, *sfeehas,* are triangle-shaped savory pastries—meat pies made with our bread dough and filled with lamb, onions, and pine nuts and then baked. These disappeared as fast as they hit the dining room table and sometimes only a few made it out of the kitchen. The flavors in *sfeeha* become more vivid as they cool, and they are even tasty eaten cold. A dollop of tart yogurt cheese (*labne*) on top of these perfect finger foods will certainly please your guests.

When made round and open-faced, this recipe becomes *lahm bi ajeen*—easier to make than the closed triangles. The vegetarian variation of these pastries, spinach pies (p. 138), are equally scrumptious! Make the bread dough, and while it rises, make the filling.

DOUGH

follow recipe for basic bread dough (p. 179)

FILLING

3 cups lamb finely chopped or coarsely ground (pp. 75–76)
2 cups onions, finely chopped
½ cup pine nuts
¾ cup yogurt cheese (*labne,* p. 36)
2 teaspoons cinnamon
1 teaspoon each salt and black pepper
2 teaspoons mild cayenne pepper
    or ½ teaspoon hot cayenne
6 whole allspice, freshly ground (½ teaspoon)
½ cup lemon juice or ½ teaspoon citric acid

FILLING

1. Cut meat, chop onions, and place in large bowl.
2. Add seasonings, pine nuts, and *labne.* Mix thoroughly; then add lemon juice or citric acid. Mother would taste the raw stuffing and adjust seasoning.

Assembly

    1. Using a rolling pin, roll out one ball of dough on a well-floured surface to about ⅛" thickness.

    2. Use a mason jar cap (3½" diameter) to cut out as many circles as possible. Put scraps of dough into a bowl with a little water; set aside.

    3. Place 1 to 2 tablespoons of filling into each circle and close into a triangle as described below, or make flat open-faced pies as directed in *lahm bi ajeen*, the next recipe.

Forming triangles

    1. Using one hand, pull up the dough from 12 o'clock and 4 o'clock on the circle of dough to the center and pinch together and hold.

    2. With your other hand at the outer edge, pinch edges of dough together all the way to the center of the circle, sealing the edge and forming the first point of a triangle.

    3. Rotate the pie holding the center with one hand while the other hand pulls up the midpoint of the remaining dough and pinches towards the center, forming the second point of the triangle.

    4. Fold in the third point, pinching together but leaving ½-inch opening at the top center of the pie.

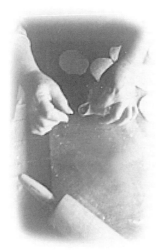
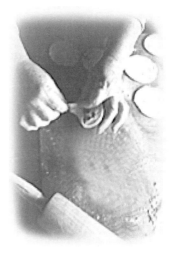

• Dust fingers slightly with flour before pinching dough so it will stay together.
• Try to keep the moist filling away from the edge of the circle and out of the joint.
•Push dough in at the point of the triangle before pinching closed to keep moisture in the pies as they cook.

BAKING

5. Place pies on oiled cookie sheet or a tray lined with baking parchment, allowing ¼" between each pie. Preheat oven to 400°F.

6. Knead dough scraps and form into a ball, dust with flour, cover and let rise again to use. If you have extra dough and no more filling, use it to make *tilme bi zaatar*, plain *tilme*, *khubz*, or a pizza! Another option is to freeze extra dough for later use: just roll it into a ball, then dust with flour, cover tightly with plastic wrap and freeze in a plastic freezer bag.

7. When cookie sheet is full, bake pies on lower rack of oven for 15 to 20 minutes or until golden brown on bottom. Move tray to upper rack and bake until top edges are golden brown, another 10 minutes or so.

8. Remove from tray and place to drain on open paper grocery bags to absorb any excess oil and to cool. *Sahteyn!*

Serves 8 to 10 as appetizers.

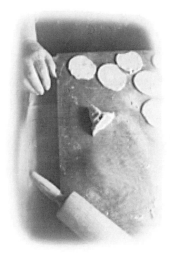

TO FREEZE PIES FOR LATER BAKING

Place unbaked pies on an ungreased tray in freezer for several hours until individually frozen. Then pack pies in freezer bags and store in the freezer. When you're ready to bake them, remove from freezer and place on cookie sheet lined with parchment. Let thaw or bake frozen, your choice. Bake in a preheated oven at 400°F as directed above in step 6.

Lahm Bi Ajeen

Lamb open-faced meat pies

◆

Almost identical to *sfeeha*, *lahm bi ajeen* is an open-faced meat pie with the addition of a little chopped tomato and a quicker cooking time. Try them both to see which you prefer. Begin with dough, and while it is rising, make the filling for *sfeeha* (p. 87) or *sambousik* filling, next recipe. You can make individual little pies for appetizers, or larger 8 to10-inch pies; it's up to you!

1. Make basic bread dough recipe (p. 179).

2. While dough is rising, follow recipe for filling on page 87, with the meat more finely chopped, or minced. Finely chopped tomato can also be added to the filling for *lahm bi ajeen*.

Assembly

1. Using a rolling pin, roll out one ball of dough on a well-floured surface to about ⅛" thickness.

2. Use a wide mason jar cap (3½" diameter) to cut out as many circles as possible; put scraps of dough into a bowl with a little water and set aside. Or you can make larger circles of dough, like pizza, or rectangles.

3. Sprinkle dough with a little water and spread one or two tablespoons of filling over each circle to ¼" from the edge. Since the lamb is uncooked, make the layer of meat no more than ¼" thick, so that the meat cooks thoroughly by the time the dough is done baking. Preheat oven to 400°F.

4. Place pies on oiled cookie sheet or a tray lined with baking parchment, allowing ¼" between each pie.

5. Knead dough scraps and form into a ball, dust with flour, cover and let rise again. If you have extra dough and no more filling, use it to make *tilme bi zaatar*, plain *tilme*, *khubz*, or a pizza! Another option is to freeze extra dough for later use: just roll it into a ball, then dust with flour, cover tightly with plastic wrap and freeze in a plastic freezer bag.

6. When tray is full, bake on lower rack of oven until golden brown, approximately 10 minutes. Move to upper rack and bake 5 to 10 more minutes, until crust is golden brown and meat is cooked.

7. Remove from tray and place on open paper grocery bags to absorb any excess oil and to cool. *Sahteyn!*

Serves 8 to 10 as appetizers.

Sambousik

SAVORY PASTRY

◆

These scrumptious savory pastries are very similar to the meat pies we grew up eating, but Mother and *Sitto* didn't make them as often as *sfeeha*. Now, this is Mother's favorite and she makes them ahead of time and freezes them, so even in her 90s, when people come over, she has something delectable to feed them! The *sambousik* are richer than *sfeeha,* as the dough is made with butter, and they too disappear as fast as they are put on the table. Perfect for *mezza* or as a side dish, *sambousik* can be served hot, warm, or at room temperature. Filling and dough can be made ahead and refrigerated. Once formed, they can be individually frozen on a tray, then put in freezer bags to later bake or fry. In Douma, they were usually fried, because people did not have ovens in their homes; today, baking them is certainly more healthful. Try both methods to see which you like best.

DOUGH

    1 cube butter, softened
    4 cups unbleached white flour
    ½ teaspoon salt
    ½ teaspoon yeast
    1 cup water

FILLING

    2 cups onions, finely chopped
    ¾ teaspoon salt
    2 tablespoons olive oil
    ½ cup pine nuts
    1 pound ground or finely chopped lamb (pp. 75–76)
    1 teaspoon cinnamon
    ¾ teaspoon black pepper
    ½ teaspoon cayenne pepper
    6 whole allspice, freshly ground (¾ teaspoon)
    ½ cup yogurt cheese (*labne,* p. 36)
    2 tablespoons lemon juice

FRYING (OPTIONAL)

    equal parts olive oil, vegetable oil, and clarified butter

ALICE'S KITCHEN
LAMB

Dough

    1. Combine butter, salt, and flour. Mix well by hand to blend completely.

    2. Dissolve yeast in lukewarm water and let proof for 5 minutes. Knead yeast thoroughly into flour mixture. Divide and roll into four balls; cover, let rest ½ hour while you make the filling.

Filling

    1. Sauté onions with salt in olive oil over medium heat until onions are translucent. Add pine nuts and sauté a few more minutes.

    2. Add meat, stirring occasionally for 10 minutes. Just before meat is fully browned, add seasonings and cook two more minutes. Remove from heat, add *labne*, and mix well. Allow to cool and then mix in lemon juice. Taste and adjust seasoning.

Assembly

    1. Roll out one ball of dough at a time on lightly floured board to ⅛" thickness. Cut into circles about 3 inches across with a canning jar cap. Roll dough scraps into a ball and set aside to rest for use if needed; it can also be frozen for later use.

    2. Fill each circle with a tablespoon or so of filling. Fold in half and pinch curved edges in well to seal, forming fat half-moons.

To fry

    Bring equal parts olive oil, clarified butter, and vegetable oil to a high heat in a deep pot with 3" or so of oil. Carefully lower in pastries and deep fry until golden, turning to the other side. Place on paper towels or bag to drain.

To bake

    Arrange pastries on a tray lined with baking parchment. If you wish, brush pastries with melted butter or a little olive oil. Bake in preheated oven at 400ºF for 15 minutes on bottom rack, then move tray to top rack for 10 minutes or until browned.

Serves 6 to 8 as appetizers.

Asabi bil Lahme Mafroume

FILO DOUGH FINGERS WITH LAMB

◆

Another delightful savory pastry that is relatively simple to prepare and is excellent served as an appetizer or entrée.

PASTRY

> 1 package filo dough
> ½ cup clarified butter, melted

MAFROUME FILLING

> 1½ pounds lamb, minced or coarsely ground (pp. 75–77)
> 2 tablespoons clarified butter
> 1 large onion, finely chopped
> ¼ cup pine nuts
> ½ teaspoon each salt and black pepper
> ¼ teaspoon cayenne
> ½ teaspoon cinnamon
> ½ teaspoon ground allspice
> 1 tablespoon lemon juice

FILLING

1. Sauté lamb in clarified butter over medium heat until well done with finely chopped onion, salt, and whole pine nuts.
2. Season with black pepper, cayenne, cinnamon, allspice, and lemon juice just before cooking is complete.

ASSEMBLY

1. On a flat tray, brush both sides of each filo leaf with butter as you layer 3 to 5 leaves on top of each other.
2. Place a 1-inch cylinder of lamb stuffing along one edge of dough and roll into a long tube the width of a cigar.
3. Cut into 3" lengths for baking. Repeat until you have used all the stuffing and filo. Start baking on bottom rack of an oven preheated to 350ºF for 10 to 15 minutes; finish on top rack for 10 minutes or until lightly browned.

Serves 4 to 6 as an entrée or 6 to 8 as appetizers.

Batata bil Sineyeh

BAKED POTATO AND LAMB PIE WITH PINE NUTS

◆

Along the lines of shepherd's pie, *batata bil sineyeh* combines the comfort of mashed potatoes with the delicacy of pine nuts accompanying the savor of a little spiced lamb. Mother's guests love it and frequently ask for the recipe. Start the potatoes cooking first, while you make the filling. This is a hearty winter comfort food—a Lebanese meat-and-potatoes dish.

FILLING

⅛ cup olive oil
2 large onions, finely chopped
½ teaspoon salt
2 pounds lamb, minced (pp. 75–77)
¼–½ cup pine nuts
¾ teaspoon black pepper
¼ teaspoon cayenne pepper
½ teaspoon cinnamon

POTATOES

10–12 medium potatoes
¼ cup milk
½ teaspoon salt
½ teaspoon black pepper
½ cup butter or olive oil
1–2 cups bread crumbs

ALICE'S KITCHEN

IF YOU MAKE IT WITH LOVE, IT WILL BE DELICIOUS!

1. Sauté onions, salt, and lamb in olive oil over medium heat until lightly browned, about 15 minutes. Add pepper, cayenne, cinnamon, and pine nuts and sauté 5 more minutes. Taste, adjust seasoning, and set aside.

2. Meanwhile, boil or steam whole potatoes in water with one tablespoon milk until tender. Milk, Mama says, brings out the flavor of potato. Drain cooked potatoes, reserving liquid for soup stock; then peel and mash them while still hot with salt, pepper, butter, and remaining milk.

3. Preheat oven to 350°F and grease an 8"x13" pan with olive oil.

4. Moisten hands with milk to keep from sticking, and spread half of the potatoes in the pan making a flat, even layer. Layer the lamb stuffing evenly over the potatoes. Cover lamb layer with remaining potatoes by making potato patties between your palms and pressing them to completely cover the filling.

5. Sprinkle top layer with bread crumbs. Bake for 45 minutes until golden brown on top. Let stand for 10 minutes before cutting and serving.

Serves 6 to 8.

Shish Barak

LEBANESE RAVIOLI IN YOGURT SAUCE

◆

These tasty homemade ravioli are filled with seasoned lamb and cooked with a yogurt sauce almost as a soup. This is a classic Lebanese dish that is served on special occasions, as there is a bit of time involved in making them, but it's well worth the effort.

DOUGH

2 cups flour
½ teaspoon salt
1 cup milk

FILLING

1 pound ground lamb (pp. 75–77)
2 onions, finely chopped
½ tablespoon clarified butter
1 cup pine nuts
½ teaspoon cinnamon
½ teaspoon black pepper
1 tablespoon parsley, finely chopped

SAUCE

4 cups yogurt (*laban*)
1 egg
1 tablespoon corn starch
3 cloves garlic
½ teaspoon salt
1 tablespoon dried spearmint or cilantro

1. Mix flour with salt in a bowl. Add milk to make dough and knead well and set aside.

2. Mix filling ingredients together in a bowl.

3. Roll out dough to ⅛" thick and cut into 3" circles using a canning jar cap. Place a heaping teaspoon of filling into the center of each circle. Fold in half and pinch edges together to seal. Fold the two corners towards each other, overlapping a little, and pinch together to form a hat-like shape, like those in the photo with our cousin Nina Sawaya al Bacha in Douma. They actually look more like Italian tortellini rather than ravioli.

4. Place them on a tray and into a preheated oven at 350ºF for 10 minutes to dry a little. Remove from oven and set aside. Or allow them to air dry.

5. To make sauce, put yogurt in a deep pot and beat in the egg and corn starch, stirring well and smoothing out any lumps. Heat over a low heat for 10 minutes, stirring frequently, being careful not to boil.

6. Mash garlic into a paste with a little salt. Stir in dried spearmint and add to the yogurt.

7. Drop ravioli into yogurt and cook over low heat for 10 to 15 minutes. At 10 minutes, test one to see if they're done, which will vary with the size you have made. Serve hot in bowls or over rice.

Serves 4 to 6.

Mfarkey

Eggplant and lamb stew

◆

Hearty and wholesome, this stew, as is the case with many Lebanese stews of meats and vegetables, is served over a bed of rice (*riz mfalfal*) and eaten with Arabic bread. Rather than salads, a fresh vegetable platter with romaine lettuce leaves, carrot strips, radishes, mint leaves, cucumber strips, and green onions makes a fine and colorful complement.

> 2 eggplants
> 3 cups lamb breast, coarsely chopped
> or ground lamb (pp. 75–77)
> ½ teaspoon salt
> 2 tablespoons clarified butter or olive oil
> 2 large onions, finely chopped
> 3 cloves garlic, finely chopped
> 3 large, ripe tomatoes
> or 1 large can whole tomatoes, chopped, with juice
> ½ teaspoon black pepper
> ¼ teaspoon cayenne pepper
> ½ teaspoon cinnamon

1. Peel eggplant and cut into 1½" cubes. Salt and place in a bowl or colander to drain. Pat them dry with a towel before cooking.

2. Meanwhile, sauté lamb with salt, onions, and garlic in clarified butter, until lightly browned; add eggplant and brown 10 minutes.

3. Add tomatoes, pepper, cayenne, and cinnamon. Cook on medium heat for 5 minutes. Stir gently with wooden spoon so that eggplant doesn't get mashed.

4. Cover, lower heat, and simmer for about 45 minutes until eggplant is thoroughly cooked, stirring gently every 15 minutes. Serve hot over rice (*riz mfalfal*) with Arabic bread.

Serves 6 to 8.

Riz ou Fassoulia

Lima beans with lamb and tomato over rice

◆

Rice and beans, *riz ou fassoulia*, are protein-rich in this delectable favorite that brings to mind memories of winter family dinners: 10 of us crowded around the dining room table, kids sometimes sitting at the kitchen table when there were guests because there was not enough room at the big table; and everyone loving the fulfilling flavors that this meal provides. Serve over rice (*riz mfalfal*) with fresh cut vegetables or steamed asparagus with lemon and garlic, and, of course, olives and Arabic bread.

2 tablespoons olive oil or clarified butter
1½ pounds lamb, cut into ¾" cubes for stewing (pp. 75–77)
¾ teaspoon black pepper
¼ teaspoon cayenne pepper
½ teaspoon cinnamon
3 medium onions, chopped
2 cloves garlic, finely chopped
½ teaspoon salt
1 can whole tomatoes, chopped, with liquid
2 packages frozen baby lima beans
    or ¾ cup dry navy beans, soaked overnight, rinsed

1. Sauté lamb in clarified butter or olive oil with seasonings, until light brown over medium heat. Add onions, garlic, and salt, continuing to sauté 5 or 10 more minutes.

2. Add tomatoes with their liquid, and beans. Cover and simmer for 20 minutes if frozen beans are used. Dry beans, soaked overnight, take about two hours of simmering to be tender.

3. Stir occasionally, adding water if necessary, until beans are done. Serve over rice (*riz mfalfal*) with Arabic bread.

Serves 6 to 8.

Bamye ou Lahm

OKRA AND LAMB

The flavors of okra (*bamye*) simmered with tomato, onion, garlic, and lamb served on a bed of rice and eaten with Arabic bread, carrot sticks, and romaine lettuce leaves make a fine supper in the summertime when okra is in season. In our village, where the summers are warm, families dry okra for use in wintertime.

2 tablespoons olive oil or clarified butter
1½ pounds lamb, cut in 1" cubes for stewing (pp. 75–77)
¾ teaspoon black pepper
¼ teaspoon cayenne pepper
½ teaspoon cinnamon
3 onions, chopped
2 cloves chopped garlic
½ teaspoon salt
1 can whole tomatoes, chopped, with liquid
1 pound fresh okra, rinsed and stemmed

1. In a deep pot with olive oil or clarified butter on a medium heat, sauté lamb with seasonings until light brown. Add onions, garlic, and salt, continuing to sauté 5 minutes.

2. Stir in tomatoes with their liquid and, very gently, the okra. Cover and simmer for 15 to 20 minutes, being careful not to overcook okra, as it will become mushy. Serve hot over rice (*riz mfalfal*) with Arabic bread.

Serves 6 to 8.

Riz ou Loubiye

STRING BEANS WITH LAMB OVER RICE

◆

This recipe brings back wonderful childhood memories of our big family dinner table, everyone joking and telling stories, all at the same time, and Mama and *Sitto* being sure we all had enough food. Serve over steamed rice (*riz mfalfal*), and scooped up with Arabic bread, with fresh cut vegetables on the side like carrots, radishes, romaine lettuce leaves, and cucumbers.

2 pounds fresh green beans, julienne-cut
1 pound lamb, cut in 1" cubes for stewing (pp. 75–77)
2 tablespoons olive oil or clarified butter
2 onions, chopped
½ cup water
1 can whole tomatoes, coarsely chopped with liquid
1 small can tomato sauce, plus one can of water
½ teaspoon salt
½ teaspoon black pepper
dash cinnamon
dash cayenne pepper

1. Rinse and cut green beans.
2. Sauté lamb in oil or butter for 5 minutes, then add onions and seasonings. Continue to stir and brown over medium heat 10 minutes.
3. Add green beans, tomatoes with their liquid, tomato sauce, and water. Cover and simmer over low heat for 45 minutes, stirring occasionally. Taste and adjust seasoning. Serve over rice (*riz mfalfal*) with bread and vegetables.

Serves 4 to 6.

Sheikh il Mihshi

STUFFED EGGPLANT WITH LAMB AND PINE NUTS

The name translates to the Sheik of Stuffed Dishes, which says it all. This is a luscious, elegant creation baked and served over rice—a memorable meal. While it is similar to *batinjan mihshi*, this recipe is served over rice (*riz mfalfal*) and the other has rice in the filling.

FILLING

1½ pounds lamb, minced or coarsely ground (pp. 75–77)
2 tablespoons clarified butter or olive oil
1 large onion, finely chopped
¼ cup pine nuts
½ teaspoon each salt and black pepper
¼ teaspoon cayenne
½ teaspoon cinnamon
½ teaspoon ground allspice
2 teaspoons lemon juice

ASSEMBLY

2 large eggplants or 12 Japanese or Arabic eggplants
¼ cup clarified butter, melted
2 cups sautéed lamb filling (above)
2 small cans tomato sauce
2 cans water
⅔ cup lemon juice, divided
½ teaspoon each salt and black pepper
¼ teaspoon cayenne
½ teaspoon cinnamon

ALICE'S KITCHEN

IF YOU MAKE IT WITH LOVE, IT WILL BE DELICIOUS!

1. Sauté lamb until well done in clarified butter or equal parts butter and olive oil with finely chopped onion, salt, and whole pine nuts. Just before cooking is complete, season with pepper, cayenne, cinnamon, allspice, and one third cup of the lemon juice, and set aside.

2. Peel eggplants and season with salt and pepper. Set aside for a few minutes to drain. Pat eggplants dry, arrange them in a deep baking dish, and baste with clarified butter on all sides. Broil until light brown and tender, turning frequently for approximately 15 minutes.

3. Cool eggplants and cut as follows:

• Medium eggplants are quartered lengthwise.

• Large eggplants are cut lengthwise first, in half, then in thirds, and finally into sixths, so you have elongated pieces. Cut a slit into the length, not all the way through—just deep enough to make a pocket, leaving ½" to 1" uncut at each end.

• If you use the elongated Japanese eggplants, just make 1 cut into length of eggplant, leaving ½" to 1" uncut at each end.

4. Return them to baking dish and stuff with lamb filling. Pour tomato sauce over the filled eggplants, and refill each can with water and pour into the tray. Season with salt, pepper, and cinnamon. Drizzle remaining ⅓ cup lemon juice over top and cover tray with foil.

5. Bake at 375ºF for 1 hour, until eggplant is tender and sauce has thickened. Serve over rice (*riz mfalfal*) with sauce (*zoum*) from the baking dish and Arabic bread.

Serves 6 to 8.

Batinjan Mihshi

STUFFED EGGPLANT WITH LAMB, TOMATO, AND RICE

◆

Very similar to *Sheikh al Mihshi*, but with subtle differences—*sheikh al mihshi* is baked and served over rice, and *batinjan mihshi* is cooked on the stovetop and has rice in the stuffing. Small eggplants, 3" to 4" in length, are not peeled in this dish as in its counterpart recipe, and the lamb is raw rather than sautéed before stuffing. Mother and *Sitto* prepared this exquisitely—it was a very special dish, when eggplants were in season. An excellent vegetarian version of this was prepared for me by my cousins in Lebanon (p. 145). Fabulous either way!

> 12 Japanese or Arabic eggplants, rinsed unpeeled

FILLING

> 2 cups coarsely ground lamb (pp. 75–77)
> ½ cup rice, soaked and rinsed
> 1 small can tomato sauce, divided
> ⅓ cup lemon juice
> ⅛ teaspoon cinnamon
> ½ teaspoon salt
> ¾ teaspoon black pepper
> dash cayenne pepper
> dash of allspice

FOR THE POT

> several lamb bones
> 1 can whole tomatoes, chopped (reserve liquid)
> ⅓ cup lemon juice
> 3–4 black peppercorns

1. Rinse and core eggplants as in *kousa mihshi* (p. 109). Place them in salted water for about 10 minutes and then drain them before stuffing.
2. Parboil lamb bones for 15 minutes and arrange on the bottom of a deep pot. In the meantime, prepare the filling.
3. In a bowl, mix lamb with rice, spices, lemon juice, and half of the tomato sauce. Stuff eggplants with filling mixture about ½-inch from the top. Arrange them on top of lamb bones in an upright position. Pour chopped tomatoes with their liquid, and remaining tomato sauce over eggplants with 2 cans of water. Season with a little more salt, pepper, and lemon juice. Cover and bring to boil.

ALICE'S KITCHEN

IF YOU MAKE IT WITH LOVE, IT WILL BE DELICIOUS!

4. Turn down heat and simmer for 1 hour or so, until eggplant is tender and sauce has thickened. Serve drizzled with tomato sauce (*zoum*) from the baking dish, Arabic bread (*khubz*), and a platter of fresh raw vegetables, including carrots, radishes, cucumbers, and romaine lettuce.

Serves 6 to 8.

Malfouf Mihshi Bi Lahme ou Riz

CABBAGE ROLLS WITH LAMB AND RICE

◆

The lemony flavor and delicate texture of *malfouf mihshi* more than compensate for the aroma of cabbage as it cooks. Whole cabbage leaves contain the filling of rice and lamb. Our Lenten vegetarian version is equally exquisite (p. 148). Serve hot, warm, or cold, with Arabic bread and fresh raw vegetables.

1 large head cabbage or 2 medium heads

STUFFING

1 pound coarsely ground lamb (pp. 75–77)
¾ cup rice, soaked and rinsed
¾ teaspoon salt
½ teaspoon black pepper
½ teaspoon cayenne pepper
½ teaspoon cinnamon
½ teaspoon allspice
⅓ cup lemon juice

FOR THE POT

several lamb bones, parboiled and rinsed (optional)
cabbage ribs, core, and small leaves
½ cup lemon juice
10–12 small garlic cloves, unpeeled
5 black peppercorns

1. Core cabbage by inserting knife point around the core from each side, towards the center of the cabbage.

2. Blanch cabbage by placing the entire head in boiling water with the core at the bottom of the pot. When leaves become slightly tender, limp, and bright green in color, remove them, one at a time, being careful not to overcook them. Blanching removes their crispness so they can be easily rolled. As they separate from the head, carefully place leaves into a colander to cool and drain for stuffing. Set aside and make stuffing.

STUFFING AND ASSEMBLY

1. Put rice, seasonings, and lemon juice in a bowl and mix thoroughly. Add lamb and mix well.

ALICE'S KITCHEN

IF YOU MAKE IT WITH LOVE, IT WILL BE DELICIOUS!

2. Open leaves flat on a clean surface and cut main rib of cabbage leaf out. Outer leaves can be cut in half if they are very large and used to make two rolls. Line bottom of a deep pot with parboiled and rinsed lamb bones or with small cabbage leaves and the rib pieces.

3. One cabbage leaf at a time, spoon several teaspoons of stuffing across one end and roll closed, tucking sides and extra parts of leaf into the center. Stack rolls in deep pot on top of leaves and ribs. When you have one layer of rolls, distribute a few whole unpeeled garlic cloves over them and continue layering in rolls, adding garlic here and there.

4. Add water to almost cover cabbage rolls: about 1 to 2 cups. Sprinkle a little salt, the lemon juice, and black peppercorns over rolls. Place a dish upside down on top of cabbage rolls to hold them intact, with a plate big enough to cover as much as possible; cover pot with a lid. Cook on high until boiling; turn down and steam for about 30 minutes.

5. Lift dish from the cabbage rolls, and continue to simmer, covered, until water has been absorbed and meat is done, another 30 minutes. Let stand in covered pot for 10 minutes or more before serving. To serve, carefully lift out tender cabbage rolls and place on a platter.

SERVING VARIATION

If all the water has been absorbed by the rice, the tradition is to put a platter on top of the pot, and holding them tightly together, briskly turn the pot upside down so the pot empties onto the platter. If you do this, be careful that there is no hot liquid to spill out! The results make for a lovely presentation.

Serves 6 to 8.

Kousa Mihshi

LEBANESE SQUASH STUFFED WITH LAMB AND RICE
◆

This was one of my favorite dishes, perhaps because I was allowed to help *Sitto* stuff the light-green Lebanese squash harvested from our garden. *Sitto* even let me try to core it using one of the corers my mother had made from brass tubing. This was tricky for me as a child and it's still tricky, because it is easy to cut through the side or the bottom of the squash—the idea is to have a very thin shell with an even thickness. Lebanese squash wasn't available in the grocery, so if we weren't raising any that year, our Lebanese friends, the McKannas, shared their crop with us. Several U.S. seed companies now sell Lebanese zucchini seeds, or you might find starts or the squash at a local farmer's market. If not, small yellow crooknecks or dark green zucchini can be used.

10 small green or yellow squash, about 4" to 6" long

FILLING

½ cup rice
½ teaspoon cinnamon
4 whole allspice kernels, ground (¾ teaspoon)
½ teaspoon each salt and black pepper
¼ teaspoon cayenne pepper
1 tablespoon lemon juice
2 cups lamb, finely chopped or coarsely ground (pp. 75–77)
1 small can tomato sauce, divided

FOR THE POT

several lamb bones, parboiled and rinsed (optional)
1 clove garlic
reserved tomato sauce
1 large can whole tomatoes, coarsely chopped with liquid
2 tablespoons lemon juice
4 whole peppercorns
3 cups water

1. Rinse and drain rice and place in a bowl. Mix in seasonings, half the tomato sauce, a tablespoon of lemon juice, and the lamb.

2. Parboil the lamb bones, rinse them, arrange them in the bottom of a deep pot, and set aside. If unavailable, place a rack on the bottom of the pot upon which to set the squash.

3. Cut off the tops and ends of the squash and core them carefully so as not to crack them or pierce the bottom: Gently insert a corer and remove the first 1½ inches of the core by rotating the corer clockwise with your dominant hand and the squash counter-clockwise with your other. As you turn, the marrow will be extruded. Ideally, there will be ⅛-inch thickness of squash around the hollow core. Save the seedy pulp for other dishes, such as squash fritters (*kousa 'raas*) and squash stew (*mfarket kousa*). Place cored squash in a bowl of salted water flavored with a clove of garlic until all are cored.

4. Take each cored squash, drain water from its center, and gently fill with lamb and rice mixture, being careful not to crack the shell, to ½-inch from the top.

5. Arrange stuffed squash upright in pot over the lamb bones. Pour in the remaining tomato sauce, the chopped tomatoes with their juice, the additional lemon juice, peppercorns, and water. Cover pot, place on stovetop with heat on high until sauce begins to boil, then reduce heat to low and simmer for approximately 1 hour until rice is done, squash is tender, and sauce is thick.

6. When serving, cut squash open and pour tomato sauce (*zoum*) from the pot over them, to the taste of the individual. Best with Arabic bread, carrot sticks, celery, cucumbers, romaine lettuce, and other cut vegetables.

Serves 4 to 6.

Waraq 'inab, Yabra', or Waraq Arish

STUFFED GRAPE LEAVES WITH LAMB AND RICE

◆

Grape leaves were such a precious commodity that a grapevine was planted in our backyard especially to meet our harvest needs. They were almost more important than the grapes, as no fruits came from this grapevine, just the young, tender, shiny leaves picked in a tidy stack, tiny stems pointing to the sky. They were taken directly into the kitchen to be filled with lamb and rice or vegetables and rice, then rolled into this famous dish, called *waraq 'inab, yabra'*, or *waraq arish*.

Toward the end of the growing season, Mother tucked stacks of fresh leaves into freezer bags and into the freezer for winter suppers when the vines were dormant. If you do not have fresh or frozen grape leaves, canned grape leaves become wilted in the canning process and roll easily straight from the jar, although they may be less tender than fresh leaves. If you pick your own, be sure they are unblemished, young, shiny, and not fuzzy. Large leaves can be picked if they are still tender, and the variety that has a broad leaf will hold more filling, but small ones are wonderful for *mezza*. Rolling grape leaves is an art worthy of mastering! A wonderful Lenten vegetarian version of this recipe is excellent (p. 148). Enjoy!

40 fresh grape leaves or 1 quart canned or frozen leaves

FILLING

2 cups finely chopped lamb (pp. 75–77)
¾ cup rice, soaked and rinsed
½ teaspoon cinnamon
4 whole allspice kernels, ground (¼ teaspoon)
½ teaspoon salt
½ teaspoon black pepper
¼ teaspoon cayenne pepper

FOR THE POT

1 pound lamb bones, parboiled and rinsed (optional)
4 cups water
⅓ cup lemon juice
5 black peppercorns

1. Place rice in large bowl and mix in seasonings. Add lamb, mix the filling well, and set aside.
2. Arrange parboiled lamb bones in a layer covering the bottom of a deep

ALICE'S KITCHEN
IF YOU MAKE IT WITH LOVE, IT WILL BE DELICIOUS!

pot and set aside. Or use grape leaves if you don't have lamb bones. Leaves that are torn or too big or small to roll are useful here.

3. Blanch fresh or frozen grape leaves in warm water briefly to wilt. Lay one leaf out on board with the leaf veins (the backside of the leaf) facing you, and the stem of the leaf toward you. Place 1 to 2 teaspoons of stuffing across the width of the leaf, to equal the thickness of your index finger. Adjust the amount of filling to the scale of the grape leaf.

4. Fold sides in over the filling and roll the leaf up like a carpet. Place each rolled grape leaf into the pot on top of the bones, side by side, forming a row. Begin the next row perpendicular to it and continue stacking them in the pot in this manner, until you use up all of the filling.

5. Add lemon juice and water to almost cover grape leaves. Place a plate on top of the grape leaves, top side down, to hold them intact and cover the pot with a lid. Cook over high heat until boiling, then reduce heat and simmer until water has been absorbed and rice is done, about 1½ hours. It is good to let them steam in the pot for 15 minutes after cooking prior to serving.

6. The traditional way to serve *waraq 'inab* is to remove the small plate and place a platter larger than the pot on top of it; then briskly turn the pot upside down onto the platter, so the lamb bones on top form a visually interesting construction with grape leaves underneath. Be sure there is no liquid left in the pot bottom before flipping it over! Serve with carrot sticks, celery, cucumbers, olives, yogurt cheese (*labne*), and Arabic bread.

Serves 4 to 6.

Ghamme ma Fatte

STUFFED LAMB TRIPE

◆

Sitto's *ghamme* or stuffed tripe recipe is an excellent example of using all parts of the lamb, creating dishes that Mother and her generation considered delicacies, but we squeamish kids didn't. It is served with crisp bread dressing.

2½ pounds lamb or beef tripe
salt and baking soda

FILLING

2 pounds lamb, finely chopped (pp. 75–77)
½ cup long grain rice, soaked and rinsed
¼ teaspoon allspice
½ teaspoon black pepper
½ teaspoon cinnamon
½ teaspoon salt
2 tablespoons lemon juice
1 onion, finely chopped (optional)
1 can garbanzo beans, drained (optional)

FOR THE POT

5 peppercorns
½ teaspoon salt

FATTE (BREAD DRESSING)

3 loaves Arabic bread, toasted to a crisp light brown
5 cloves garlic
¼ teaspoon salt
1 cup vinegar

1. Place rice in a mixing bowl, add seasonings, and lemon juice; mix well. If you wish to use onion and garbanzo beans, mix them in. Add ground lamb, mix well, and set aside.

2. Sprinkle salt and baking soda liberally over tripe; rinse it well and allow to drain. Tie one end of tripe with string to close it. Using a funnel, loosely stuff it with the filling, allowing room for rice to expand in cooking. Fill each section, leaving room to tie end, and then tie the end closed.

3. Puncture each length of stuffed tripe every 12" with a fork. Place in a deep pot and fill with water to cover. Add peppercorns and salt. Cover and bring

to a boil. Reduce heat and simmer for 1 to 1½ hours. Test to see if it is done by cutting a little section.

4. While it is cooking, prepare *fatte* (bread dressing) to serve over it. Toast bread until light brown and crispy. When cool, crush bread into ½" pieces. In a bowl, mash garlic into a paste with salt. Stir in vinegar. Place bread in a bowl and sprinkle with a few drops of broth from the pot of *ghamme*. Pour vinegar and garlic sauce over bread and toss well.

5. Serve tripe cut into 4-inch sections topped with bread pieces (*fatte*). A Lebanese delicacy, to be sure.

Serves 8 to 10.

Kebab or Kibbe 'Raas

BAKED *KIBBE* BALLS WITH PINE NUTS

◆

K*ibbe nayye* that is leftover can be made into a variety of dishes. One is *kibbe bil sineyeh* that is traditionally eaten with tart yogurt cheese (*labne*) and Arabic bread. Another version of it takes on a different shape in *kibbe 'raas*: football-shaped balls stuffed with sautéed lamb, onions, and pine nuts that are then baked. The *kibbe nayye* and the filling need to be made ahead.

2½ cups *kibbe nayye* (p. 83)
½ cup #1 bulgur (*burghul*), soaked and rinsed
a bowl of ice water for dipping your hands
⅓ cup olive oil
¼ cup clarified butter, cold, divided

FILLING

1 recipe of sautéed lamb (*mhamsa*, p. 78)

1. Coat the inside of an 10"x13" baking dish evenly with olive oil. Pre-heat oven to 400°F.

2. Put bulgur in a bowl and mix thoroughly with *kibbe nayye* using your hands to blend it completely.

3. Take about two tablespoons of the *kibbe* mixture and roll into a ball with your hands. Using your index finger, press into the ball, hollowing out the center to make room for filling.

4. Carefully spoon a tablespoon or so of filling into the hollow, and then pinch the ball closed, rolling between your palms to smooth it out, making points at two ends, shaping into a football shape. Dipping your hands in cold water helps smooth the meat.

5. Place each ball in the baking dish with ½" of space in between them, and complete roll-ing and stuffing until using up the meat.

6. Bake in lower shelf of oven for about 15 minutes, until browned; turn the balls over to bake and brown other side.

Serves 8 to 10.

DJEJ

◆

CHICKEN

Mama remembers eating chicken, for dinner or *ghada*, the main meal of the day in Douma on Sundays. *Sitto* butchered the chicken and then washed it well with baking soda and salt. In the village, every family raised their own chickens because they efficiently consumed kitchen food scraps and consistently converted them into eggs. Chickens were a special Sunday dinner entrée in a mostly vegetable and grain-based diet. To carry on the village tradition in our affluent Los Angeles neighborhood during the 1950s, we risked disregarding prevailing conventions and kept chickens—briefly— until the rooster's crowing became too dissonant and the neighbors complained.

I'll never forget the day I came home from elementary school to find *Sitto* chasing one of the chickens in the back yard, while brandishing a big kitchen knife. Sure enough, she caught the chicken, and chopped off its head. Needless to say, I could not eat the chicken we had for dinner that night, knowing it was one I had loved.

Rural Lebanese continue to catch wild birds that are eaten as a delicacy and Mother remembers how tasty these birds were. Now for many years a vegetarian, I am grateful we weren't presented with little birds to eat when I was a child! The recipes here are the favorite dishes Mother and *Sitto* made frequently when we were growing up. They washed the chicken well with salt and baking soda before cooking it, and removed and discarded the skin and fat prior to cooking—wise practices to follow. Whenever possible, it is best to buy sustainably farm-raised, free-range, organically fed chickens. This is the closest we can come to the good, old days when everything was natural and organic, which is best for our earth and our health.

Djej Mihshi

STUFFED CHICKEN WITH LAMB AND RICE

◆

Here is our authentic Lebanese recipe for special-occasion chicken stuffed with a rice and lamb filling. Mother and *Sitto* made two types of rice for chicken—one that was stuffed inside the chicken and a slightly different version that is cooked on the side to provide enough for extra guests. Recipe for the additional side dish of rice follows. Be sure to make the sautéed nuts for garnish.

> 1 whole chicken

LAMB STUFFING

> 2 cups lamb, minced or coarsely ground (pp. 75–77)
> ½ cup rice, soaked and rinsed
> ½ teaspoon cinnamon
> ¼ teaspoon allspice
> ½ teaspoon each salt and black pepper
> ¼ teaspoon cayenne pepper

FOR THE POT

> ⅛ cup olive oil
> salt and ground black pepper
> 3 cups water or vegetable stock
> 5 whole peppercorns

1. Mix stuffing ingredients together well. Preheat oven to 350ºF.

2. Remove and discard skin and fat; then rub chicken with salt and baking soda to clean it; rinse well with cold water. Stuff chicken with lamb and rice mixture. Close with small skewers, place in a roaster, and rub with olive oil, salt, and pepper. Add water and peppercorns; cover pot.

3. Bake the stuffed chicken approximately 1 to 2 hours, depending upon the size of the chicken.

4. In the meantime, prepare extra rice, if needed, and sauté nuts for garnish as this tops it off beautifully!

5. Test chicken for doneness: a fork will easily pierce the leg when the chicken is done. Remove from oven and place stuffing in a platter alongside cut pieces of roasted chicken; garnish with sautéed nuts. Serve with Arabic bread, additional rice, and yogurt (*laban*).

Serves 6 to 8 with additional rice side dish.

RICE SIDE DISH

½ pound ground lamb or finely chopped lamb (pp. 75–77)
2 tablespoons clarified butter
¼ cup pine nuts
½ teaspoon salt
½ teaspoon black pepper
½ teaspoon allspice
¼ teaspoon cinnamon
2 cups chicken broth
1 cup rice, soaked and rinsed

GARNISH

½ to 1 cup blanched, slivered almonds and/or pine nuts
1 tablespoon butter or olive oil

1. Sauté lamb in clarified butter. Add pine nuts and brown. Stir in seasonings. Add chicken broth, cover, and bring to a boil.

2. Add rice, cover, and steam 20 minutes if using white rice, or 45 minutes if using brown rice. When rice is done, stir with fork, cover, and let stand for 10 minutes before serving.

3. While rice is cooking, sauté nuts in butter. Serve rice with chicken pieces and garnish with browned nuts. Scrumptious!

Makes 4 cups.

Sha'yriyeh ou Riz ma Djej

ORZO WITH RICE AND CHICKEN

◆

The very flavor and texture of this dish made it one of my top ten childhood favorites. Chicken, rice, orzo, yogurt (*laban*), and bread . . . it is a great combination. Moist chicken and rice with tangy yogurt. Mmmm. And it's very easy to make!

1¼ cups rice, soaked and rinsed
1 cup *sh'ayriyeh* (Italian pasta called rosa marina or orzo)
3 tablespoons clarified butter
6 pieces of chicken or 1 whole chicken, cut up
2 whole allspice kernels
3 cinnamon sticks
1 bay leaf
3 whole black peppercorns
½ teaspoon salt

1 quart plain yogurt, for the top

1. If chicken is whole, cut it into six pieces. Remove and discard skin and fat; then rub chicken with salt and baking soda. Rinse well in cold water. Place in a deep pot with water to cover. Add cinnamon sticks, bay leaf, allspice, peppercorns, and salt. Cover pot and bring to a boil. Skim top, removing and discarding any residue that forms. Turn down heat and simmer until tender, about ½ hour. Remove chicken from heat and set aside.

2. In a deep pot over medium heat, melt butter and add *sh'ayriyeh* to it. Stir and brown it for about 10 minutes. Add rice; continue browning and stirring for 3 minutes.

3. Remove chicken from broth and wrap in foil to keep warm. Strain hot chicken broth (about 3½ cups) over rice and stir. Cover pot and cook over high heat for about 10 minutes until boiling. Lower heat and simmer for 15 minutes more and turn off heat. Let stand for 15 minutes.

4. Stir with fork; taste and adjust seasoning. Serve chicken over rice with yogurt (*laban*). A platter of fresh vegetables, such as cut radishes, carrots, lettuce, and Arabic bread round this into a complete meal.

Serves 4 to 6.

ALICE'S KITCHEN
IF YOU MAKE IT WITH LOVE, IT WILL BE DELICIOUS!

Djej Mishwi

BARBEQUED CHICKEN WITH GARLIC MARINADE

◆

No explaining needed here . . . just be sure to make the garlic mayonnaise (*toum ou zeit,* p. 44) ahead of time, because this is what really makes this summer barbeque spectacular!! Serve with Alice's *salata* and french fries. In Lebanon, the very popular french fries are made with their local huge white potatoes from the Bekaa Valley and are delicious, deep-fried in vegetable oil. Use your local counterpart seasonally available from your farmers' markets. An alternative to deep-frying is to brush thinly sliced potatoes lightly with olive oil and bake them.

> 1 whole chicken cut into parts, or 8 pieces of chicken
> 7 cloves garlic
> ½ teaspoon salt
> 1 cup lemon juice
> ⅛ cup olive oil
> ½ teaspoon black pepper
> ¼ teaspoon cayenne pepper

1. Remove and discard skin and fat; then rinse chicken pieces with water and rub them with baking soda and salt. Rinse again, drain, and place in a bowl.
2. In a small bowl, mash garlic into a paste with salt. Add olive oil, lemon juice, and pepper. Pour into bowl with chicken pieces, and toss so that pieces are completely coated with marinade. Cover bowl and refrigerate for 2 hours or more.
3. Prepare barbeque or grill, preheating it.
4. Place chicken on a hot grill and barbeque for 7 minutes on each side until golden brown or as you like. Serve with fabulous garlic mayonnaise (*toum ou zeit*), salad (*salata*), and french fried potatoes—a summer favorite.

Serves 4 to 6.

Djej Mhammar

BROILED CHICKEN WITH GARLIC MARINADE

◆

Recently I made this specialty of Mother's for a New Year's dinner party, and my guests were licking their fingers and asking for the recipe. Make the superb garlic mayonnaise (*toum ou zeit*, p. 44) for dipping ahead of time! The mayonnaise used in the marinade is the plain, store-bought kind. Excellent either baked or broiled.

> 1 whole chicken cut into parts, or 8 pieces of chicken
> 7 cloves garlic
> ½ teaspoon each salt and black pepper
> ½ cup lemon juice
> ¼ teaspoon cayenne pepper
> ⅛ teaspoon each cinnamon and allspice
> ½ cup plain mayonnaise
> ¼ cup olive oil
> 1 teaspoon paprika

1. Remove and discard skin and fat; rinse chicken with water, and rub with baking soda and salt. Rinse well with water and drain.

2. In a large bowl, mash garlic into a paste using a little salt. Add lemon juice, spices, mayonnaise, and olive oil and mix well. Add chicken pieces to marinate, coating each piece thoroughly; cover and refrigerate for an hour or more.

3. Follow instructions for baking or broiling.

BROILING

Preheat oven to broil. Put chicken in a roasting pan and place under broiler to brown for 7 minutes. Sprinkle with paprika; turn over, add paprika, and brown the other side. Sprinkle with water, cover with foil, reduce heat to 325°F, and bake for 5 to 10 minutes more, or until the chicken is done.

BAKING

Preheat oven to 375°F. Put chicken in a baking dish lined with parchment; sprinkle with paprika; and place on bottom oven rack for 15 to 20 minutes. Turn over with a fork; add paprika; move to top oven rack; bake until chicken is done.

Serve with garlic mayonnaise (*toum ou zeit*), *salata*, and potatoes: french fried, Lebanese potato salad, or Lebanese mashed potatoes.

Serves 4 to 6.

ALICE'S KITCHEN

IF YOU MAKE IT WITH LOVE, IT WILL BE DELICIOUS!

Shish Taouk

GRILLED CHICKEN WITH GARLIC MARINADE

◆

In Lebanon, *shish taouk* is a popular grilled kebab made with luscious strips of marinated chicken. It is served with rice or lentils, *hommus*, and salad such as *tabbouli, fattoush,* or our refreshing basic *salata*. Alternatively it can be served in a pita with a dab of our tantalizing garlic mayonnaise (*toum ou zeit*, p.44), onions and tomatoes with pickled turnips (*lifit*) on the side. Marinate chicken for a few hours for the best results.

2 chicken breasts, cut into 2" strips
7 cloves garlic, minced
½ teaspoon salt
½ cup lemon juice
½ teaspoon black pepper
¼ teaspoon cayenne pepper
1 teaspoon paprika
⅛ cup olive oil
1 onion, cut in half and then ⅓ (optional)

5–7 metal or bamboo skewers (soak bamboo in water first)

1. Remove and discard skin and fat, then rinse chicken with water, and rub with baking soda and salt. Rinse well with cold water and drain.
2. Place chicken strips in a large bowl, add garlic, salt, lemon juice, spices, and olive oil and mix well, coating each piece thoroughly. Cover bowl and refrigerate to marinate for a few hours.
3. Prepare barbeque or grill. Skewer chicken, alternating with onions after every two chicken pieces, and place on grill for about 5 minutes. Turn to other side, and grill a few more minutes until done.
4. Serve with garlic mayonnaise (*toum ou zeit*), *salata,* and french fried potatoes, or in pita bread as described above.

Serves 4 to 6.

Riz bi Tfeen

UPSIDE-DOWN RICE

◆

Simple and yet very satisfying and easy to make, this one-pot meal featuring chicken or lamb shanks, with garbanzo beans, rice, and onions, is flavorful and nutritious. I've cooked a meatless version of this which is great; just eliminate the meat and follow the recipe using vegetable stock.

4 chicken pieces or 2 lamb shanks
3 yellow onions, julienne-cut
2 tablespoons clarified butter or olive oil,
    or equal parts of each
1 can garbanzo beans, drained
1 cup rice, soaked and rinsed
½ teaspoon salt
3 whole peppercorns
¼ teaspoon ground allspice
½ teaspoon ground cinnamon
4 cinnamon sticks

1. Remove and discard skin and fat; then rub chicken with baking soda and salt and rinse well. If using lamb shanks, rinse them. Drain chicken or lamb and place in large pot. Cover with water, add seasonings and bring to a boil. Simmer 20 minutes. Let cool. Strain and reserve broth.

2. Sauté onions in clarified butter or olive oil in a deep pot until they are translucent. Add garbanzo beans and continue to sauté about 5 minutes.

3. Remove meat from bone and layer pieces over onions and beans. Stir in a little more salt, pepper, allspice, and ground cinnamon. Add broth to cover the chicken or lamb. Add rice on top without stirring. Cover and bring to a boil, then reduce heat to low and simmer until rice is done, about 30 minutes or longer if using brown rice.

4. Let stand for 10 minutes and then loosen rice from edges of pot. Place a large round platter on top of pot and briskly and carefully turn the pot upside down emptying the one-pot meal onto the platter. Serve with Arabic bread, yogurt (*laban*), and fresh cut vegetables.

Serves 4 to 6.

Burghul Mfalfal

CHICKEN WITH BULGUR

◆

Similar to the lamb recipe of the same name, this dish uses chicken instead of lamb, with garbanzo beans and onions. Also similar to *riz bi tfeen*, this is made with bulgur instead of rice. The protein of a small amount of meat with wheat can feed a large family, and serving this with yogurt (*laban*) adds even more protein. Our traditional seasonings of cinnamon, allspice, salt, and pepper give it its Lebanese signature and great flavor.

1 whole chicken, cut into pieces, or 8 pieces of chicken
2 quarts water or vegetable stock
3–4 whole cinnamon sticks
½ teaspoon salt
6 whole peppercorns
6 whole allspice kernels
1 cup #4 bulgur (*burghul*), soaked and rinsed
¼ cup clarified butter
1 can garbanzo beans, drained
1 onion, chopped
⅛ cup olive oil

1. Remove and discard skin and fat; then rub chicken with baking soda and salt. Rinse well with water and drain.

2. Place chicken into a deep pot with water, cinnamon sticks, salt, peppers, and allspice; cover pot and bring to a boil, then lower heat and simmer for about 30 minutes. Set aside to cool, reserving broth.

3. Place bulgur in another deep pot and brown for a few minutes, stirring constantly, before adding butter. Add clarified butter, stirring until brown.

4. Meanwhile, in a sauté pan, sauté onion in olive oil until translucent. Add garbanzo beans and continue to cook about 5 minutes. Set aside.

5. Strain broth from chicken and add 3 cups broth to *burghul*. Cover and steam for 15 minutes, adding more broth if needed.

6. Remove chicken from bones and add to *burghul*, layering in onions and beans. Steam 10 more minutes. Turn off heat and let stand for 15 minutes before serving with yogurt (*laban*), Arabic bread or pita chips, carrot sticks and other fresh vegetables or salad.

Serves 4 to 6.

Bamye ou Djej

OKRA AND CHICKEN

◆

Okra (*bamye*) gently simmered with tomato, onion, garlic, and chicken makes a light, flavorful stew that is served on a bed of rice (*riz mfalfal*) and eaten with Arabic bread, carrot sticks, and romaine lettuce leaves. Perfect for supper in the summertime when okra is in season.

> 2 tablespoons olive oil or clarified butter
> 1½ pounds lamb, cut in 1" cubes for stewing
> ¾ teaspoon black pepper
> ¼ teaspoon cayenne pepper
> ½ teaspoon cinnamon
> 3 onions, chopped
> 2 cloves chopped garlic
> 1 teaspoon salt
> 1 can whole tomatoes, chopped, with liquid
> 1 pound fresh okra, rinsed and stemmed

1. Brown chicken pieces in clarified butter or olive oil with seasonings over medium heat, until light brown. Add onions, garlic, and salt, continuing to sauté 5 minutes.

2. Stir in tomatoes with their liquid and, very gently, the okra. Cover and simmer for 15 to 20 minutes, being careful not to overcook okra as it will become mushy. Serve hot over rice with Arabic bread.

Serves 4 to 6.

Samak

◆

Fish

Since Douma is a high mountain village, in Mama's days there in the early 1920s, it was a long journey to the Mediterranean, even though its waters were clearly visible from the town's 3000-foot elevation. Because of the distance and the lack of good refrigeration, fish was not a frequent part of our family repertoire. In Los Angeles, fish remained a minor part of our diet. The exception was canned tuna fish for Fridays and Lent, which was lavished with lemon juice, as we preferred all of our fish dishes.

Lebanese coastal people have fresh fish as a much more significant part of their diet—a typical example of the regional differences in our cooking. In the Lebanese mountains, there are local rivers but these are not vast like the Pacific Northwest rivers that I'm familiar with; they are more like creeks. Though few in number, these zesty fish recipes are delectable.

Whenever possible, buy freshly caught fish that is local and in season, or from sustainably run farms if it is farm-raised. This is for environmental as well as health reasons. Talk to your local natural foods store and ask them about the best fish choices, and ask them or your local supermarket to buy their fish from sustainable sources, which is beneficial to all.

Samak Bil Furn Ma Taratour

BAKED FISH WITH TAHINI

◆

Lemon juice, onions, and flavorful tahini (*taratour*) sauce are the classic Lebanese accompaniments to fish. Sautéed pine nuts (*snobar*) add an elegant touch as a garnish plus crunch!

1 whole fish, 12" to 14"
olive oil
¼ teaspoon salt
¼ teaspoon pepper
1 large onion, finely chopped
⅓ cup lemon juice

GARNISH

taratour sauce (p. 42)
½ cup parsley sprigs
2 lemons, cut into wedges
½ cup sautéed pine nuts

1. Preheat oven to 350ºF. Rinse fish, pat dry, and rub with olive oil, salt, and pepper. Wrap tightly in brown paper or baking parchment and place on baking dish. Bake for 20 to 30 minutes, depending upon the size and thickness of the fish, using the rule of thumb of 10 minutes per inch of thickness.

2. Meanwhile, sauté onion in olive oil for about 15 minutes. Set aside. Make *taratour* sauce and sauté pine nuts for garnish.

3. Remove and discard the paper, skin, and bones of the fish. Arrange pieces of fish on a platter. Spread sautéed onion over the top. Drizzle with *taratour* sauce and lemon juice. Garnish with parsley, lemon wedges or slices, and sautéed pine nuts.

Serves 4.

IF YOU MAKE IT WITH LOVE, IT WILL BE DELICIOUS!

Kibbet Samak

BAKED FISH AND BULGUR WITH PINE NUT FILLING

◆

K*ibbe*, the "national dish" of Lebanon, usually refers to lamb ground with bulgur and onions, which is eaten raw (*nayye*) or baked (*bil sinneyeh*). When visiting Lebanon, I discovered many kinds of *kibbe* besides lamb and bulgur—beef, fish, potato, pumpkin, and walnut—all mixtures of a main ingredient with equal parts of bulgur and onion. Mother's fish *kibbe* recipe is complemented with the addition of orange zest, great with fish. This recipe is scaled down from a big recipe for our large family.

1 pound halibut filet, deboned
1 onion, quartered
1 cup #1 bulgur, soaked and rinsed
½ teaspoon each salt and black pepper
½ teaspoon cayenne pepper
½ teaspoon ground coriander
2 tablespoons lemon juice
2 tablespoons orange zest

FILLING

1 onion, julienne-cut
½ cup pine nuts
½ cup olive oil
½ teaspoon salt

1. Remove skin and bone from fish and rinse. Preheat oven to 425°F.

2. Grind fish with quartered onions in food grinder or processor. Mix in seasonings and grind again, mixing with bulgur.

3. Sauté julienne-cut onions, salt, and pine nuts in olive oil until light brown. Lift nuts and onions from pan with slotted spoon and reserve oil.

4. Lightly oil an 8"x8" baking dish; spread half the fish mixture making an even layer ½" thick. Spread onion filling evenly over this; cover with remaining *kibbe*, smoothing out the surface with your hand.

5. Cut into diamonds. Pour olive oil from sauté evenly over the top of the *kibbe*. Bake for 15 minutes in lower oven rack; move to top oven rack to brown the top. Serve hot or cold with *salata*.

Serves 4 to 6.

Samak Miqli Ma Taratour

Fried fish with tahini sauce

◆

Fish is always best when it's fresh. Frying makes it tasty with the addition of our zesty lemon and *taratour* sauce for a great summer meal. Serve it with *tabbouli*, *fattoush*, or *salata*, and french fries!

> 2 pounds halibut or rock bass filets
> salt and pepper
> ¼–½ cup olive oil, for frying
> ½ cup flour
> ¼ cup lemon juice
> ¾ cup tahini *taratour* sauce (p. 42)
> 2 lemons, cut into wedges for garnish

1. Rinse fish filets in water and pat dry. Season with salt and pepper. Put flour on a plate and pat filets in flour to coat both sides. Heat olive oil in a skillet and lay fish filets in skillet.

2. Fry for about 5 minutes on each side until golden brown but still tender. Remove from heat and drain on a paper towel. Serve on a platter drizzled with lemon juice and *taratour* sauce, surrounded by lemon wedges.

Serves 4 to 6.

ALICE'S KITCHEN

If you make it with Love, it will be Delicious!

'Raas Samak

FISH PATTIES

◆

Nowadays, we're becoming more health conscious and aren't eating so much fried food. Once in a while, however, it's okay to indulge! Serve this with healthy *tabbouli*, and you'll feel no guilt!

1½ pounds fish, rinsed, skinned, and boned
2 small potatoes, boiled
2 small onions, quartered
1 egg, separated
½ teaspoon salt
½ teaspoon black pepper
¼ teaspoon cinnamon
½ teaspoon cumin
1 teaspoon vinegar
½ cup flour
1 cup bread crumbs
½ cup olive or vegetable oil, for frying
¾ cup *taratour* sauce (p. 42)
2 lemons, cut into wedges for garnish

1. Grind fish together with potatoes and onions in food grinder two times, or in food processor until it is finely minced. Place mixture in a bowl and add egg yolk, seasonings, and vinegar. Mix well. Stir egg white in a flat bowl. Place flour into a flat plate.

2. Form fish into patties or rounds and dip into flour first, then into egg white and then bread crumbs.

3. Heat oil in skillet and fry patties on each side until light brown. Remove from skillet and drain on paper towel. Serve hot or at room temperature with *taratour* sauce, lemon wedges, and *salata*.

Serves 4 to 6.

Samak Mishwi

BROILED OR GRILLED FISH WITH TAHINI SAUCE

◆

Generously dotted with minced garlic and moistened with lemon juice, a simple piece of fish is elevated to gourmet heights. The secret is not to overcook the fish. Serve it with or without the tahini (*taratour*) sauce—it's great either way.

> 2 pounds halibut or rock bass filets
> olive oil
> salt and pepper
> 3 cloves garlic, minced
> ½ cup lemon juice
> ½ cup *taratour* sauce (p. 42)
> 2 lemons, cut into wedges for garnish

1. Heat oven to broil or grill. Rinse fish in water and pat dry. Rub with olive oil and season lightly with salt and pepper. Lay filets in a broiling pan and sprinkle with minced garlic and lemon juice.

2. Broil for about 5 minutes on each side until just golden brown and still tender. Remove from heat and serve on a platter with lemon wedges and *taratour* sauce.

Serves 4 to 6.

AKL SIYEME

◆

VEGETARIAN ENTRÉES

Because my book is about family and preserving our culinary traditions, it has been a labor of love. Although I have been a vegetarian for most of the past 25 years and the recipes in this section are the ones I use the most, the question of whether to include our meat recipes in this book didn't take long to answer. With food trends going to extremes from vegan to all-meat diets, our Lebanese cuisine remains a healthy and moderate way of eating.

The Lebanese diet is a Mediterranean diet: well-balanced with small amounts of meat, eggs, lots of fresh, raw vegetables, grains, and fresh fruits, with small amounts of healthy fat from sheep and goat milk yogurt and cheeses as well as olive oil. Our village, Douma, sits 3000 feet above the Mediterranean Sea, on a steep mountain slope, terraced with olive trees, some of which are 2000 years old! Our spiritual heritage is Eastern Catholic and follows Lenten practices that allowed for the creation of a myriad of vegetarian dishes. Over the years, these continue to be my favorites (especially *mjaddrah*), along with soups, salads, and the classic appetizers of *hommus* and *baba ghannouj*. The Arabic word *Siyeme* means Lenten, which is basically a meatless, fasting, typically springtime menu.

When visiting Lebanon in 1996 as a vegetarian, my cousins were thrilled to make meatless dishes for me. As a result, I was blessed to be introduced to several new recipes to add to my family's already grand repertoire of vegetarian dishes. You'll find a pumpkin *kibbe* as well as a potato and walnut *kibbe*. Mother and *Sitto* knew these dishes but didn't make them, instead making us many other fabulous dishes, from easy to elaborate: stuffed and rolled vegetables, lentil and rice dishes, stews, spinach pies, omelettes, and even a recipe for *falafel*. All are delectable and nutritious so enjoy! Mother remembers strangers asking her what she fed her children since we looked so healthy!

Mjaddrah

LENTILS AND RICE WITH CARAMELIZED ONIONS

◆

This is a favorite from childhood, when my gardening passions were budding and I used to pretend that the brown *mjaddrah* was the earth and the green salad served on top of it as the vegetables I was growing. The combination is perfect with bread and provides rich proteins. Caramelized onions lacing the top elevate this simple, nutritious food to gourmet status. Best with *salata* and scooped up with Arabic bread, it is one of our easiest recipes to make, and is a potluck favorite, with everyone vying for the sweet and flavorful carmelized onions.

1 cup onions, chopped to sauté
3 onions, julienne-cut, to caramelize
⅛ cup olive oil
½ cup brown or white rice, soaked and rinsed
1 cup lentils, rinsed
4 cups water or vegetable stock
½ teaspoon salt
¼ teaspoon cayenne pepper

1. Sauté chopped onions in oil until slightly brown in a soup pot.
2. Meanwhile, rinse lentils and rice. If you use brown rice, add both lentils and rice to onions and sauté a few minutes more. Add water, salt, and cayenne. Cover, bring to a boil and simmer for 1½ hours. With white rice, add it to the pot after lentils have simmered for nearly an hour.
3. Stir from time to time and add water if necessary: *mjaddrah* can be made as dry as rice or as wet as a thick porridge.
4. While the lentils and rice simmer, julienne-cut three onions and sauté them in olive oil in a cast iron or sauté pan, first on high heat, stirring constantly, then on low, until they are golden brown, about 30 minutes.
5. Let *mjaddrah* stand for 15 minutes after it is done before putting it onto a serving platter. Delicious hot, at room temperature, or cold, heaped on a platter with the caramelized onions lacing the top.

Serves 4 to 6.

Mjaddrah ma Burghul

LENTILS AND BULGUR WITH CARAMELIZED ONIONS

◆

Made with bulgur instead of rice, this variation on *mjaddrah* has a hearty wheat flavor and is just as nutritious, providing a protein-rich combination of lentils and bulgur (*burghul*) that is medium to coarse in size.

1 cup chopped onions
3 onions, julienne-cut, to caramelize
⅛ cup olive oil
½ cup bulgur, soaked and rinsed
1 cup lentils, soaked and rinsed
4 cups water or vegetable stock
½ teaspoon salt
¼ teaspoon cayenne

1. Sauté chopped onions in oil until slightly brown in a soup pot.

2. Add lentils, water, salt, and cayenne to onions. Cover, bring to a boil and simmer for an hour.

3. Stir in bulgur; check water level and add water if needed; continue to simmer for 20 minutes, or until done.

4. In the meantime, julienne-cut three onions and slowly sauté in olive oil in a cast iron or sauté pan until golden brown, about 30 minutes.

5. Serve *mjaddrah* on a platter with caramelized onions lacing the top, with *salata* and Arabic bread. May be eaten hot, at room temperature, or cold.

Serves 4 to 6.

Mdardarah

Lentils and Rice with Caramelized Onions

◆

And yet another variation on *mjaddrah,* this one has more rice to lentils than *mjaddrah* and a drier consistency—more like steamed rice. Quite delicious, as are the other variations, *mdardarah* is also served with *salata* and Arabic bread and of course, the flavorful carmelized onions. Serve hot, at room temperature, or cold in the summer for a picnic.

> 1 cup chopped onions
> 3 onions, julienne-cut, to caramelize
> ⅛ cup olive oil
> ½ cup brown (or white) rice, soaked and rinsed
> ½ cup lentils, rinsed
> 3 cups water or vegetable stock
> ½ teaspoon salt
> ¼ teaspoon cayenne

1. Sauté chopped onions in olive oil until slightly brown.
2. Meanwhile, rinse lentils and rice. If you use brown rice, add both lentils and rice to onions and sauté a few minutes more. Add water, salt, and cayenne. Cover, bring to a boil and simmer for 1½ hours. If you use white rice, add it to the pot after the other ingredients have simmered for nearly an hour.
3. Check water level and stir about midway, adding water if needed so that it does not stick.
4. In the meantime, julienne-cut three onions and slowly sauté in olive oil until golden brown.
5. When *mdardarah* is done, let it stand for 10 minutes before transferring it to a serving platter. Scatter the caramelized onions over the top and enjoy.

Serves 4.

ALICE'S KITCHEN
IF YOU MAKE IT WITH LOVE, IT WILL BE DELICIOUS!

134

Riz ou Kousa

RICE AND SUMMER SQUASH

◆

S*itto,* my dear grandmother, made this excellent summer dish when summer squash (*kousa*) were abundant. Simple to prepare and tasty, it is one of the first dishes I was able to cook on my own. Let your child try it with your guidance! It makes a great summer potluck dish, served hot, at room temperature, or cold, scooped in Arabic bread with fresh cut vegetables or a salad alongside.

1 onion, finely chopped
¼ cup olive oil
5 yellow squash or small zucchini, chopped into 1" cubes
3 stalks celery (optional)
¾ cup rice, soaked and rinsed
3 fresh tomatoes, chopped, plus ½ cup water
    or 1 large can whole tomatoes, chopped, with juice
    or ½ small can tomato sauce plus 1 cup water
½ teaspoon each salt and black pepper
dash cayenne pepper

1. In a deep pot, sauté onion in olive oil for 10 minutes and then add seasonings, squash, celery, and tomato. Sauté 10 minutes over medium heat. Add rice and water as needed to create a cup of liquid with tomatoes. Cover and bring to boil, then reduce heat and simmer for ½ hour or until rice is done. Brown rice takes twice as long as white rice.

2. Stir occasionally and check to see if more water is needed—the correct consistency is like that of a moist rice. Let stand in pot for 10 minutes before serving. Present on a colorful platter with Arabic bread.

Serves 4 to 6.

Burghul ou Kousa

Bulgur and summer squash

◆

In this variation on *riz ou kousa* using medium-sized bulgur, the wonderful flavor of wheat comes through as well as its nutty texture. Serve with Arabic bread and fresh cut vegetables.

¼ cup olive oil
2 onions, chopped
2 celery stalks, chopped
4 yellow squash or small zucchini, chopped into 1" cubes
¾ cup bulgur (*burghul*), soaked and rinsed
3 fresh tomatoes, chopped, plus ½ cup water
    or 1 large can whole tomatoes, with liquid
    or ½ small can tomato sauce plus 1 cup water
½ teaspoon salt
¼ teaspoon black pepper
¼ teaspoon cayenne pepper
dash cinnamon

1. In a deep pot, sauté onion in olive oil for 10 minutes; then add celery, squash, and chopped tomato. Sauté 10 minutes over medium heat.

2. Add bulgur, water as needed to create a cup of liquid with tomatoes, and seasonings. Cover and bring to boil, then reduce heat and simmer for ½ hour, until bulgur is done. Stir occasionally and check to see if more water is needed. Let stand in pot for 10 minutes before serving.

Serves 4.

ALICE'S KITCHEN
IF YOU MAKE IT WITH LOVE, IT WILL BE DELICIOUS!

Mfarket Kousa

SUMMER SQUASH STEW

◆

Stews are typical of the one-pot meals essential to our Lebanese cuisine. Quick to prepare, served over rice, and eaten with Arabic bread, this particular one is nutritious, tasty, and satisfying, using the cores or squash marrow from stuffed summer squash (*kousa mihshi*) or finely chopped fresh squash. The flavors of this are deliciously reminiscent of the stuffed squash with lamb, yet without the meat. Serve over rice (*riz mfalfal*) with Arabic bread and fresh cut vegetables.

⅛ cup olive oil
1 onion, minced
1 clove garlic
1 large can whole tomatoes, chopped
    or 3 chopped fresh tomatoes with their juice
3 cups yellow or green squash marrow from cored
    zucchini or finely chopped squash
½ teaspoon salt
¼ teaspoon black pepper
¼ teaspoon cayenne pepper
¼ teaspoon cinnamon

1. Sauté onion and garlic in olive oil over medium heat in a deep sauté pan. When onion is transparent, stir in the tomatoes.

2. If using squash marrow, squeeze out and set aside liquid for use in soup stock. Stir squash and seasonings in with onions and tomatoes. Cover and simmer until squash is done, about 25 minutes.

Serves 4.

Fatayir bi Sbanikh

SPINACH PIES

◆

Better tasting after they have cooled from the oven, spinach pies were difficult to get enough of when Mother and *Sitto* baked them. As a child, I loved trying to make these and am grateful to Mother and *Sitto* for this early opportunity to develop a skill and love for making them. They are even more fun to make when there are two or three people involved in the production—chatting, rolling dough, filling, and pinching—the time flies when making these labor-intensive delicacies. They are formed similarly to meat pies (pp. 88–89), except spinach pie triangles are totally closed; both make great appetizers.

At the end of the recipe are variations if you don't have time to make small pies and a Greek variation with feta cheese crumbled into the filling. First, prepare the dough following the basic bread dough recipe, and while it rises, make the filling.

DOUGH

follow recipe for basic bread dough (p. 179)

FILLING

2 bunches of spinach, rinsed and dried
    or 1 package of frozen spinach
1 bunch parsley, rinsed, stemmed
2 cups fresh spearmint, rinsed and stemmed
1 bunch green onions
2 small white onions
½ cup celery tops
2 small zucchini, grated (optional)
1 teaspoon salt
½ tablespoon black pepper
½ teaspoon cayenne pepper
⅓ cup lemon juice
    or ¼ teaspoon citric acid to minimize liquid
2 tablespoons olive oil

FILLING

1. Chop onions and put in large bowl. Stir in salt, pepper, and cayenne.
2. Finely chop green onions, spinach, parsley, mint, celery tops, and grated

ALICE'S KITCHEN
IF YOU MAKE IT WITH LOVE, IT WILL BE DELICIOUS!

138

zucchini and mix in thoroughly. Add citric acid or lemon juice and oil just before filling the dough. Taste and adjust seasoning.

1. Using a rolling pin, roll out one ball of dough on a well-floured surface to about ⅛" thickness.

2. Use a mason jar cap (3½" diameter) to cut out as many circles as possible; put scraps of dough into a bowl with a little water and set aside.

3. Place 1 to 2 tablespoons of filling into a circle, leaving ½" of dough exposed to join the dough together and close it into a triangle as explained on pp. 88–89 for meat pies, with one difference—the dough on spinach pies is pinched totally closed.

Secrets of forming triangles filled with spinach

• Keep the wet filling away from the seam, and keep your fingers dry and floured while pinching dough so the seam stays sealed in baking.
• Add a tablespoon of wheat germ or flour to filling if too much liquid accumulates in bowl.
• Fill pie as much as possible because spinach shrinks with cooking.
• Push in the point of the triangle before pinching edge closed; this keeps juices from escaping in baking.

4. Place pies on oiled cookie sheet or tray lined with baking parchment about ¼" to ½" apart. Preheat oven to 375°F.

5. Knead dough scraps and form into a ball, dust with flour, cover and let rise again. If you have extra dough and no more filling, use it to make *tilme bi zaatar*, plain *tilme, khubz,* or a pizza! Or freeze extra dough for later use: just roll it into a ball, then dust with flour, cover tightly with plastic wrap and freeze in a plastic freezer bag.

6. Bake pies on lowest oven rack until bottoms are golden brown, for about 10 to 12 minutes. Move tray to top rack until tops are lightly browned, another 10 minutes.

7. Remove from trays and drain on opened paper bags to absorb oil and cool. Save some for the guests!!!

To freeze pies for later baking

Place unbaked pies on ungreased tray in freezer for several hours until individually frozen and then pack in freezer bags to store for a month or so. Or freeze baked pies for reheating prior to serving.

• Make dough ahead and freeze, by wrapping orange-sized balls tightly in plastic and placing in a freezer bag. Remove from freezer and place dough in a warm place allowing a few hours for it to thaw and rise. It can also thaw in the refrigerator overnight.

• Instead of small circles of dough, form pastry into 6" to 8" circles of dough, and use proportionately more filling, thus having fewer large triangles—the type available in restaurants because they are quicker to make. In Lebanon, these are served with a lemon squeezed over the top or *zaatar* sprinkled on to add a bit of flavor and zest.

• A dear Syrian friend of mine, *Sitt* Amine, forms her spinach pies as one large rolled-out piece of dough, places it on a cookie sheet, and puts spinach filling 1" thick covering one-half of the dough to ½" from the edge. She folds the other half of the dough across to cover the filling, rolls over it lightly with the rolling pin and then bakes it as one big piece, with a little olive oil brushed across the top. She doesn't seal the edges, which allows some of the juices to seep out. After baking, cool and cut into small, easy-to-hold sections. This is a much easier method than individual pies.

• Precook fresh spinach filling in a sauté pan before stuffing to reduce the moisture content and compact it. Mother, in recent years, is using this method, and although it is somewhat easier, I prefer the fresh, once-cooked spinach.

• Add ½ pound crumbled feta cheese to spinach filling.

Serves 8 to 10 for appetizers.

ALICE'S KITCHEN
IF YOU MAKE IT WITH LOVE, IT WILL BE DELICIOUS!

'Ijjeh

Omelette with Parsley, Mint, and Onion

◆

Atasty frittata-like omelette, *'ijjeh*, is light, flavorful, and simple to make. Even in the coldest of Oregon winters, I find parsley and mint in my garden for this tasty dish. It's served for breakfast, brunch, lunch or dinner, tucked into a round of pocket bread—with additional pocket bread, feta cheese or *jibn*, olives, cucumbers, and fig jam served alongside. Of many variations for *ijjeh*, here's our favorite.

1 small white onion, finely chopped
½ teaspoon salt
¼ teaspoon black pepper
dash cayenne pepper
½ teaspoon cinnamon
2 tablespoons flour
1 teaspoon baking powder
4 green onions, finely chopped
½ bunch parsley, finely chopped
4 eggs
¼ cup clarified butter and oil, equal parts
¼ cup fresh spearmint, finely chopped (optional)
½ cup celery tops, finely chopped (optional)
¼ cup grated zucchini (optional)

1. Place white onions in bowl; stir in spices, flour, and baking powder.
2. Mix in green onions, parsley and, if desired, mint, celery, and zucchini. Crack eggs over the top and mix well with a fork.

3. Heat butter and oil in skillet to medium high. Pour in mixture and spread it out evenly. Cook until golden brown and top is not runny, about 5 to 10 minutes. Flip over carefully and brown other side.

A SIMPLE WAY TO FLIP *'IJJEH:*

Place a dish over the skillet that is larger than the skillet; using pot holders, hold the plate flat onto the skillet and briskly turn the skillet upside down, transferring the omelette onto the plate. Then slide the omelette off the plate back into the skillet to brown other side. Cut into quarters or sixths. Serve hot, warm, or cold inside pocket bread.

Serves 4.

142

ALICE'S KITCHEN
IF YOU MAKE IT WITH LOVE, IT WILL BE DELICIOUS!

Kousa Mihshi Siyeme

SUMMER SQUASH STUFFED WITH RICE

◆

Our vegetarian alternative to *kousa mihshi* stuffed with rice, garbanzo beans, parsley, and tomato, is satisfying and wonderfully seasoned. If the light green, very tender, Lebanese summer squash are unavailable, use small yellow crooknecks or dark green zucchini. Mexican squash varieties are very similar to Lebanese and might be found in farmers' markets. Seeds for Lebanese squash are available through a few seed companies, if you care to grow your own. This tasty summer dish can be made with or without garbanzo beans; mint is also an optional ingredient.

10 small Lebanese squash (*kousa*), yellow crookneck,
   zucchini, or Mexican squash

FILLING

1 cup canned garbanzo beans, drained
   or ½ cup dry garbanzo beans, soaked overnight
1 cup rice, soaked and rinsed
2 bunches parsley, finely chopped
1 bunch spearmint, finely chopped (optional)
1 bunch green onions, finely chopped
2 stalks celery with tops, diced
1 teaspoon salt
1 teaspoon black pepper
¼ teaspoon cayenne pepper
1 can whole tomatoes, chopped, with liquid
   or 1 pound fresh tomatoes, finely chopped
⅓ cup lemon juice
¼ cup olive oil, divided

1. If using dry garbanzo beans, soak overnight in a pot. Drain water and add fresh water to cover. Cover pot, bring to a boil, then simmer for about 20 minutes. Cool, drain, and remove skins from beans, by rolling beans gently with a rolling pin on a towel.

2. In a bowl, mix together rice, beans, seasonings, chopped greens, and one half of the olive oil.

3. Core squash according to directions on page 109. Fill with rice mixture to ½" from top and arrange stuffed squash upright in a pot, propped up next to one another.

4. Cover with tomatoes with their liquid, lemon juice, remaining olive

oil, and one cup water. Cover and bring to boil over high heat on the stovetop, then lower heat and simmer approximately 45 minutes, until rice is done, squash is tender, and sauce (*zoum*) is thick.

   5. Split each *kousa* in half on individual plates and pour on a little sauce. Serve hot with Arabic bread and fresh cut vegetables.

Serves 4 to 6.

ALICE'S KITCHEN

IF YOU MAKE IT WITH LOVE, IT WILL BE DELICIOUS!

Batinjan Mihshi Siyeme

Stuffed Eggplant with Rice, Tomato, and Parsley

◆

Made for me by our cousins Nicole and George Sawaya in Lebanon, this vegetarian version of stuffed eggplant *(batinjan mihshi)* is truly excellent! Small eggplants, 3" to 4" in length, are stuffed just as in *kousa mihshi,* stuffed squash.

12 small Japanese or Arabic eggplants, rinsed, unpeeled

FILLING

½ cup rice, soaked and rinsed
3 tomatoes, finely chopped
1 bunch green onions or 1 Spanish onion, finely chopped
½ bunch parsley, finely chopped
½ bunch spearmint, finely chopped
⅓ cup lemon juice
½ teaspoon salt
¼ teaspoon pepper
¼ teaspoon cayenne

FOR THE POT

1 small can tomato sauce
¼ cup olive oil
⅓ cup lemon juice
2 cups water

1. Rinse and core eggplants as in *kousa mihshi* (p. 109). Place them in salted water for 10 minutes and then drain.
2. In a bowl, mix together rice, tomatoes, greens, lemon juice, and spices. Taste and adjust seasoning.
3. Fill each eggplant with rice mixture to ½" from top and arrange upright in a deep pot, propped against one another.
4. Pour tomato sauce over them plus 2 cups of water, olive oil, and lemon juice. Cover and bring to boil. Turn down heat and simmer for an hour or so, until eggplant is tender and sauce has thickened.
5. Serve with sauce (*zoum*) and Arabic bread.

Serves 4 to 6.

Malfouf Mihshi Siyeme

VEGETARIAN STUFFED CABBAGE ROLLS

◆

Absolutely delectable, this vegetarian version of lamb-stuffed cabbage rolls (*malfouf mihshi*) is labor-intensive but well worth the effort! It is a tasty seasonal springtime one-pot meal that my mother and *Sitto* made with love during Lent or on meatless Fridays! Serve it with Arabic bread and fresh cut vegetables.

1 large or 2 medium heads cabbage

FILLING

¾ cup garbanzo beans, soaked overnight,
    halved and skins removed (see step 3)
1 bunch parsley, finely chopped
½ bunch spearmint, finely chopped
3 green onions
1 Spanish onion
½ cup rice, soaked and rinsed
½ head of celery, tops and stalks
½ teaspoon salt
¼ teaspoon black pepper
¼ teaspoon cayenne pepper
¼ cup lemon juice
⅛ cup olive oil

FOR THE POT

10–12 small cloves of garlic, unpeeled
2 cups water
¼ cup olive oil
⅓ cup lemon juice
salt

1. Core cabbage by inserting knife point around the core to about 4" deep, circling it, and removing it.

2. Blanch whole cabbage by placing core-side down in a pot of boiling water for a few minutes until slightly tender, limp, and bright green in color. Separate leaves one at a time as they wilt enough to be flexible to roll. Gently place leaves in a colander to cool and drain for stuffing.

3. Place soaked garbanzo beans on a clean kitchen towel and roll gently with a rolling pin to break them in half and to separate them from their skins.

ALICE'S KITCHEN
IF YOU MAKE IT WITH LOVE, IT WILL BE DELICIOUS!

4. In a bowl, mix together the rice, garbanzo beans, salt, pepper, lemon juice, and olive oil.

5. Finely chop parsley, mint, onions, and celery; mix them into rice mixture. Taste and adjust seasoning.

6. Open cabbage leaves flat on a clean, flat surface and cut main rib out. Line bottom of a deep pot with small leaves and rib pieces. Large outer leaves can be cut in half and used to make two rolls.

7. One cabbage leaf at a time, spoon several teaspoons of stuffing across one end and roll tightly closed, tucking sides and extra parts of leaf into the center. Stack rolls in pot on top of leaves and ribs. When you have one layer of rolls, distribute whole unpeeled garlic cloves over them and continue layering in cabbage rolls and garlic.

8. Pour water, a little salt, lemon juice, and olive oil over the top. Place a plate upside down over rolls to hold them intact and cover pot with lid. Cook on high until boiling, then turn down heat and steam until rice is done, about 1 hour. Remove plate after cooked half way, about 30 minutes, and continue cooking. Let stand for 15 minutes before serving.

Serves 6 to 8.

Waraq ʿInab or Waraq Siliq

VEGETARIAN STUFFED GRAPE LEAVES OR CHARD LEAVES

◆

Rolled grape leaves, either with meat and rice, or rice and vegetables, are one of the finest of Lebanese dishes. Please see recipe on page 110 about picking fresh grape leaves, which make the best stuffed grape leaves in summertime. Fresh chard leaves are a perfect winter or springtime substitute in this nutritious and delectable vegetarian composition. Make more than you think you'll need, as they're fantastic the next day, either reheated, at room temperature, or cold.

40 fresh or frozen grape leaves
    or 1 quart canned grape leaves
    or 10–20 chard leaves (red or green)

FILLING

1 cup rice, soaked and rinsed
1 bunch green onions or 1 Spanish onion, finely chopped
1 bunch parsley, finely chopped
½ bunch spearmint, finely chopped
1 cup tomatoes, finely chopped
½ cup garbanzo beans, precooked or canned (optional)
½ teaspoon salt
½ teaspoon black pepper
¼ teaspoon cayenne pepper
¼ cup lemon juice
⅛ cup olive oil

FOR THE POT

4 cloves garlic
½ cup lemon juice
3 cups water
⅛ cup olive oil

1. In a large bowl, add seasonings to rice and mix well; add lemon juice and olive oil. Mix in chopped vegetables and beans. Taste and adjust seasoning.

2. Blanch fresh or frozen grape leaves in warm water for a few minutes to wilt them, or they will wilt just left out a few hours. Canned grape leaves are

148

ALICE'S KITCHEN
IF YOU MAKE IT WITH LOVE, IT WILL BE DELICIOUS!

wilted enough to roll easily. Place extra or torn grape leaves to cover the bottom of a deep pot and set aside. If using chard leaves, follow the same procedure, except in step 3, remove the central chard rib and stem, placing the ribs at the bottom of the big pot. Cut chard leaves in half or quarter so they're 4" to 5" wide.

3. Lay one leaf out on a board with veins facing you and the stem towards you; place stuffing about the thickness of your index finger across the width of the leaf. Fold sides in covering the filling, and roll the leaf up tightly like a carpet. For larger chard leaves, you can use more filling.

4. Place each rolled grape leaf into the pot side by side, forming a row. Begin the next row perpendicular to it and continue stacking them in the pot in this manner, until you have used up all of the filling. Nestle whole garlic cloves in between them.

5. Pour water, lemon juice, and olive oil over them and place a plate on top of the grape leaves, top side down. Cook over high heat until boiling, then simmer until rice is done, approximately 45 minutes. Let stand for 15 minutes before serving.

6. Serve with carrot sticks, celery, cucumbers, olives, yogurt cheese (*labne*), and Arabic bread.

Serves 6 to 8 as an entrée or 8 to12 for appetizers.

Masbahit il Darwish

EGGPLANT POTATO STEW

◆

Here is the original Lenten version of Monk's Rosary that our family ate and loved. Simple, hearty, and nutritious as so many of our one-pot dishes are, this stew can be served on its own or over steamed rice (*riz mfalfal*) with Arabic bread.

> 1 onion, julienne-cut
> 2 potatoes, small cubes or wedges
> 2 garlic cloves, chopped
> 4 zucchini or yellow squash, cut on diagonal
> 1 eggplant, cut into 1" cubes
> 1 can garbanzo beans, drained
> 1 can whole tomatoes
> > or 4 fresh tomatoes, peeled, chopped, with juice
> ½ teaspoon salt
> ¼ teaspoon cayenne pepper
> ¼ cup olive oil

1. Preheat oven to 375°F. Layer the above ingredients into a stew pot in the order presented above. Cover and bake for 30 minutes.

2. Stir and continue to bake uncovered at 350°F until liquid is absorbed, potatoes are cooked, and sauce thickens—approximately 15 minutes more. Serve hot with Arabic bread and fresh cut vegetables.

Serves 4 to 6.

Masbahit il Darwish

MONK'S ROSARY

◆

The name of this implies that it is a poor person's food because it is meatless—in the past, eating meat was a sign of wealth. Times have changed, with many people choosing a vegetarian diet for health reasons, regardless of economic status. This is Mother's newer version of this stew, with more vegetables than the one on the previous page, served on its own or over steamed rice (*riz mfalfal*) with Arabic bread. This recipe makes a large pot, enough to feed a family, and because it's just a matter of chopping vegetables, it's easy to prepare.

1 eggplant, cut into large cubes
1 cup celery, diced
2 potatoes, diced
3 carrots, cut on diagonal
1 can garbanzo beans, drained
3 zucchini or yellow squash, cut on diagonal
2 green or red peppers, cut into 1-inch chunks
5 garlic cloves, chopped
3 onions, julienne-cut
1 can whole tomatoes
  or 4 fresh tomatoes, peeled and chopped, with juice
5 peppercorns
½ teaspoon salt
¼ teaspoon cayenne pepper
¼ teaspoon cinnamon
½ cup olive oil

1. Preheat oven to 375°F. Layer the above ingredients into a stew pot or casserole with lid in the order presented above. Cover and bake for 30 minutes.

2. Stir and continue to bake uncovered at 350°F until sauce thickens and potatoes are cooked, approximately 15 minutes more. Serve hot with Arabic bread and fresh cut vegetables.

Serves 6 to 8.

Riz ou Fassoulia Siyeme

LIMA BEANS OR WHITE BEANS WITH TOMATO OVER RICE

◆

Here I have adapted a dish made traditionally with small bits of lamb into a vegetarian version. The rice and beans, *riz ou fassoulia*, are a protein-rich combination seasoned with the same spices as the lamb version and just as wonderful. Serve over steamed rice (*riz mfalfal*) with fresh cut vegetables and Arabic bread.

2 tablespoons olive oil
2 medium onions, chopped
3 cloves garlic, chopped
½ teaspoon salt
¾ teaspoon black pepper
¼ teaspoon cayenne pepper
½ teaspoon cinnamon
1 can whole tomatoes, chopped, with liquid
2 packages frozen lima beans
    or ¾ cup dry navy beans, soaked overnight
    plus 2 cups water

1. In a deep pot, sauté onions, garlic, and seasonings in olive oil over medium heat for about 15 minutes, stirring frequently.

2. Add tomatoes, with their liquid and the beans. Turn heat up, cover pot, and bring to a boil. Then reduce heat to low and simmer for 20 minutes if frozen beans are used. Dry beans, soaked overnight, take 2 hours or more of simmering to be tender, and need the additional water.

3. Stir occasionally, adding water if necessary, until beans are done. Serve over rice with Arabic bread.

Serves 4 to 6.

Falafel

FAVA AND GARBANZO BEAN PATTIES

◆

Although I don't remember eating this as a child, it is a food that I love and frequently make. This new recipe, inspired by a recent trip to Lebanon, incorporates Mother's recipe, suggestions from friends, and comes with a warning: it can be addictive! Serve as in Beirut: folded in a pocket bread with *lots* of *taratour* (tahini sauce), tomatoes, spearmint, parsley, onions with sumac, and pickles; pickled turnips (*lifit*) on the side. Luscious! Make *taratour* sauce ahead and refrigerate. (p. 42)

A food processor makes this very easy to make; a food grinder would also work. An alternative to frying *falafel* is to broil or bake them as flat patties, with a coating of sesame seeds. This method allows for much less oil absorption. Read notes at the end of the recipe before beginning.

> 1 cup dry fava beans, soaked 24 hours
> 1 cup dry garbanzo beans, soaked 24 hours
> ½ onion, minced
> 5 cloves garlic, minced or mashed into a paste
> ½ teaspoon salt
> ½ teaspoon black pepper
> 1 tablespoon ground coriander
> 2 teaspoons cumin
> ½ teaspoon paprika
> ¼ teaspoon cayenne pepper
> ½ teaspoon baking soda
> ½ cup parsley, minced
> ½ cup fresh cilantro, minced
> 1 or 2 tablespoons flour (if needed)
> ½ cup sesame seeds (in mixture or rolled on outside)
> vegetable oil, for frying
> fresh chopped spearmint, parsley, tomatoes, green onions
>   or onions with sumac, for garnish

    1. Rinse beans and soak them in 1 quart of water for 24 hours. Canned beans may be substituted for dry beans. Drain beans and rinse. Grind beans in a food processor or put them through a food grinder twice.

    2. Add onion, garlic, and spices, baking soda, minced parsley, and cilantro, mixing well. Add sesame seeds to mixture, or place them on a plate.

3. Form a spoonful of the mixture into a ball. If the consistency is correct, and the ball holds together, proceed. If not, mix in water or flour, so that you can form a ball or patty in the palm of your hands.

4. Roll ball in sesame seeds if you haven't added them to mixture. If you have a *falafel* tool, add the sesame seeds to the mixture and carefully drop the *falafel* into the heated oil with the *falafel* ejecting tool (*qalb*), as described below.

To fry

Heat oil about 2" deep in a wok or skillet to 450-475ºF. Fry *falafel* in hot oil until golden brown on both sides. Remove with slotted spoon and drain. It is possible to fry them in a small amount of oil instead of deep frying; I have made it both ways. Serve in pocket sandwiches with fresh vegetables and plenty of tahini or *taratour* sauce.

To bake or broil

Preheat oven to 350ºF to bake or 475ºF to broil, and place *falafel* on baking parchment or an oiled baking dish. Bake for 20 minutes on each side. Broil for 5 to 10 minutes on each side, checking frequently so as not to burn.

Notes on successful *falafel* making

• The secret to *falafel* holding together in balls or patties is the consistency of the mixture. If it is too dry, it will fall apart, so add water; if it is too moist, add a little flour. Ideally you can roll it into a ball, or shape it into a patty in your hand, and it will hold together.

• Slipping the skins off the fava beans before grinding takes time and results in a perfectly textured mix in the food processor. When I did not remove the skins, the mixture was drier and needed to have some flour and water added to hold it together, but the taste was nuttier and flavorful, and perhaps more nutritious.

• If using a blender to grind the beans, add water to make them purée. The mixture then becomes too wet, so add some flour to make it bind together.

• If using canned beans, it may be necessary to add flour, also.

• Make a batch or a double batch of *falafel*, form them into patties, and then freeze them individually by placing patties on a cookie sheet and into the freezer until hard, approximately an hour. Remove from freezer, place into a plastic freezer bag and back in freezer for use later, 1 or 6 at a time, for a quick meal.

Serves 4 to 6; 8 to 10 for appetizers.

Kibbet Batata ou Jouz

POTATO, WALNUT, AND BULGUR KIBBE

◆

Another vegetarian version of *kibbe*, the "national dish" of Lebanon: potato and walnut with bulgur is tasty, unusual, and easy to make. This was served to me in Lebanon; I'm sharing my version of it here! It's a unique vegetarian dish to take to a potluck that can be served warm, at room temperature, or cold, and can be made quickly in a food processor.

3 cups potato, boiled
1 onion, minced (or chopped for food processor)
1 cup #1 bulgur, rinsed
1 cup walnut meats, chopped
1 teaspoon salt
½ teaspoon black pepper
1 teaspoon marjoram
2 tablespoons fresh spearmint (optional)
1 fresh rose geranium leaf (optional)

GARNISH

walnut halves, spearmint or rose geranium leaves, olive oil

1. Boil potatoes until tender; save water for soup stock.
2. Pour ½ cup of hot water over bulgur in a bowl and set aside.
3. Mash potatoes with minced onions or put potatoes and onions into the food processor and pulse, removing lumps.
4. Add potato mixture, walnuts, and seasonings to bulgur, mixing well.
5. Taste and adjust seasonings, adding more if needed.
6. Using a spatula, transfer *kibbe* to a platter, forming a smooth mound. Decorate by pressing a design into the surface with a fork; garnish with walnuts and mint leaves. Drizzle a little olive oil over the top of the *kibbe*.

Serves 4 to 6.

Kibbet Jlunt

BAKED PUMPKIN AND BULGUR WITH PINE NUTS

◆

K*ibbe*, the "national dish" of Lebanon, usually refers to lamb ground with bulgur and onions that's eaten raw (*nayye*) or baked (*bil sinneyeh*). When visiting Lebanon, I discovered many kinds of *kibbe* besides lamb with bulgur—especially vegetarian versions such as potato, pumpkin, and walnut—all mixtures of a main ingredient with bulgur and onion. Pumpkin *kibbe* made with pumpkin or butternut squash is unusual, simple to make, and was really enjoyed at a recent dinner party!

> 2 cups pumpkin or butternut squash
> 1 onion, quartered
> 1 cup #1 bulgur, rinsed
> 1 teaspoon salt
> ½ teaspoon black pepper
> dash cayenne pepper
> 1 teaspoon ground coriander
> 2 tablespoons fresh cilantro

ONION PINE NUT LAYER
> 1 onion, julienne-cut
> ½ cup *snobar*, pine nuts
> ⅓ cup olive oil, divided

1. Preheat oven to 425°F. Bake pumpkin or squash until tender.
2. Pour 1 cup of hot water over bulgur in a bowl and set aside.
3. Meanwhile, sauté julienne-cut onions, salt, and pine nuts in half of the olive oil until light brown. Spread the sauté mixture evenly over the bottom of an 8"x8" glass baking dish and set aside.
4. Remove pumpkin pulp from skin and grind with quartered onion in food grinder or processor, making a pureé. Add pumpkin and seasonings to bulgur, mixing thoroughly.
5. Spread the pumpkin mixture over the onions and pine nuts, making an even layer, smoothing out the surface with your hand or a spatula.
6. Cut into diamonds. Drizzle remaining olive oil evenly over the top of the *kibbe*. Bake for 15 minutes in lower oven rack; move to top oven rack to lightly brown the top. Serve hot, warm, or cold.

Serves 4 to 6.

ALICE'S KITCHEN
IF YOU MAKE IT WITH LOVE, IT WILL BE DELICIOUS!

156

KHUDRA
◆
VEGETABLES
BEANS & GRAINS

Vegetables, beans, and grains are truly the heart of our cuisine, making Lebanese cooking one of the most popular for vegetarians and carnivores alike, and so healthy!

For all bean dishes, it is best to use organic dry beans and soak them overnight before cooking. Rice, also organic, is soaked for 20 to 30 minutes before cooking, with a good rinsing afterwards. Pre-soaking rice, beans, and grains is part of traditional wisdom in that it deactivates enzyme inhibitors making nutrients more available and digestable, as well as decreasing cooking time. The grain becomes more alive, absorbing moisture as in sprouting.

This section begins with our basic buttery rice that serves as a base for so many of our dishes, *riz mfalfal.* Then come our all-time favorites: *hommus, baba ghannouj,* and other dips that are perfect for appetizers (*mezza*). The serving size described is for serving as a side dish or as one of many appetizers. Steamed, sautéed, and grilled vegetables of all sorts follow with our garlic lemon sauce or with tahini sauce, and are perfect eaten warm in the cool season, or cold in the summertime. Tasty vegetable patties and squash fritters make quick meals. A great grilled red pepper and walnut dip recipe (*mhammara*) is another new addition to our book. Enjoy!

Riz Mfalfal

STEAMED RICE WITH BUTTER

◆

Buttery and rich, *riz mfalfal* was one of our family staples, the base upon which so many of the stews made with beans, vegetables, and perhaps small bits of lamb were laid. Scooped up with a triangle of Arabic bread and followed by crunchy fresh vegetables, the nutritional value is excellent, especially if made with brown rice. This recipe is based on quicker cooking white rice, so increase the cooking time 20 minutes if you use brown rice. The quantity is enough to serve our large family, so adjust the recipe in half or otherwise, unless you want a lot of leftovers!

¼ cup clarified butter
5 cups water
¼ teaspoon salt
3 cups rice, soaked 1 hour, rinsed and drained
¼ teaspoon cinnamon

1. Heat clarified butter until hot. Carefully add water—it will sizzle and splatter—and salt; bring to a rolling boil in a pot with a lid.

2. Stir in rice, cover, and cook on medium high heat about 10 minutes or until most of the surface water has evaporated and air bubbles form through the rice.

3. Reduce heat to low and cook for 10 minutes more, unless it's brown rice, which takes 20 minutes longer.

4. Turn off heat and let sit for 10 minutes, then stir with fork to fluff up. Let stand covered 15 minutes. Serve on platter with the surface smoothed out and sprinkled with ground cinnamon.

Serves 6 to 8.

ALICE'S KITCHEN

IF YOU MAKE IT WITH LOVE, IT WILL BE DELICIOUS!

Hommus bi Tahini

GARBANZO BEAN PURÉE WITH TAHINI

◆

Our family loves *hommus bi tahini* best when it is tangy, the way Mama and *Sitto* made it. We garnish it with sprinkled paprika, parsley sprigs, and a little olive oil. In Lebanon, pomegranate seeds, whole garbanzo beans, and a drizzle of olive oil might be the garnish. Chopped fresh mint and olive oil also make a lovely garnish. A Palestinian friend made a minced fresh jalapeño, garlic, salt, lemon, and parsley sauce served atop the *hommus* that was hot and surprising! Instead of dipping with the traditional Arabic bread, try pita chips or fresh cut carrot or cucumber strips. A jazzy variation of *hommus* with sautéed lamb, onions, and pine nuts (*mafroume*, p. 78) spread lightly across the top, can be made ahead.

In the photo, Mama is mashing the garbanzo beans (*hommus*) by hand—the traditional way, which of course takes time. For those in a super hurry, the very quick food processor or blender methods using canned garbanzo beans are listed first, followed by the traditional method using dry beans.

> 2 cups dry garbanzo beans, soaked overnight
>   or 2 cans garbanzo beans
> ½ teaspoon baking soda (for traditional method)
> 4 heaping tablespoons tahini
> 3 cloves of garlic
> ½ cup lemon juice
> ½ teaspoon salt
> 2 tablespoons olive oil (optional)

QUICK BLENDER *HOMMUS* METHOD:

Blend garlic, salt, and lemon juice in the blender. Pour into a bowl. Blend the canned or cooked garbanzo beans (drained) one cup at a time with ⅛ cup water. Stir this into the bowl. Stir in tahini, ¼ cup warm water, and olive oil. Taste and add more lemon or salt, if necessary. Serve and enjoy!

QUICKEST FOOD PROCESSOR *HOMMUS* METHOD:

Using drained canned garbanzo beans, put all ingredients, minus the baking soda, into food processor and pulse or blend; add a little warm water; taste, and add more water, lemon juice, tahini, salt, or garlic to suit your own taste buds!

Traditional method for making *hommus*

Dry bean method

Drain soaked beans, put in large pot, cover with twice as much water. Bring to boil and simmer over medium heat for 45 minutes. Add baking soda. Cook over low heat, removing any froth that forms, until very tender. Set aside to cool. Drain and reserve water.

Canned bean method

Drain liquid from can. Place beans in a pot with water to cover; bring to a boil, reduce heat, add baking soda, and simmer for 15 to 20 minutes until tender, removing any froth that forms. Set aside to cool. Drain and reserve water.

1. Mash garlic with salt into a smooth paste in a bowl; stir in tahini. Gradually stir in ¼ cup warm water or the bean cooking water, which thickens the tahini; stir in lemon juice and garlic paste.

2. Set aside a few whole garbanzo beans for garnish and put the remaining beans through a food mill or mash them through a strainer, blender, or food processor. Add some of the cooking water to blend. Mix puréed beans into tahini mixture. Add ¼ cup olive oil; taste and add more lemon, salt, or garlic as needed.

3. Spread into a thin layer on a flat plate, making a swirl in the surface with the back of a spoon. Then garnish with whole chick peas, parsley, paprika or mild cayenne, and olive oil drizzled over the top. Serve with Arabic bread, pita chips, or carrot, celery, and cucumber sticks.

A tip for quickly cooking dry garbanzo beans

After soaking uncooked beans overnight with a little baking soda, rinse and drain. Place 2 cups of uncooked beans into a freezer bag and freeze for later use. Freezing soaked beans breaks them down, which speeds up cooking time significantly, which means *hommus*, now! And less cooking preserves more nutrients and saves time! Thanks to my dear Douma–Portland friend and great cook Adnan Haddad for this tip.

Serves 6 to 8 for appetizers.

Alice's Kitchen

If you make it with Love, it will be Delicious!

Baba Ghannouj

Eggplant with Tahini

◆

Along with *hommus*, *baba ghannouj* is one of the most popular Lebanese dishes and is becoming available in non–Middle Eastern venues, such as supermarket delis, because it is so tasty. The secret to its distinctive flavor comes from charring the eggplant directly over a flame. Dried mint and a bit of yogurt adds an extra touch to our already divine family recipe, from our Douma friends, the Haddads. A must for appetizers (*mezza*), *baba ghannouj* sprinkled with pomegranate seeds, a loaf of Arabic bread, cucumber spears, and olives make for a perfect light meal. *Baba* can also be whirled in a food processor, combining steps 2 and 3.

> 2 medium–large eggplants
> 1 tablespoon olive oil
> ¼ cup lemon juice
> 3 cloves garlic
> ½ teaspoon salt
> ½ cup tahini
> 1 teaspoon dried spearmint (optional)
> ¼ cup yogurt (optional)
> fresh parsley or pomegranate seeds, for garnish

1. Set whole, unpeeled eggplant over flame until totally charred, about 15 minutes per side—when one side is done, gently hold eggplant with wooden spoons on each end to turn it without piercing it. The marvelous charred flavor is most easily done directly over the flame of a gas stove burner—I set eggplant directly on the burner grating—or on a barbeque grill, or under a broiler.

2. Chop garlic, place in a medium-sized bowl,. and mash into a paste with salt. When eggplant is cool, carefully slice it in half lengthwise and use a spoon to scoop pulp into the bowl, discarding large seeds and charred skin. Mash it into the garlic paste until the mixture is smooth.

3. Mix in tahini, lemon juice, and olive oil. Add dried mint and yogurt if you wish. Taste and adjust seasoning.

4. Spread into a thin layer on a flat plate, making a swirl in the surface with the back of a spoon. Garnish with parsley, pomegranate seeds, or finely ground dried mint; drizzle with olive oil. Serve warm or cold with snippets of Arabic bread or pita chips. Heaven!

Serves 6 to 8 for appetizers.

Batinjan Mtabbal

EGGPLANT WITH GARLIC, OIL, AND LEMON

◆

Essentially, this is *baba ghannouj* without tahini, so it is somewhat lighter with less fat, yet it's equally delicious.

2 medium to large eggplants
1 tablespoon olive oil
¼ cup lemon juice
3 cloves garlic
½ teaspoon salt

GARNISH

½ cup fresh parsley sprigs
⅛ cup pomegranate seeds

1. Set whole, unpeeled eggplant over flame until totally charred, about 15 minutes per side—when one side is done, gently hold eggplant with wooden spoons on each end to turn it without piercing it. The marvelous charred flavor is most easily done directly over the flame of a gas stove burner—I set eggplant directly on the burner grating—or on a barbeque grill, or under a broiler.

2. Chop garlic, place in a medium-sized bowl, and mash into a paste with salt. When eggplant is cool, carefully slice it in half lengthwise and use a spoon to scoop pulp into the bowl, discarding large seeds and charred skin. Mash it into the garlic paste until the mixture is smooth.

3. Add lemon juice and olive oil, mixing thoroughly. Taste and adjust seasoning, adding more lemon, garlic, or salt as needed.

4. Transfer to a lovely bowl and garnish with parsley or pomegranate seeds and drizzle with a little olive oil. Serve warm or cold with snippets of Arabic bread or pita chips, and fresh cut vegetables.

Serves 4 to 6.

ALICE'S KITCHEN
IF YOU MAKE IT WITH LOVE, IT WILL BE DELICIOUS!

Ful Mdammas

FAVA BEANS WITH GARLIC AND LEMON

◆

Fava beans grow in the snow and seem to withstand the weather well. They grow from Spain and France through Egypt, a springtime protein-rich staple of Mediterranean diets. There are two common varieties of fava beans, both are eaten fresh and dried: huge, dried beans are used in making *falafel*; a smaller fava, used for this dish, is made from a smaller variety of beans, either dried or canned. My garlic-laden recipe is lemony tart and very hearty, ready for scooping with bread.

An even smaller variety of fava is used in gardening as a cover crop, which, when turned into the earth, adds nitrogen-fixing bacteria into the soil, enriching and fertilizing it for subsequent plantings. The fava bean flower is a beautiful white blossom dotted with black, imparting a gorgeous fragrance. So if you have an opportunity to do a fall planting for spring harvest, you can enjoy fresh fava beans right out of the pod, just like in the old country.

> 1 large can fava beans
>   or 2 cups small dry fava beans, soaked overnight
> 6 cloves garlic, peeled
> ½ cup lemon juice
> 2 tablespoons olive oil
> ½ teaspoon salt
> dash of cayenne pepper
> ½ cup chopped fresh parsley for garnish

   1. If using canned beans, add 1 cup of water and garlic to beans and heat slowly for about an hour. For dried beans, rinse soaked beans, place in a pot, and add a quart of water, salt, and garlic cloves. Bring to a boil, then reduce heat, and simmer for about 3 hours.

   2. Check and stir frequently, so that beans thicken but do not stick or burn, adding water if necessary. Some beans will break down into a very thick, soupy consistency and others remain whole.

   3. Just before serving, add parsley, lemon juice, and olive oil; taste and adjust seasoning. Lots of lemon and garlic make this a heavenly dish. Garnish with a little more parsley and serve with Arabic bread for appetizers (*mezza*), breakfast, a hearty winter lunch, or supper.

Serves 4 to 6.

Loubiye bi Banadura ou Zeit

STRING BEANS WITH TOMATO AND OLIVE OIL

◆

String beans with tomatoes are simply flavorful and easy to make; they appeared regularly, to our delight, on our dinner table—with or without lamb—served over rice (*riz mfalfal*) or as a side dish in a variety of forms, this one with tomato and olive oil. A classic Lebanese family vegetable offering in the summer using garden fresh beans or in the winter using frozen beans from the summer harvest.

> 2 medium onions, chopped
> ¼ cup olive oil
> 1½ pounds string beans, french cut, rinsed
> 1 medium can whole tomatoes, chopped
> ½ teaspoon salt
> ¼ teaspoon black pepper
> dash cayenne pepper

1. Sauté onions with oil and salt in a deep skillet or sauce pan over medium heat until translucent.

2. Add string beans, black pepper, and cayenne. Cover and cook 5 minutes. Lower heat and steam for 15 minutes. Add tomatoes and simmer on medium heat until tender, about 20 minutes. These beans are well-cooked, like a stew, rather than today's trend towards crunchy vegetables.

3. Serve hot or warm over rice (*riz mfalfal*) with Arabic bread (*khubz*). In the summer, it is delicious served cold with bread.

Serves 4 to 6.

164

ALICE'S KITCHEN
IF YOU MAKE IT WITH LOVE, IT WILL BE DELICIOUS!

Bamye ou Riz

OKRA WITH RICE

◆

Made in the summer when fresh okra are in season, this well-seasoned tomato and okra combination is served over steamed rice (*riz mfalfal*).

2 pounds okra, rinsed and stemmed
3 onions, julienne-cut
2 cloves garlic, chopped
⅓ cup olive oil
2 small cans tomato sauce
1 teaspoon ground coriander seed
½ teaspoon salt
¼ teaspoon black pepper
dash cayenne pepper
¼ cup lemon juice
1 cup water

1. Rinse and carefully stem okra. Dry them and brush with olive oil. Broil until lightly browned on both sides, about 5 to 10 minutes.

2. Meanwhile, sauté onions lightly in remaining oil. Add okra, garlic, tomato sauce, water, lemon juice, and seasonings. Stir very gently, leaving the okra intact; cover and simmer for 30 minutes. Serve over rice (*riz mfalfal*), with Arabic bread and fresh cut vegetables or *salata*.

Serves 4 to 6.

Khudra Makhluta

SAUTÉED VEGETABLES WITH *TARATOUR* SAUCE

◆

Tasty vegetables, sautéed to a golden brown that brings out their sweetness and flavor, are served over steamed rice and drizzled with tahini garlic sauce—simply fabulous! If you make this dish in the winter, you can use another winter vegetable such as broccoli or golden beets instead of summer squash.

> ¼ cup olive oil
> ½ cauliflower, cut into florets
> 2 carrots, sliced on the diagonal
> 2 Italian zucchini or Lebanese squash, sliced
>   on the diagonal, when in season
> onion or other vegetables (optional)
> tahini or *taratour* sauce (p. 42)
> ¼–½ cup pine nuts (optional)

1. Heat olive oil in a large skillet over medium heat. Stir in cauliflower and carrots, coating them with oil. Sauté for 10 minutes, stirring frequently until they begin to brown.

2. Add squash and mix well, continue to sauté and brown. Cover, reduce heat, and steam for about 10 more minutes.

3. Meanwhile, make tahini or *taratour* sauce.

4. Serve vegetables over rice or as a side vegetable, with tahini sauce. As an extra treat, garnish with pine nuts lightly sautéed in a tablespoon of olive oil.

Serves 4.

Kousa 'Raas

SQUASH FRITTERS

◆

An excellent summer side dish or appetizer—a fine use for some of that extra squash from the garden or the squash pulp cored from stuffed squash (*kousa mihshi*). If using grated squash, add an egg or two to hold the mixture together.

2 cups grated squash or squash marrow
    from cored zucchini *kousa mihshi*
2 green onions, chopped
2 sprigs spearmint, finely chopped
½ bunch parsley, finely chopped
2 stalks celery, finely chopped
¼ teaspoon salt
¼ teaspoon black pepper
¼ teaspoon cayenne pepper
⅓ cup flour
2½ teaspoons baking powder
½ cup olive oil, for frying, or use a non-stick pan
1 or 2 eggs for grated squash mixture (otherwise optional)

1. Grate squash into a bowl. If using squash marrow from cored squash for *kousa*, drain squash in a colander and reserve liquid for soup stock.

2. Squeeze mint and parsley to remove excess water and add with chopped green onions and celery to bowl. Mix it all together along with seasonings, flour, baking powder, and eggs, if using grated squash.

3. Heat skillet with olive oil. When it is hot, spoon out a tablespoon of mixture and flatten into round patties about ½" thick and 3" across. Fry on both sides until golden brown.

4. Drain on paper towels. Garnish with parsley; serve for appetizers (*mezza*), brunch, or as a side dish with Arabic bread (*khubz*).

Serves 4 to 6.

Batata Madqou'a Siyeme

LEBANESE MASHED POTATOES

◆

If you love mashed potatoes, you will love this recipe. These potatoes are fabulous, either served hot, warm, or cold. Traditionally made during Lent in the spring before Easter, we enjoyed this dish through the summer months, as they are a "light" version of mashed potatoes without butter and milk or cream—instead, using a bit of healthy olive oil, and flavorful lemon and garlic. I use organic potatoes, and value the nutrition in them so I don't peel them. Mother would, of course, peel them for purely aesthetic reasons.

> 6–8 medium potatoes, peeled and quartered
> ⅓ cup olive oil
> ⅓ cup lemon juice
> 3 cloves garlic
> ½ teaspoon salt
> 3 tablespoons dried spearmint

1. Boil potatoes until tender. Meanwhile, in a small bowl, mash chopped garlic with salt into a paste; add oil and lemon juice and set aside.

2. When potatoes are tender, remove them from cooking water and reserve it. Place potatoes in a deep bowl and mash them while they are warm. Mix in garlic sauce and a little water from cooking the potatoes. The remaining potato water can be saved for soup stock.

3. Crush dried mint between your palms over the mixture and mix thoroughly. Taste and adjust seasoning. Serve hot, warm, or cold.

Serves 4 to 6.

ALICE'S KITCHEN
IF YOU MAKE IT WITH LOVE, IT WILL BE DELICIOUS!

Shmandar, Sbanikh, or Siliq Miqli

Sautéed beet greens, spinach, or chard

◆

Spring or summer brings another excellent Lenten dish from my dear Mother, Alice, that complements the mashed potato recipe on the previous page, lentil soups, or more elaborate meals. Greens are a great source of Vitamin A, iron, and other minerals plus in this recipe, they're lemon and garlicky delicious. String beans sautéed in this way are equally satisfying.

> 2 bunches spinach or greens, rinsed and drained
> 1 onion, julienne-cut
> 2 cloves garlic, minced
> 2 tablespoons olive oil
> ¼ teaspoon salt
> ⅓ cup lemon juice

1. Chop stems of greens to 2" lengths and tear greens into pieces. Sauté onions and garlic lightly in olive oil with salt until light brown. When onions are translucent, add stems of chard or beet greens and continue to sauté for about 5 to 7 minutes.

2. Add leafy greens, stir, and cover. Steam for 10 to 15 minutes on low. Add lemon juice. Taste and adjust seasoning. Serve hot, warm, at room temperature, or cold.

Serves 4 to 6.

Loubiye Mtoume

String beans with garlic, lemon, and olive oil

◆

Whether the vegetable is string beans, spinach, asparagus, chard, beet greens, or potatoes, the garlic-laden lemon sauce poured over them is superb and can be served warm or at room temperature. Young, fresh-picked, homegrown string beans can be cooked to just tender, while more mature beans need to steam longer. The old-fashioned way of cooking until vegetables are limp and dark green is really not necessary. So cook these to your own taste. My mother julienne-cut our beans so they would cook to tenderness. If the beans are quite young, steam them whole.

1½ pounds string beans, julienne-cut
2–3 cloves garlic
¼ teaspoon salt
2 tablespoons olive oil
¼ cup lemon juice

1. Steam string beans in a covered pot or vegetable steamer with a cup of water until tender.
2. Meanwhile in a small bowl, mash chopped garlic into a paste with salt. Mix in lemon juice and olive oil.
3. Reserve bean water for cooking rice or for soup stock. Place drained beans in a bowl and pour garlic sauce over them. Toss, taste, and adjust seasoning.

Serves 4 to 6.

ALICE'S KITCHEN

If you make it with Love, it will be Delicious!

Kousa or Batinjan Miqli

FRIED SQUASH OR EGGPLANT

◆

Almost anything fried is yummy. But memories of Mother and *Sitto* frying up squash and eggplant down in the basement, on the special stove used for baking bread so the kitchen wouldn't get so hot in the summertime, make me long for this comfort food again. Salting and draining the vegetables ahead of time draws out the liquid and keeps them from absorbing as much oil in frying. These finger-licking, quick-to-disappear rounds were served with fish or *mjaddrah* during Lent or on Fridays. We ate them tucked into Arabic bread with our meal, or as a cold sandwich the next day, in the unlikely event that any were leftover.

Mother's latest technique is to grill, broil, or bake the squash brushed with just a tiny bit of oil. That recipe is on the next page.

> 2 large eggplants or 5 Japanese eggplants, unpeeled
> or zucchini, unpeeled
> salt
> ½ cup olive oil for frying or a non-stick pan
> and the slightest amount of oil

1. Slice zucchini or eggplant into ¼" thick rounds, leaving the skins intact—as they're quite tasty. Sprinkle with salt on both sides. Place in a bowl or colander for an hour to drain. Remove from bowl, discard liquid, and pat them dry with a paper or cotton towel.

2. Heat olive oil in a skillet; when it is hot, deep fry rounds until golden brown on each side, turning them with a fork. Place on paper towels to drain. You may need to add oil between batches; be sure it is hot before putting them in. Serve hot, warm, or cold with Arabic bread (*khubz*).

Serves 4 to 6 for appetizers.

Kousa Mishwi

GRILLED, BROILED, OR BAKED SQUASH

◆

If you're looking for a low-fat alternative to the fried squash recipe on the previous page, my dear, brilliant mother, Alice, has come up with a wonderful solution! Her latest culinary technique is to grill, broil, or bake the squash brushed with just a tiny bit of oil and sprinkled with a little salt. The simplicity of this is no indication of how good it tastes. This is a great way to use up some of those giant zucchini that inevitably present themselves every summer.

An inexpensive natural bristle paint brush that is 1–2" wide dedicated to kitchen tasks is a great way to apply the olive oil and washes easily with soap.

> 2 large zucchini or Lebanese squash
> salt
> olive oil

1. Preheat oven to 400ºF or light up your grill.
2. Slice zucchini in half lengthwise, and then into long, thin strips. Place on a baking dish. Brush lightly with olive oil, or drizzle a little on.
3. Bake, broil, or grill for 5 to 10 minutes. Sprinkle with a little salt. Serve hot, warm, or cold—finger-licking good!

Serves 4.

ALICE'S KITCHEN
IF YOU MAKE IT WITH LOVE, IT WILL BE DELICIOUS!

Ijjet Khudra

VEGETABLE PATTIES

◆

Mother's variation on her yummy summer squash fritters and our Lebanese omelette (*'ijjeh*) are these excellent party appetizers—vegetable patties. They can easily be made ahead and served at room temperature, or warm from the stove. Other ways to serve them: as a side dish, snack, or for a light lunch.

2 cups grated summer squash
1 grated potato (optional)
2 green onions, finely chopped
2 sprigs spearmint, finely chopped
½ bunch parsley, finely chopped
2 stalks celery, finely chopped
½ teaspoon each salt and black pepper
¼ teaspoon cayenne pepper
⅓ cup flour
2 teaspoons baking powder
2 eggs
½ cup olive oil, for frying or less, using a non-stick pan

1. Grate squash and potato into a bowl.
2. Add mint, parsley, chopped green onions, and celery to bowl. Mix all together and then add seasonings, flour, baking powder, and eggs.
3. Heat skillet and add olive oil. When it's hot, spoon out a tablespoon of mixture and flatten into round patties about ½" thick and 3" across. Mother places several 3" canning jar caps in the hot oil, then fills them with the mixture. She removes the caps to flip them. Fry on both sides until golden brown.
4. Drain on paper towels. Garnish with parsley; serve hot, warm, or cold for appetizers (*mezza*), brunch, or as a side dish with Arabic bread (*khubz*).

Serves 4 to 6 for appetizers.

Hommus Mtabbal

GARBANZO BEANS WITH GARLIC AND LEMON

◆

Hommus really means garbanzo beans, but in Lebanon *hommus bi tahini* is the name for the extremely popular *hommus* that is being sold in all kinds of versions, from red pepper to spinach, spelled in so many ways—one that even makes me think of my garden (humus)!

The recipe here is for garbanzo beans served warm, with lemon juice, garlic, and olive oil—most of the ingredients of *hommus* but without the sesame seed purée, *tahini*. It is best made with dry garbanzo beans soaked overnight. This same dish is also called *balila* and *hommus mtoum*—the three different names shows that it's a popular village food—beans with their broth and garlic—a healthy comfort food!

> 2 cups dry garbanzo beans, soaked overnight
> or 2 cans garbanzo beans
> 1 quart water
> ½ teaspoon baking soda
> 3 cloves of garlic
> ½ cup lemon juice
> 1 teaspoon salt
> 2 tablespoons olive oil

1. Drain soaked beans, put in large pot, cover with twice as much water. Bring to boil and simmer over medium heat for ¾ hour. Add baking soda. Cook over low heat until very tender, discarding any froth that forms.

2. Mash garlic with salt into a smooth paste in a bowl; stir garlic paste, lemon juice, and olive oil into the beans with their broth.

3. Taste and add more lemon, salt, or garlic as needed and serve in bowls with Arabic bread or pita chips or crackers, and vegetables or salad.

Serves 4 to 6.

Mhammara

GRILLED RED PEPPER AND WALNUT DIP

◆

A fabulous spread was laid out before us on a twenty-foot long table at our lunch (*ghada*) stop in the Lebanese mountains. Mother and I were guests on a bus tour of Lebanese monasteries with the Greek Orthodox choir and pastor from the Douma church. Departing our hotel before dawn, all was quiet, but for the birds, and people sipping their morning coffee, talking softly on the bus. By mid-morning, it was as far from quiet as could be. The choir singing, a drummer drumming, and all, including the driver, clapping to the music along windy mountain roads and congested Beirut traffic, in joyful song: at first Church music, and then folk songs! Even Mother was clapping and singing, remembering songs from her childhood! A great trip topped by a Lebanese feast. Oh, yes, the *mhammara*! A red pepper dip that I'd never before tasted was one of the delicacies on that table and here for your pleasure—quickly made in a food processor! Our friends love it!

3 red bell peppers, roasted or grilled until blackened
1 cup walnuts
1 tablespoon pomegranate syrup
1 tablespoon chili paste
3 cloves of garlic
2 tablespoons lemon juice
1 teaspoon salt
½ teaspoon cayenne pepper (optional)
2 tablespoon sesame seeds
2 tablespoons bread crumbs, or more as needed

1. Place whole red peppers over a grill, or broil until blackened on all sides. This only takes a few minutes. Put hot peppers into a paper bag and close, to cool. This makes them easy to peel, under running water, removing all the blackened skin. Cut in half and remove seeds. Juices from the peppers can be used in the dip.

2. Put peppers and all of the remaining ingredients into a food processor, and pulse just until the consistency is minced but not puréed.

3. Taste and add seasonings or bread crumbs as needed. Serve with Arabic bread, pita chips, or crackers.

Makes 2 cups of dip, serving 8 to 10 for appetizers.

'Arnabit Miqli

SAUTÉED CAULIFLOWER WITH *TARATOUR* SAUCE

◆

In winter, spring, summer, or fall, whenever cauliflower was available, Mother and *Sitto* fried or sautéed it to a golden brown, bringing out its flavor. Wonderful served over rice and laced with tahini or *taratour* sauce, it can also be served on its own, or accompanying *mjaddrah* or fish, with a squeeze of fresh lemon juice.

¼–½ cup olive oil
1–2 cauliflowers, cut into florets
tahini or *taratour* sauce (p. 42)
lemon (optional)

1. Heat olive oil in a large skillet over medium heat. Stir in cauliflower florets, coating them with oil. Sauté for 10 minutes, stirring frequently until they begin to brown. Either continue to fry or sauté until done; or cover, reduce heat, and steam for about 10 more minutes.

2. Meanwhile, make tahini or *taratour* sauce.

3. If cauliflower is fried, lift florets from oil and place on paper towel to drain before serving on a platter.

4. Serve over rice or as a side vegetable with sauce and lemon wedges.

Serves 4–6.

KHUBZ

◆

BREADS

Bread is an essential part of every Lebanese meal, central to our diet and our culture. Traditionally, Lebanese foods are eaten with torn pieces of bread formed into a triangle held with three fingers in the form of a scoop. Some foods are rolled into a sandwich or stuffed into the bread's pocket. Eating fresh baked bread, hot from the oven, is an almost universal pleasure—plain, with honey, butter, jam, yogurt, cheese, olives, or with the *zaatar* herb mixture.

Arabic bread takes on a variety of forms and shapes, depending upon how it is to be baked and eaten, and the recipe, style, and village of the baker. *Khubz marqouq,* big flat paper-thin round loaves, is baked in an oven. In the old country, there was a *tannour,* like the Indian tandoor, in which the bread was baked against the vertical walls of the oven. When the bread was done, it would fall toward the fire below, requiring the baker's unwavering attention as she caught it in the nick of time. Now there are only a few remaining *tannour* ovens in Lebanon. In Douma, Marie Talalai baked Mom and me some fabulous *tannour khubz.* The *furn* is the prevailing oven for baking breads; it is much like pizza ovens fired by either gas or wood.

Saj bread is baked over a *saj,* an open fire with a domed metal disk placed over it, like an upside-down wok; this ancient method of baking is being revived and becoming popular at sidewalk take-out restaurants in Beirut. Lebanese thick breads (*tilme*) and meat or spinach pies are baked in *furn* ovens or regular home ovens.

Nowadays, commercial bakeries in the cities and larger towns produce mountains of the big, flat *khubz marqouq* loaves on a conveyor belt system, much like the ones I've seen in Mexico for producing corn tortillas. In the Christian Syrian town of Sidnaiye, it was interesting observing people lined up waiting for bread, just as I remember Mexicans lining up for their daily tortillas coming off the conveyor belt.

Yet homemade breads are where my passions lie. Armenian flat breads called *lavosh* are similar to our *khubz marqouq*. Commercially available pita bread is a reasonable substitute for homebaked Arabic bread. When I was growing up, we called our bread Syrian bread. Mama's papers said she came from Douma, Syria.

In this section, I share our family recipes for baking bread, the method Mother devised for baking in our classic old Wedgewood gas stove. In those days, people weren't baking pizzas at home, and baking peels—the big flat wooden boards that pizza bakers use to slide the dough in and out of the oven—weren't readily available to buy, so Mother had a local woodworker make her two: one big and one small. If you're interested in baking our flat bread or pizza, a pizza peel is very useful and makes authentic kitchen wall decor when you're not using it!

Precious family recipes include *tilme,* a thick, foccacia-like bread with special herb toppings, and dough for savory pastries, such as spinach pies. The dough may be frozen before rising for later use. Typically, I bake bread once or twice a month and freeze the baked loaves for quick thawing over an open gas flame on my kitchen stove—just a few seconds on each side and the bread is hot and softened, as though it was freshly baked.

When I bake as Mother did (pp. 4, 6, 179), I make one recipe of basic bread dough and divide the balls into various sizes for bread, *tilme bi zaatar, tilme bi kishk,* and plain *tilme* (recipes on the following pages). First, I bake the flat or pocket bread in the hot gas oven without the baking racks on the oven floor; then I turn the heat down, put the racks back in, mix a small batch of *zaatar* and/ or *kishk* and bake the thick breads. If I run out of toppings, I bake more bread, plain *tilme,* or freeze the remaining dough for later use.

New recipes include pita chips—a great alternative to fattening commercial snack chips or to bread for dipping, and an excellent cracker recipe like Armenian crackers with sesame seeds. Baking bread truly nourishes the soul as much as eating it nourishes the body. I hope you enjoy baking your own bread with these recipes, and choose organic grains if you're able.

Good eating! *Ma'koul il hana!*

Khubz Marqouq

BASIC BREAD DOUGH

Mother and *Sitto's* basic time-honored bread recipe is the one we use for baking Arabic bread, either big flat loaves, or smaller, thicker pocket bread, called pita bread (*kmaaj*), or a foccacia-like bread called *tilme*, for *tilme bi zaatar, tilme bi kishk*, or for spinach or meat pie dough. I even use it to make Italian style pizza. If you're baking our thin, flat bread or pita (pocket) bread, you'll need a baking peel, and a baking stone is a great help. This recipe makes approximately a dozen 8" flat loaves or 5" pocket loaves; plus 7 thick 8" *tilme* loaves for plain *tilme, zaatar,* or *kishk*.

> 3 cups warm water
> 3 tablespoons dry yeast
> 1 teaspoon salt
> 1 tablespoon sugar (optional)
> ¾ cup wheat germ (if using only white flour)
> 8 cups flour (I use 3 cups whole wheat and
>   5 cups unbleached white)

    1. Dissolve yeast in lukewarm water in a large bowl. Add sugar and let proof for 5 minutes. With your hand, mix in salt and 3 cups of the flour, removing lumps. Continue adding flour a cup at a time, kneading as you go and scraping flour from the sides of the bowl with your hand. Add more water as needed.

    2. When the dough is thoroughly mixed and has a smooth, moist consistency that does not stick to your hands, divide it into 5 to 6 parts and shape into orange-sized balls for thick loaves of tilme or for spinach or meat pies. To make small loaves, roll into walnut-sized balls. To freeze, see below.

    3. Roll balls in flour and place on a cloth-covered flat surface allowing space between them to double in size. Cover with a damp cloth or plastic wrap and place in a warm spot to rise for one hour or until doubled. Preheat oven to 475°F.

4. On a clean, dry, floured surface, roll out a ball of dough with a rolling pin, sprinkling flour on the loaf and rolling pin. Roll as thick as you like: ⅛" for *khubz marqouq* or ¼" for pocket bread (*kmaaj*)—using flour to keep the dough from sticking. Here's where the twirling and tossing in the air comes in. I watch pizza bakers to learn their tricks and vividly remember Mother's arms performing her bread dance from the days when she baked every two weeks. It's a matter of gently passing the bread from hand to hand or arm to arm; and if you're courageous, tossing it in the air and catching it! Another way is to hold the dough circle at one end, and drape it over your hand, gravity stretching it as you round the circle. Dough is very forgiving, so try it! Place the rolled-out loaf onto the baking peel sprinkled with flour. While one loaf is baking, begin rolling out the next one.

5. Baking our bread happens quickly and requires undivided attention. Every oven is different, so be watchful, get to know your own oven and what works best. The hotter the oven, the quicker it puffs up and the pocket forms.

IN A GAS STOVE: Slide dough off baking peel directly onto the bottom of hot oven either onto a baking sheet, a piece of foil, or better yet, onto a baking stone, for about 3 to 5 minutes, until bread puffs up or forms air bubbles. Use peel to lift out and slide into broiler for a minute or less, until puffy and lightly browned on top. Watch carefully as it can burn quickly!

IN AN ELECTRIC OVEN: Place dough on a tray on the bottom oven rack until bread puffs up. Move to top rack briefly to lightly brown top.

6. Stack bread loaves as they come out of the oven in a damp towel to cool and soften, or eat hot and crispy, with butter and honey. Heaven!

These loaves will keep several days in a ziplock bag in the fridge, or you can freeze the bag of loaves and reheat them just before serving. I place small loaves right on the gas burner of my classic gas stove to reheat, flipping them on each side for 10 seconds, wrapping them in a towel to keep warm for the table.

TO FREEZE DOUGH

Roll dough balls in flour; wrap each tightly in plastic; freeze in ziplock bags. To thaw and rise: remove from bag, dust again with flour, leave at room temperature 2 hours to rise; roll out and bake as above. Or leave dough in plastic in refrigerator overnight to rise; then dust in flour and let rise at room temperature.

Tilme bi Zeit

THICK ARABIC BREAD WITH OLIVE OIL

◆

T*ilme* can refer generally to bread but also refers to a thick, foccacia-like bread that is eaten with cheese and olives or for dipping and all the usual ways bread is eaten in our cuisine. It is made with the same basic bread dough and differs in the thickness, the method of forming the loaf, and a lower baking temperature. This recipe is for plain *tilme*; for the herbed *zaatar* or *kishk* variety, see the next recipes. I use this same recipe for making pizza, foccacia, or *tilme*. This plain *tilme* will dry out quickly and is best eaten the same day it is baked.

> basic Arabic bread dough (p. 179)
> olive oil
> water

1. Follow basic dough recipe, making dough balls as large or as small as you like—including small individual-sized rounds, through step 3. An orange-sized ball will make a tilme about 8" across. To make tiny appetizer servings, roll balls the size of a walnut. Roll dough in flour and place on a tray in a warm place to rise. Preheat oven to 375ºF.

2. Place raised ball of dough on an oiled baking sheet or a tray lined with baking parchment. Using your hand, dipped into water or olive oil, pat and flatten dough to ½" thick, spreading dough out from the center, leaving edges slightly thicker to make an 8-inch round. Leave space between them for rising in baking.

3. Let dough rest 10 minutes and then bake on lower oven rack until slightly browned on the bottom. Move to top oven rack until top is very lightly browned. Serve warm or cool.

This recipe makes approximately 16 thick, 8-inch plain *tilme* loaves; or vary with savory toppings of *zaatar* or *kishk*; or make flatbreads; or freeze dough for later use.

Tilme bi Zaatar or Manaqish

LEBANESE BREAD WITH *ZAATAR*

◆

One of the most unique flavors of our cuisine is *zaatar*, a savory combination of spices and dried herbs mixed in Lebanese villages. The mixture, composed of *zaatar*—variously defined as thyme, oregano, or savory!—with sumac and sesame seeds, is baked on bread dough, and served hot or at room temperature for breakfast, lunch, appetizers, or dinner. So delicious! In Lebanon, *tilme bi zaatar,* or *manaqish,* is eaten for breakfast right from the oven or filled with tomatoes, fresh mint leaves, green onions, or yogurt cheese (*labne*) and eaten like a sandwich. Our family enjoyed it simply, with delicious *zaatar*. For more on *zaatar*, see page 225.

basic Arabic bread dough (p. 179)
⅔ cup *zaatar* sauce, for 6 big loaves (p. 44)
3–4 tablespoons sesame seeds
⅔ cup olive oil

1. Follow basic dough recipe through step 3, making dough balls as large or as small as you like, even small individual-sized rounds for appetizers (*mezza*). An orange-sized ball will make a tilme about 8" across. To make tiny appetizer servings, roll balls the size of a walnut. Roll dough in flour and place on a tray in a warm place to rise. Preheat oven to 375ºF.

2. While dough is rising, place *zaatar* in a small bowl and stir in sesame seeds. Stir in olive oil and set aside.

3. Place a raised ball of dough on an oiled baking sheet or a tray lined with baking parchment. Flatten dough with your hand to 1" thick, spreading it out from the center, leaving edges thicker, making an 8" circle.

4. Spoon 2 tablespoons *zaatar* sauce onto center of dough circle (or 1 teaspoon on tiny loaves); press into dough and spread mix to ½" from the edge—the dough now about ¼" to ½" thick. Fill baking sheet, leaving space between each *tilme* to rise in baking. If there is extra dough, make plain *tilme* (*tilme bi zeit*) or *tilme bi kishk* or freeze the dough.

5. Let dough rest 10 minutes. Bake on bottom oven rack for 10 to 15 minutes, until bottom is slightly browned. Move to top rack until lightly browned on top. Remove from oven; cool and serve. Cut into small triangles for *mezza* or larger pieces, or serve whole, as you like. To me, *tilme bi zaatar* is addictive!

Makes 6 to 8 big loaves plus 24 tiny individual 3" loaves.

Tilme bi Kishk

LEBANESE BREAD WITH *KISHK*

◆

Kishk is a traditional Lebanese food made by villagers in the summer for winter use. Made of bulgur (*burghul*) combined with yogurt (*laban*), the mixture is sundried, then is laboriously ground between the palms of the hand into coarse flour. This is a method of preserving a protein-rich food for winter use. Here, it is applied to *tilme* and makes a pizza-like savory bread that is excellent. The first time I tasted this, it was made by my cousins in our village, Douma, in Lebanon. Mama and *Sitto* didn't make this for some reason but made *kishk* soup, which wasn't a big favorite. On *tilme*, I love it and make it regularly!

Another recent *kishk* recipe discovery has it sautéed with olive oil, onions, and garlic, to be eaten like *hummus* with bread when it has cooled—fabulous as made by my Tripoli friend Rima. *Kishk* can be purchased in Middle Eastern stores or online.

> basic Arabic bread dough (p. 179)
> 3 cups *kishk* (for 6 big loaves)
> 1 cup olive oil
> 1 onion, minced
> 2 cups tomato, minced
> ¼ to ½ teaspoon cayenne pepper (optional)

1. Follow basic dough recipe, making dough balls as large or as small as you like—including small individual-sized rounds, through step 3.

2. Preheat oven to 375°F. Place *kishk* in a small bowl and stir in olive oil, onion, tomato, and cayenne. Mix well and set aside.

3. Place a raised ball of dough on an oiled cookie sheet or a tray lined with baking parchment. First flatten dough with your hand to 1" thick, spreading it out from the center, leaving edges slightly thicker.

4. Spoon a couple of tablespoons *kishk* mixture and press into dough, spreading to ½" from the edge, flattening dough to about ¼" to ½" thick. Continue filling tray with loaves, leaving space between each *tilme* to rise in baking.

5. Let dough rest 10 minutes. Bake on bottom oven rack for 10 to 15 minutes or until bottom is slightly browned. Move to top rack until lightly browned on top. Remove from oven, cool or serve hot from oven. Cut into small triangles for *mezza* or larger pieces, or serve whole, as you like. Mmmm!

Makes 6 to 8 big loaves plus 24 tiny individual 3" loaves.

Qurban

HOLY BREAD

◆

Aspecial bread traditionally made by families for the forty-day Mass for the dead. The family baked the bread, bringing a few loaves to the priest, who blessed it and offered it to congregants after Mass. The special dough for this slightly sweetened bread begins with our regular bread dough and has the addition of *mahlab*, a unique Lebanese spice, which creates its distinctive flavor. *Qurban* is stamped before baking with a handcarved woodblock (*tabi*) bearing a sacred Greek inscription in a round design, centered with a cross. In our Eastern Catholic rite, this bread is used for the Holy Communion Bread and is dipped in Sacramental Wine.

> basic Arabic bread dough (p. 179)
> 2 teaspoons *mahlab*, ground with 1 teaspoon sugar

1. Follow step 1 of the basic bread dough recipe, making the dough for *qurban* on the stiff side.

2. When the dough is thoroughly mixed and has a smooth, moist consistency that does not stick to your hands, divide it into 5 to 6 parts and shape into orange-sized balls for thick loaves.

3. Roll balls in flour and place on a cloth-covered flat surface, allowing space between them to double in size. Cover with a damp cloth or plastic wrap and place in a warm spot to rise for 1 hour or until doubled. Preheat oven to 350ºF.

4. Place raised ball of dough on an oiled cookie sheet or a tray lined with baking parchment. Using your hand, pat and flatten dough to ½" thick, spreading dough out from the center to make an 8" round. Press stamp design into the middle of dough round; using a wooden matchstick, poke holes around the design on the top of the loaf to prevent rising.

5. Let dough rest 5 minutes. Bake on lower oven rack until slightly browned on the bottom. Move to top oven rack until top is very lightly browned. Remove from oven and using a brush or your hand dipped in water, wipe the hot loaf, which will make it shiny. Cool and serve.

This recipe makes 6 to 8 thick 10-inch loaves of *qurban*.

ALICE'S KITCHEN

IF YOU MAKE IT WITH LOVE, IT WILL BE DELICIOUS!

Kaak ma Simsum

Armenian-style Crackers with Sesame Seeds

◆

Although this is not one of our family recipes from my childhood, it is a favorite recipe that I've adapted for sesame seed crackers that go very well with our foods, as an alternative to bread or pita chips. If you love to bake, you'll love these; they're amenable to many variations. My friend Karen's creative example: she transformed them into garlic-tomato pesto-parmesan crackers that people love. So this recipe is a good place to start, and you can create your own modifications by just adding ingredients to the dough. They keep well for weeks in airtight tins, if they last that long! Excellent with jam, *hommus* or *baba gannouj*, red pepper dip, yogurt cheese, and appetizers. A pizza cutter, a squirt bottle filled with drinking water, a rolling pin, and baking parchment are useful tools for making these.

> 1 cup water (lukewarm)
> 1 tablespoon yeast
> 1 teaspoon salt
> ¼ cup olive oil or melted butter
> 3¼ cups flour (2 cups white and 1 cup whole wheat)
> ½ cup sesame seeds

1. Dissolve yeast in lukewarm water in a medium-sized bowl. Let proof for 5 minutes. Add olive oil or butter. With your hand, mix in salt, flour, and sesame seeds, removing lumps, kneading and scraping flour from the sides of the bowl with your hand, blending it well.

2. Divide it into 8 balls by dividing it in half, then quarters, then eighths. Roll balls of dough in flour and place on a tray in a warm place to rise to double in size. Cover with a dry towel. Preheat oven to 350ºF.

3. Place raised ball of dough on a well-floured surface; roll out with a rolling pin as thinly as possible. Carefully transfer to a cookie sheet lined with parchment. Using a pizza cutter or a knife, cut dough into strips 1" to 2" wide and then cut crosswise into 4" lengths on the cookie sheet. Squirt dough with water; place on lower oven rack for 10 minutes until slightly browned on the bottom.

4. Squirt again with water and move to top oven rack for 10 minutes until top is lightly browned and crackers are crisp. Cool and serve. Cool completely before storing in airtight tins, to keep crisp. If they're a little soft, they can be placed in the oven to crisp after it has cooled down a bit, and left until until they're cool.

Makes approximately 6 to 8 dozen crackers.

Khubz Mhammas

PITA CHIPS

◆

Either homemade Arabic flat bread (*khubz marqouq*), pita bread, or store-bought pita bread can be used for this simple low-fat chip, that works perfectly for dipping into *hommus*, *baba ghannouj*, yogurt, or for *fatte* and *fattoush* recipes. Use both whole wheat and white bread if you're having a dinner party or serving appetizers, so your guests can have their choice. It is possible to brush the bread lightly with olive oil, or to drizzle a little oil over the bread on the tray before putting it in the oven, if you care to add a little fat. Add minced garlic or garlic paste to the olive oil and you'll end up with garlic pita chips!

In baking these, use a hotter oven if you have little time and are able to keep your eye on them so they don't get overdone. A low temperature works well also; it takes a little longer for the bread to crisp up.

> 6 loaves Arabic or pita bread
> olive oil (optional)

1. Preheat oven to 250ºF to 350ºF.
2. Slice pita bread along the seam all the way around, splitting it in half. With a pair of kitchen scissors, cut bread into small triangles, 2 or 3 at a time.
3. Spread bread pieces in a single or double layer on a baking sheet and place in oven for 10 to 30 minutes, depending upon the oven temperature. Use 2 baking sheets, putting one tray on the top shelf, and the other tray on the bottom, switching the trays about halfway through, and mixing the chips on the tray, so they get evenly crisped.
4. Serve warm or cool. Cool completely before storing in airtight tins, to keep them crisp.

Makes lots of pita chips—enough for a big party!

ALICE'S KITCHEN
IF YOU MAKE IT WITH LOVE, IT WILL BE DELICIOUS!

HILOU

◆

SWEETS

Dessert in the Middle East typically consists of a platter of fresh or dried fruit such as dates, a bit of feta or yogurt cheese, olives, or a dab of fig jam on a snippet of Arabic bread, rather than cakes, cookies, and pies. Figs, grapes, and all fruits in season are the traditional way to finish a meal.

Nevertheless, we do have an amazing variety of sweets and pastries that are customarily eaten during the holidays, or are offered to guests with Arabic coffee, later in the evening after dinner. Certain sweets are often associated with celebrating specific holidays, holy days, or family events.

Our pastries range from a myriad of filo dough variations on baklava (*baklawa*) filled with pistachios, almonds, walnuts, or pine nuts, to rice pudding, or cookies that are hard to resist. You will even find a recipe for our distinctive Lebanese ice cream! Nut-filled *mamouls* are a Lebanese specialty, as are cookies filled with dates or rolled in sesame seeds. Flavoring with rose water or orange blossom water makes these sweets fragrant, tantalizing, and satisfying. These and other special flavorings such as *sahlab, mahlab,* and *miski* are available in Middle Eastern stores or online. Several recipes, such as our scrumptious Lebanese crepes (*'atayif*), or *baklawa* call for a special syrup, *'attar*, which is made ahead and chilled.

Some of our sweets are very easy to make, and others take more time, as do many good things. Usually we use unbleached white flour and white sugar, because these are eaten sparingly—they're special treats, not an everyday indulgence. Baking on baking parchment makes cleanup much easier, saving time. Enjoy these Lebanese pastries and desserts with your friends and families, imagining you're in the souks of Tripoli or Beirut, or in the mountains of Lebanon.

'Attar

SIMPLE FRAGRANT SYRUP

◆

'A*ttar*, our light, fragrant syrup, divinely scented with orange blossoms or roses, is used in many of our dessert recipes. Make some ahead of time to have on hand in the refrigerator, as our recipes require it chilled. This recipe makes approximately a cup of syrup, which is the perfect amount for the recipes in **Alice's Kitchen**.

> 1½ cups sugar
> 1½ cups water
> ⅓ cup lemon juice
> 1 teaspoon orange blossom water (*may zahar*)
>   or rose water (*may warid*)

    1. Put water, sugar, and lemon juice in a saucepan and cook over low to medium heat. Stir frequently, until mixture thickens into a syrupy consistency, about 30 to 45 minutes, being careful not to let it burn.

    2. Cool and add *may zahar* or *may warid*. Decant into a glass bottle and chill. This will keep refrigerated for several months.

Makes approximately 1 cup syrup.

ALICE'S KITCHEN
IF YOU MAKE IT WITH LOVE, IT WILL BE DELICIOUS!

'Atayif bi Jouz

Lebanese crepes with cheese or walnut filling

◆

$\mathbf{S}$imilar to French crepes, yet diminutive in size, these excellent warm Lebanese filled pastries can be enjoyed as evening desserts or, as they are typically served in Lebanon, for breakfast or brunch. There are two different fillings: one cheese and the other walnut. Make both to see which you prefer, using half the filling recipe below for each. The delicate orange blossom water (*may zahar*) flavor makes them irresistible. 'Atayif can be made ahead, stored in the freezer, and fried or baked at the last minute. Make 'attar syrup ahead and chill.

1 cup 'attar syrup, cold (p. 188)

Cheese filling

> 1 pint ricotta cheese
> > or 2 cups unsalted 'arishe (p. 35)
> 1½ cups grated jack cheese
> 1½ tablespoons sugar
> 1 tablespoon orange blossom water (*may zahar*)

Walnut filling

> 2 cups chopped walnuts
> 2 tablespoons sugar
> 2 tablespoons orange blossom water (*may zahar*)

Dough/batter

> 2 cups flour
> 2½ cups water
> ½ tablespoon yeast
> 1 teaspoon sugar

⅛ teaspoon baking soda
½ teaspoon salt
vegetable oil and clarified butter (p. 39)
    for frying or baking

1. Dissolve yeast in lukewarm water with sugar and let proof 5 minutes in a deep mixing bowl. Combine salt and baking soda with flour and gradually stir into water, removing any lumps that form. The correct consistency is like a thin pancake batter. Cover and place in a warm place to rise for ½ to 1 hour or until doubled in size.

2. Meanwhile, make either cheese or nut filling by mixing ingredients in a bowl. If making both kinds, make half as much of each filling.

3. Heat a griddle coated lightly with olive oil to medium temperature. If batter is too thick, thin it with a little water. Pour batter into 4" rounds, about ⅛" thick. Cook only on one side until the surface has air bubbles and is not wet or shiny and the bottom is golden brown, like a pancake. Set them on a plate side by side, or slightly overlapping each other and cover with a tea towel. Fill those that are done as described in step 4, while others are cooking on the griddle.

4. Fill each dough circle with a heaping teaspoon to tablespoon of either cheese or nut filling on the uncooked side and pinch edges firmly together to seal closed, forming a fat half-circle. Set aside to fry or place overlapping each other into a glass baking dish to bake.

To deep fry

Heat equal parts oil and butter in a frying pan to ½" deep. When it is hot, drop in 'atayif and brown on each side for about 3 to 4 minutes. This may take longer if they were frozen (use directly from freezer without thawing). Lift out and drain on paper for a moment. Place on a platter and drizzle cold 'attar syrup over while they are still quite hot. Serve immediately. Yum!

To bake

Preheat oven to 350ºF. Place 'atayif in a glass baking dish dotted with a little clarified butter. Bake for about 30 minutes. If they have been frozen, bake for 45 minutes. Remove from oven and immediately drizzle cold 'attar syrup over them and serve right away. Divine!

To freeze for later use

Place individual pastries on a cookie sheet and freeze. When frozen, transfer them to freezer bags for use later. When ready to bake, follow instructions above.

Makes approximately 60 small pastries, about 8 to 10 servings.

ALICE'S KITCHEN
IF YOU MAKE IT WITH LOVE, IT WILL BE DELICIOUS!

190

Mamoul

WALNUT FILLED COOKIES

◆

These traditional Easter cookies are made in Lebanon in press molds, called *'aalib*. Mother and *Sitto* preferred to devise their own method of decorating these scrumptious nut-filled cookies—Mother says it was out of love to make them more beautiful! She commissioned a sheet metal worker to cut out and form several pincers (*malqat*) to use for decorating *mamouls* and date-filled cookies. Most likely you'll use a *mamoul* mold.

Mamouls are not difficult to make, but like all good things, they take time, so invite some friends over or bring your children 'round you and have fun filling, pinching, and decorating together! The first step of dough is done 5 hours ahead. Once they are baked, eating them will be as pleasing as making them, only much faster! The special ingredient, Cornell cherry kernel (*mahlab*), is available from Middle Eastern stores or online, as is a *mamoul* mold. Both methods of making *mamouls* are described. If you have access to an old-fashioned nut grinder, this is the best way to grind nuts to the desired coarseness, and avoids overgrinding in the food processor.

FILLING—MIX TOGETHER

        3 cups finely chopped walnuts
        2 tablespoons orange blossom water (*may zahar*)
        ⅓–½ cup sugar

DOUGH

        2 cups farina (*smeed*) or cream of wheat
        1¼ cups melted clarified butter (*samne*)
        ½ teaspoon *mahlab,* ground with 1 teaspoon sugar
        ½ cup milk
        ½ tablespoon dry yeast
        1½ cups flour
        ½ cup sugar
        2 tablespoons orange blossom water (*may zahar*)

TOPPING

        ½ cup powdered sugar

1. In a mixing bowl, pour warm melted butter over farina and *mahlab*. Let stand approximately 5 hours.

2. Then, dissolve yeast in ¼ cup of warm milk. Heat remaining milk almost to boil, pour over farina mixture and let cool for 10 minutes.

3. Mix flour into farina mixture. Knead in yeast and milk mixture. Add orange blossom water (*may zahar*) and knead well to achieve a uniform, elastic, moist dough, adding more flour if needed. Cover and put in a warm place to rest for one-half hour before forming cookies.

4. Preheat oven to 350ºF.

5. Roll a ball of dough 1½" in diameter in the palm of your hands. Support the dough in one hand while depressing a hollow into the ball creating an even thickness using your other index finger.

6. Place roughly 1 teaspoonful of filling into hollow and pinch closed, reshaping it into a round form between your palms. Use *malqat* (pincers) to make a design on cookie, place on cookie sheet, and bake for ½ hour until ever so slightly brown. Bake for 10 minutes on bottom rack; move to the top oven rack until light golden, about 5 to 10 minutes.

7. Cool cookies completely and then sift powdered sugar over the tops and serve. Or store in airtight tins for up to two weeks, and dust with powdered sugar before serving.

IF USING *MAMOUL* MOLD (*'AALIB*)

Follow step 5; then fill with nuts and pinch closed, forming a sphere. Press sphere into the mold, flattening the bottom; gently tap the mold to release the cookie into your hand or onto the cookie sheet. Continue baking as described in step 6.

Makes about 4 dozen cookies.

ALICE'S KITCHEN
IF YOU MAKE IT WITH LOVE, IT WILL BE DELICIOUS!

192

Kaak bi Simsum

Sesame Cookies

◆

Sesame-covered, crisp and light, with the subtle richness of *mahlab* flavor–we couldn't get enough of these cookies! *Sitto* and Mother let me help make them— rolling dough, lifting the fragile dough circles out of a pool of milk, and dropping them onto the beach of sesame seeds. Our sesame cookies are a perfect accompaniment to tea or coffee, and are a great baking project to do with children, who love to cook, given the opportunity.

Topping

½ cup milk
¼ cup sugar
1–2 cups sesame seeds

Dough

3 cups flour
2 teaspoons baking powder
¾ cup sugar
1 teaspoon *mahlab*, ground with 1 teaspoon sugar
¾ cup clarified butter (p. 39)
    or ½ pound butter, melted
1 egg
¾ cup milk

Topping

1. Mix milk and sugar together in a bowl and set aside.
2. Put sesame seeds in a wide shallow bowl and set aside.

Dough

1. Mix dry ingredients including *mahlab*, together in a bowl. Pour in melted butter and mix thoroughly.
2. Beat egg with milk and knead into dough. Consistency desired is moist, not sticky. Add flour if needed to achieve this.
3. Preheat oven to 350ºF.
4. Take a small piece of dough and roll it between your palms to form a pen-like shape, ⅓" by 6" long. Pinch ends of the dough together, with ½" overlap, making a circle about 2" to 3" across, with a hole in the center.
5. Place circle of dough into milk-and-sugar mixture for a moment, coating the dough. Carefully lift it out with a fork and lay it onto the sesame seeds;

Alice's Kitchen
Sweets

gently lift and turn it over, covering entire cookie with seeds, which adhere to the surface. Using the fork, place cookie onto a cookie sheet lined with parchment, and shape it into a circle again, leaving a little space between each cookie to rise. The dough is soft, pliable, and is easily shaped at this stage.

6. Bake for 10 to 15 minutes until lightly browned and crisp. Cool completely before storing. These will store for a few weeks in an airtight container, if they are kept out of sight!

Makes about 5 dozen cookies.

194

ALICE'S KITCHEN
IF YOU MAKE IT WITH LOVE, IT WILL BE DELICIOUS!

Kaak bi Haleeb

ANISE COOKIES WITH MILK

◆

The flavors of anise and *mahlab* impart subtle fragrance to another Lebanese classic pastry. Dense, thick cookies that are more like cake or bread, *kaak bi haleeb* have a wonderful olive oil flavor and a chewy texture. They are simple both in their making and in their elegance; they are not frequently seen outside Lebanese circles, so they would be an interesting and easy dessert to make for guests.

1 tablespoon yeast
¼ cup warm water
½ cup sugar
1 cup olive oil (a light olive oil is best)
2 tablespoons aniseeds, finely ground
½ teaspoon *mahlab,* ground with 1 teaspoon sugar
½ teaspoon salt
3 cups flour
¼ cup milk

1. Dissolve yeast in lukewarm water and set aside to proof.
2. Meanwhile, in a mixing bowl, cream together oil with sugar. Add *mahlab*, aniseeds, salt, and flour, mixing thoroughly with your hands. Knead in yeast and water mixture. Slowly mix in enough milk so that the consistency becomes smooth but not sticky. Cover and let rest ½ hour.
3. Divide dough into 3 balls and let rest another ½ hour. Preheat oven to 350ºF.
4. With your hands, form dough into little balls, about the size of a walnut, and then flatten to 2" to 3" wide circles that are ¼" thick. Pinch edges like a pie crust and press a fork across the top, to create a design on the surface and keep the cookie flat. Place on cookie sheet lined with parchment and bake for 15 minutes: about 7 minutes on the bottom oven rack and finishing on the top rack, until lightly golden in color. Cool thoroughly and enjoy. When cool, store in an airtight container. These cookies are best eaten within a few days of baking.

Makes about 2 dozen cookies.

Ghraybe

SHORTBREAD COOKIES

◆

Crisp and light, these classic Lebanese shortbread cookies melt in your mouth! Our tradition is to have cookies only during the Christmas holidays, served with tea or Arabic coffee. Every year in the weeks before Christmas, Mother still bakes up a storm and puts together beautiful gift boxes that include these and a variety of her other sweets, stuffed dates and homemade candies. `

> 1 cup clarified butter, softened
> 1 cup superfine sugar
> 1½ cups flour
> 1 egg white
> 1 cup blanched almonds, split in half
>   or whole pistachio or pine nuts, for top

1. Cream the butter until fluffy. Gradually add sugar and then egg white, continuing to blend. Add flour and mix well, adding more flour as needed so dough doesn't stick to your hands.

2. Preheat oven to 325°F.

3. Shape into balls the size of a walnut and place on ungreased cookie sheet. Make an indentation in the center of each by pressing half of a blanched almond into the top, flattening the cookie a little. Or roll into a coil and join ends forming a small donut shape with a hole in the center.

4. Bake lightly for 15 to 20 minutes in center oven rack until bottoms are ever so slightly golden; the tops remain white. Cool for 10 minutes before moving from cookie sheet and then cool thoroughly before storing or serving. Store in airtight tins to keep crisp.

Makes about 3 dozen cookies.

Nus Qamar

ALMOND CRESCENT MOONS

◆

Mother's secret recipe, these exquisite almond crescent moons are so light and crispy, they are irresistible! And these are very simple to make. The best way to grind the almonds to the right size is with an old-fashioned nut grinder. They might get too pulverized in a food processor, becoming more like almond meal.

¾ pound butter
¾ cup sugar
1 teaspoon vanilla extract
1 teaspoon almond extract
3 cups sifted flour
2 cups minced or finely chopped almonds

1. Cream butter and sugar. Add vanilla and almond extracts, and gradually stir in flour and almonds, mixing well with your hands. Add more flour if dough sticks to your hands.

2. Preheat oven to 325ºF.

3. Roll a tablespoon of dough between your palms to elongate it. Pinch the edges to slight points and place on cookie sheet, curving it into a crescent moon shape, each one about 2" long by ½" across at the thick center. Fill tray with moons, leaving ½" between each to expand, as they do get bigger in baking.

4. Bake on center oven rack for 15 to 20 minutes until lightly golden; watch these carefully so they don't burn. Cool completely before storing, although these will disappear before you know it!

Makes about 4 dozen cookies.

Harist il Louz or Nammoura

GROUND ALMOND AND FARINA PASTRY

◆

Moist, dense and cake-like, this almond-rich pastry, *nammoura*, is easy enough for a child to make and tastes terrific. Even though it will keep, this pastry is at its best when freshly made. Make *'attar* syrup ahead and chill.

1 cup cold *'attar* syrup, for top after baking (p. 188)

4½ cups farina
1 cup finely ground almonds, ground in blender
1¾ cups sugar
3 teaspoons baking powder
1 tablespoon orange blossom water (*may zahar*)
2 cups milk
1 cup clarified butter, warm (p. 39)
3 tablespoons sesame tahini oil
    or sesame oil, to grease 13"x18" baking dish
½ cup almonds, blanched and split in half,
    to decorate top

1. Preheat oven to 375ºF. Mix dry ingredients well.
2. Add orange blossom water (*may zahar*) to milk and pour into dry in-gredients. Mix well and stir in butter, mixing thoroughly. Spread mixture into greased baking dish, smoothing out top with a spatula, about ½" thick. If a smaller baking dish is used, the cookies will be thicker. Cut into small diamonds, the same as for *kibbe*, page 86. Place a blanched almond half into each diamond.
3. Place tray on lower oven rack and bake for about 15 minutes, until edges just begin to brown.
4. Move to top oven rack for 10 minutes so top will turn a light golden brown. Remove from oven and quickly recut. Immediately drizzle cold *'attar* syrup evenly over the top of pastry while still hot. Let cool for an hour or so and then serve.

Makes about 30 cookies.

Asabi bi Ajwe

Date fingers

◆

In these luscious cookies, dates, figs, or any other fruit preserve fill a buttery short dough. Following is the recipe for date filling, but two or so cups apricot, quince, or fig jam would nicely substitute for dates. Sometimes Mother uses a mixture of jams, whatever she has on hand—mmmmm! At the end of the recipe, I'm including a quicker alternative way to shape these cookies in a log, for those who don't have time like our mothers and grandmothers did, to make these the traditional way. They still taste great.

Date filling
>3 cups chopped dates
>2 cups water
>2 tablespoons clarified butter, unmelted

Dough
>1 pound softened butter (not clarified)
>¾ cup sugar
>2 eggs
>1 jigger (2–3 tablespoons) brandy
>½ teaspoon ground *mahlab*
>5 cups flour

Date filling

1. Cook dates in saucepan with water for 20 minutes over medium heat, stirring occasionally.

2. Stir in butter and add a little more water if necessary, cooking until it becomes a thick paste. Set aside to cool, while making dough.

Dough

1. Cream together butter and sugar in a mixing bowl. Beat in eggs and stir in brandy and *mahlab*. Slowly stir in flour, mixing well until dough does not stick to your hands but is not dry or stiff, adding flour as needed.

2. Preheat oven to 325°F.

3. Roll a piece of dough into a walnut-sized ball in the palm of your hands. Holding dough cupped in the palm of one hand, press the index finger of your other hand into the ball, making a hollow in the dough, forming an even ⅛ thick-

ness of dough. This is similar to *mamoul*, pictured on pages 191–192, except it is an elongated shape rather than round.

4. With a small spoon or fork, place approximately one teaspoon of filling into the dough and pinch it closed. Gently roll the filled dough between your palms, into an elongated shape, with pointed ends and a thick middle.

5. Use pincers (*malat*) to squeeze the top of the dough, creating tiny decorative ridges. Place on cookie sheet and bake for 15 minutes on bottom oven rack until slightly golden on the bottom, then on top rack for another 5 to 10 minutes to tinge the top lightly golden. Cool thoroughly before storing or serving.

QUICK ALTERNATE METHOD OF MAKING DATE COOKIES (STARTING FROM STEP 2)

1. Use a rolling pin to roll an orange-sized piece of dough into a rectangular sheet about ⅛" thick.

2. With a fork or spoon, mound jam, which needs to be thick rather than runny, into a long cylinder along edge of dough about ½" from the edge.

3. Using both hands, roll the edge of the dough, tightly like a carpet, just enough to enclose the jam inside it. Cut this away from the remaining dough, leaving the remaining dough flat on the table.

4. Carefully seal the edge of the cookie log by pinching the dough together. Gently use both hands to roll the log back and forth, which will round it out and elongate it even more. At this point it's fine to cut it into 2 sections, which you can carefully lift onto the tray lined with baking parchment.

5. Starting on one end of the log, use a sharp knife and make a series of cuts through the top of log 1" apart going almost all the way through. The log will stay connected, but after baking, you can easily separate these into little rounds of dough filled with jam.

6. Continue making logs of jam until you've used up your dough.

7. When you've filled your cookie sheet, bake for 15 minutes on bottom oven rack until slightly golden on the bottom, then on top rack to brown for another 10 minutes or so. Cool thoroughly before separating into little cookies and before serving or storing.

Makes about 4 dozen cookies.

200

ALICE'S KITCHEN
IF YOU MAKE IT WITH LOVE, IT WILL BE DELICIOUS!

Zlabye

LEBANESE FRITTERS

◆

Mother's Lebanese fritters are eggless and light. Powdered sugar dusting the top imparts a delicate sweetness to a remarkably basic but nonetheless satisfying treat. Taste them both ways—with powdered sugar and without, to see which you prefer.

4 cups flour
½ teaspoon salt
3 teaspoons baking powder
3 tablespoons olive oil
1 cup warm water
½–1 cup vegetable oil, for frying
½ cup powdered sugar, for top

1. Mix dry ingredients together. Add olive oil to water and mix with dry ingredients to make dough, adding a little more water or flour as needed.

2. Form 4 balls of dough the size of an orange. Roll each ball in flour; place on a tray, cover with a cotton cloth, and let rest in a warm place for ½ hour.

3. On a clean dry surface, roll out one ball of dough to ¼" thick and cut into 1"x3" strips. Continue with each ball of dough.

4. Heat oil in a frying pan. As strips deep fry in hot vegetable oil, they puff up and turn light golden brown. Turn to brown other side.

5. Place on paper towel to drain; sprinkle with powdered sugar on all sides while warm and serve. Only cook as many as you will serve at a time. The remaining dough can be refrigerated for several days or frozen for later use.

Makes about 4 dozen fritters.

'Awamat

FRIED LEBANESE DOUGHNUTS

◆

'**A**wamat are an unusually sweet and decadent winter holiday treat that our family loves. The potato flour used in Mother's recipe makes the dough light. The root of the word *awamat* means floating, since when they are fried, they float to the top of the pot. They are lighter than doughnuts or fritters, and are dipped quickly into cold '*attar* syrup, which is made ahead and chilled. Serve with Arabic coffee or tea. *Mshabbak* is a variation on this made by drizzling the batter into the oil with a funnel, overlapping itself like a pile of rope.

2 cups '*attar* syrup, chilled (p. 188)

3 cups water, lukewarm
1 tablespoon yeast
1 teaspoon sugar
3 cups flour (2 cups unbleached white and 1 cup potato flour)
¼ teaspoon baking soda
½ teaspoon salt
2–3 cups equal parts olive oil and vegetable oil, for frying

1. Dissolve yeast in lukewarm water with sugar in a deep mixing bowl and let proof for 5 minutes.

2. Combine salt and baking soda with flour. Gradually stir this into the yeast mixture, until a pancake batter consistency is achieved. Cover and let rise for a half hour or until doubled in size.

3. Heat oil in a deep skillet to quite hot. Drop spoonfuls of dough into oil to fry until lightly browned. An oiled spoon allows the batter to slide right off.

4. Lift '*awamat* from oil with a slotted spoon and immediately dip for a moment into bowl of cold '*attar* syrup. Serve on a platter either while warm or at room temperature.

Makes about 3 dozen pastries.

Baklawa

BAKLAVA

Unlike the weighty, honey-laden, sticky, and too-sweet baklava one finds commercially outside of the Middle East, our *baklawa* is so light and scrumptious that it is difficult to eat just one. Our recipe is very simple, flavored only with orange blossom water, and without the cinnamon that some families use. It's rather easy to create, so if you've never baked this heavenly dessert, give it a go! Our family traditionally enjoyed *baklawa* during the Christmas season. Tins filled with *baklawa* continue to be treasured holiday gifts shared with friends and neighbors.

Make *'attar* syrup ahead and chill. If you have access to an old-fashioned nut grinder, this is the best way of grinding nuts to the desired coarseness, which avoids the overgrinding that may happen quickly in a blender or food processor.

> 1 cup cold *'attar* syrup (p. 188)
> 1 package filo dough, at room temperature

FILLING

> 3 cups walnuts or pistachio nuts
> 1 pound clarified butter, melted
> ½ cup sugar
> 2 tablespoons orange blossom water (*may zahar*)

    1. Coarsely grind nuts and place in a bowl. Stir in sugar and orange blossom water (*may zahar*).

    2. Preheat oven to 225°F.

    3. Butter 8"x13" baking dish, using a pastry brush. Divide filo dough into 2 equal parts, cutting it in half so that one sheet fits the size of your baking dish.

Begin layering individual sheets of filo dough into the baking dish, brushing each layer with butter. Continue until ½ of the filo dough remains.

4. Spread the nut filling evenly to the edge, covering the filo. Cover the nut layer with a sheet of filo and continue layering the remaining filo, brushing each sheet with butter as above. With a sharp knife, cut the pastry into diamond shapes, beginning with lengthwise strips about 1½" wide, being sure to cut through all layers to the bottom of the tray. Then make another series of parallel cuts at 45 degrees, also 1½" wide creating diamond shapes.

5. Bake slowly in middle rack of oven for 2 hours or until golden brown on top and bottom. Remove from heat and immediately drizzle cold syrup evenly over the top. Cool and reslice to serve.

Makes about 2 dozen cookies.

ALICE'S KITCHEN
IF YOU MAKE IT WITH LOVE, IT WILL BE DELICIOUS!

Bouza

LEBANESE ICE CREAM

◆

If you have ever tasted Lebanese ice cream, you've experienced its incomparable flavor and texture. During hot Los Angeles summers, Mother and Dad pulled out the ice-cream maker, the rock salt, and the precious *sahlab* and *miski* in little packets from Lebanon and began the magical process. The distinctive flavor of *sahlab* is slightly more subtle but no less unusual than that of *miski*, the pine resin from Lebanon's magnificent pine trees (*snobar*). *Miski*, pictured right, in addition to imparting a resonant flavor, also creates the resinous, gummy texture unique to Lebanese ice cream. There is nothing like it this side of Beirut.

I remember we first used an old hand-crank, labor-intensive ice-cream maker and a huge block of ice that we chipped with an ice pick—a very fun summer event for kids! But eventually Dad bought us an electric spinning model and bags of ice cubes. Whichever method you use, *sahteyn!* Before you begin, check the size of the ice cream maker; if it holds a gallon of ice cream, you can triple this recipe and fill the ice cream maker to three-quarters full. If you only want a half-gallon of ice cream, just double the recipe. This recipe makes a quart.

> 1 quart whole milk
> 1 tablespoon *sahlab*
> 1 cup sugar
> ½ teaspoon *miski,* ground with 1 tablespoon sugar
>
> ice cream maker
> 2 cups rock salt
> 3 bags of ice cubes or 2 blocks of ice

    1. Heat milk slowly in a deep pot. Mix sugar and *sahlab* and add slowly to warm milk, stirring constantly until it thickens.

    2. Meanwhile, grind *miski* with sugar with a mortar and pestle until fine. Put through a strainer to remove coarse pieces and add gradually to thickened custard, mixing well and removing lumps. Cook 5 more minutes and remove from heat. Cool.

    3. Put custard in ice cream maker to ¾ full; put in dasher and close tightly.

Pack freezer compartment alternately with rock salt and ice per instructions for ice-cream maker. Allow the pack to stand for 3 minutes before you start turning. Churn for 15 minutes, adding more ice and salt, keeping it filled to the top. Be sure to keep your eye on the electric ice-cream maker through the process, because as soon as the ice cream hardens enough, the machine stops turning, and it must be un-plugged or the motor will burn.

4. Pour off the salt water and wipe off lid. Remove the dasher carefully, keeping salt or water from getting into the ice cream. Place a cork in the lid where the dasher was and replace the lid. Repack the container in the freezer, adding more salt and ice; cover with newspapers. Let stand for an hour or two. Transfer to pint or quart containers and put in freezer to harden. Enjoy!

Makes 1 quart ice cream.

206

ALICE'S KITCHEN
IF YOU MAKE IT WITH LOVE, IT WILL BE DELICIOUS!

'Amah

WHEAT BERRY PORRIDGE

◆

Cold winter nights by the fire accompanied by a bowl of 'amah warms the spirits and the soul. 'Amah means wheat in Arabic, but traditional American hot cereals do not compare with this brothy blend, perfumed with aniseeds (*yensoon*), that can be a nutritious winter evening dessert, with the leftovers easily heated for a quick, hearty breakfast. Our family loved it in winter as we sat cozily by the fire in the den telling stories or playing *basra* (a card game my *Sitto* taught us!). Our Melkite church in Los Angeles served it already sweetened in paper cups with nuts at Easter and at memorial Masses—a tradition going back to ancient Egyptian mourning rites. Symbolizing the resurrection of the dead as well as spring renewal and growth, it is also served to celebrate births, New Year's Day, and the fall feast of St. Barbara, which coincides with Halloween.

'Amah is very easy to make and the consistency can vary from as dry as steamed rice to a soupy broth—terrific any where in-between. Nuts and raisins added after cooking, by each person, provide a protein-rich combination plus iron, while the aniseeds impart flavor and help digestion.

> 1½ cups whole wheat berries ('*amah*), rinsed
> 4 cups water
> 1 tablespoon aniseeds (*yensoon*)
> ½ cup walnut pieces
> ½ cup raisins
> sugar or honey
> pine nuts or pistachio nuts (optional)

    1. Put wheat berries in a medium-sized pot with water and aniseeds. Cover and bring to a boil. Reduce heat and simmer for 1½ to 2 hours, stirring occasionally, and adding water if necessary.

    2. When wheat berries are fully cooked and tender, serve in bowls with cooking broth. Sugar, honey, walnut pieces, and raisins are offered in bowls to each person so they may sweeten their '*amah* to taste, and add walnut pieces, other nuts, and raisins, as they choose.

Serves 4 to 6.

Knafe bi Jibn

Filo cheesecake with orange blossom water syrup

◆

In her 1926 coming-to-America story, my dear mother, Alice, tells of a delightful stop on their way from their village of Douma to Beirut, where they would embark to Italy, then on to America in another ship. My *Sitto*, with her three children: Adib, Alice, and Edmond, went out of their way to the northern city Tripoli (*Trablos*), to a special place: the *Hallab* bakery for a famous pastry—*knafe bi jibn*. Mother and *Sitto* recreated their American version of *knafe bi jibn*, which is out of this world! The pastry dough is a shredded filo, available by the name of *kataify* or *'ataayif*. It can be found in Middle Eastern food stores. On one of my trips to Lebanon, I managed to find the *Hallab* in Tripoli, still there after all these years, serving their celebrated *knafe bi jibn*. In 1998, returning to Lebanon with Mother for her first time since 1926, we had to go there and eat *knafe*; and we did! It was out of this world!

> 1 pound shredded filo dough, *kataify'* or *'atayif*
> ¾ cup clarified butter, melted
> 1 cup cold syrup, *'attar* (p. 188)

FILLING

> 2 pints ricotta cheese or 4 cups *'arishe* (p. 35)
> 1½ pounds jack cheese, grated
> 3 tablespoons sugar
> 1 teaspoon each orange blossom water (*may zahar*)
>   and rose water (*may warid*)

1. Cut shredded dough into 1" lengths with scissors or a knife into a bowl. Drizzle warm clarified butter over dough, thoroughly blending butter into the dough between your palms—Mother says for at least 5 minutes.

2. Spread half of the dough into an 8"x13" glass baking dish.

3. Preheat oven to 350ºF.

4. Combine filling ingredients together in a bowl and mix well. Gently spread filling to cover the bottom layer of dough. Add remaining dough to cover filling. Bake for 35 to 45 minutes, until top is light brown.

5. Remove from heat and immediately drizzle cold *'attar* syrup evenly over the top. Serve at once. Superb!

Makes 12 servings.

208

ALICE'S KITCHEN
IF YOU MAKE IT WITH LOVE, IT WILL BE DELICIOUS!

Riz ib Haleeb

RICE PUDDING

◆

Comfort food if there ever was one, *riz ib haleeb*, a classic Mediterranean pudding with Lebanon's fragrant flavorings: orange blossom water, rose water, and cinnamon. Cool and refreshing, our recipe is not too sweet. Steam rice ahead of time. If white processed sugar or dairy products are not a part of your diet, substituting soy or rice milk, brown rice, and agave syrup for the sugar works very well!

> 2 cups steamed white short grain rice, without salt
> 1 quart milk
> 2 tablespoons cornstarch
> ½ cup sugar
> pinch salt
> 1 teaspoon each orange blossom water (*may zahar*)
>   and rose water (*may warid*)
> 2 teaspoons ground cinnamon, for topping

    1. Mix together all ingredients except fragrant waters (*may zahar* and *may warid*), and cinnamon in a sauce pan. Separate grains of rice with a spoon or fork.

    2. Cook on stove top stirring frequently over medium heat, until milk thickens, for about ½ hour. Remove from heat and add *may zahar* and *may warid*.

    3. Pour into individual pudding dishes and cool. Then refrigerate to set the pudding.

    4. Serve chilled with a dusting of powdered cinnamon or ground pistachio nuts on the top.

Makes 12 half-cup servings.

Mhallabiye

ROSE WATER PUDDING

◆

Perfumed with orange blossom and rose waters, this smooth, cool, delicate pudding is sprinkled with cookie crumbs and crunchy ground nuts. It is an unusual, refreshing and memorable Middle Eastern dessert that can be made to jell in one big glass tray or in individual glass pudding bowls.

> 1 quart milk, divided
> ½ cup cornstarch
> 1 cup sugar
> one packet of plain gelatin powder (optional)
> 1 teaspoon each orange blossom water (*may zahar*)
>   and rose water (*may warid*)
> 2 cups butter cookie crumbs, for topping
> 2 cups ground pistachio nuts or walnuts, for topping

1. Blend 2 tablespoons of milk with cornstarch in a small bowl.

2. Put cornstarch mixture into a sauce pan with the remaining milk and the sugar. Heat over low heat, stirring until the mixture thickens, about 20 minutes. If it doesn't thicken, dissolve a packet of plain gelatin powder into the milk.

3. Remove from heat and stir in fragrant waters of *may zahar* and *may warid*. Pour into a glass tray or into individual pudding dishes. Sprinkle a thin layer of cookie crumbs over the top followed by a sprinkling of ground pistachio nuts or walnuts on the top. Refrigerate to set pudding. Serve chilled.

Makes 12 half-cup servings.

MURABBA

◆

PRESERVES

Mama and *Sitto* seasonally made superb jams and preserves—a regular feature on our table along with bread, cheese, and olives. They used the fruits from the abundant trees in our garden: fig, apricot, lemon, and orange; quince came from our friends in the San Fernando Valley, the McKannas, who had a big orchard with almonds and many fruits. The making of jams, fruit preserves, and molasses are traditional methods to preserve fruit, as is drying. In Douma, many houses had flat roof tops, which were warm and dry through the summer months; here, garden vegetables, grains, herbs, fruits, seeds and nuts were dried for winter use on woven drying trays or strung to hang and dry indoors.

Dried herbs such as spearmint, thyme, *zaatar*, and sumac (pictured above) were used often. Since Lebanon was on the Spice Road between the Far East and Europe, many East Asian spices came into Lebanese culinary use, such as cinnamon and peppers, that were not native to western Asia. Vegetables like okra, eggplant, pumpkin seeds, and tomatoes were dried. Tomatoes were also made into a paste, dried and stored in earthenware crocks. Vegetables and fruits were pickled to preserve them—from turnips and eggplants to watermelon rind sweetened with sugar.

Grains and legumes like corn, fava, and garbanzo beans, and lentils, too, were made to last through the winter. Some were cooked whole like wheat (*'amah*), which was also taken to the mill (*baidar*) and ground into bulgur or flour. The grain mill was near the olive mill (*maasra*), next to Uncle Ishaac l'Hage's home, where olives were

pressed into oil, a fabulous preservation alternative to salt curing, and so useful in that delectable form. The pits from the pressed olives are packed into blocks and are still used by villagers as winter home heating fuel. Ancient stone terraces hold soil and olive trees that cascade down the mountainsides and provide the oil and fruits so cherished by our people. In a town near Douma are olive trees with trunks that span six feet wide and said to be 2000 years old.

Fruits and nuts, brought in from the coast, the desert, or the south, such as fresh dates (*bahlah*)—quite divine, and tamarind (*tamr hind*), dried dates, pistachio nuts (*fistuq*), apricots (*mish moosh*), bananas, oranges, and other citrus rounded out what was not grown in the mountains. Figs (*teen*), apples, quince, walnuts, persimmons, pomegranates, and pears are abundant in Douma, as are grapes, which are eaten fresh and made into raisins or *dibis* (grape molasses) and eaten on bread, or are fermented to make aniseed liquor (*arak*). Other types of molasses enjoyed in Lebanon are carob (*dibis kharnoub*), date (*dibis tamr*), and pomegranate (*dibis rimman*) which are used to make beverages by adding water, and as with *dibis rimman,* used for tartness in salads.

Being in Lebanon in the early fall allowed me fabulous first-taste experiences—fresh dates, grape molasses, pomegranate juice, and fresh pistachio nuts brought in from the east, whose gorgeous magenta sleeve enveloping the fresh nuts are the inspiration for the red dye on some pistachio nut shells sold in the U.S.—Aha!

Recipes for preserves included in this section are our most loved jams, of which a teaspoonful spread onto a snippet of Arabic bread, makes for a fine yet modest dessert. The secret of these jams is in using fresh, tree-ripened fruit and in some recipes, using *miski*, found in Middle Eastern food shops. *Miski* is a mastic resin from pine trees that is ground with sugar in a mortar and pestle. We use it in making preserves of figs and quince, where it imparts its distinctive flavor as well as acting as a preservative. Enjoy!

ALICE'S KITCHEN
IF YOU MAKE IT WITH LOVE, IT WILL BE DELICIOUS!

Teen Ma'qoud

FIG JAM WITH ANISEED AND WALNUTS

◆

Along with the aromatic flavor of aniseed, the most important secret of our recipe is to use tree-ripened figs. They can be dried first and they can be figs of any color. Once I thought that any fig is a good fig, but I must say I have tasted fresh figs in this country that were not so good; there are so many varieties. A rule of thumb is: if the figs taste good fresh, they'll make a great jam; if they don't taste great, the jam won't either.

Our jam, which is not as overly sweetened as tradition might have it, is perfect on Arabic bread, pita chips, or sesame crackers for breakfast or dessert. It is also an excellent alternative for filling date cookies (*asabi bi ajwe*).

> 10–20 ripe figs (2–4 cups)
> ¼–½ cup sugar
>   use less if figs are really oozy sweet (*dablouni*)
> ½–1 tablespoon aniseeds
> 2 tablespoons lemon juice
> ½ cup chopped walnuts (optional)
> ¼ teaspoon *miski,* ground with 1 teaspoon sugar (optional)
> 2 tablespoons sesame seeds (optional)

    1. Cut off stems and chop figs into quarters, and place into a 2-quart sauce pan. Sprinkle sugar and aniseeds on top of figs without stirring. Cover and let stand overnight, forming a syrup in the bottom.

    2. Add lemon juice and stir. Begin to cook slowly over low heat for several hours, until figs make a thick paste, stirring from time to time.

    3. Remove from heat and set aside to cool overnight.

    4. Cook again on low heat for ½ to 1 hour more, stirring frequently to avoid burning or sticking. Add walnuts, sesame seeds, and *miski,* if available, and cook for 10 more minutes.

    5. Can in sterile jars or cool and place in clean jars and refrigerate or freeze. Refrigerated jam can be stored several months, if enough moisture has been removed from figs during the cooking process. Jam can be frozen for later use.

Makes approximately 2 pints of jam.

Sfarjel Ma'qoud

QUINCE JAM

◆

Quince are very high in natural pectin and our preserves are appealing, thick and beautifully colored reddish-brown. Quince, like the apple, is a member of the rose family. Similar to an apple in appearance, but larger, and yellow when ripe, quince is not a fruit you can just bite into like an apple—it is very tart and mouth-puckering because of its high pectin content, which makes it great in preserves.

> 6 quince, rinsed
> 3 cups sugar
> 3 cups water
> 3 tablespoons lemon juice
> ¼ teaspoon *miski*, ground with 1 teaspoon sugar (optional)

1. Peel and core quince, reserving peelings and core; chop quince into shoestrings or matchsticks about ⅛" thick and 2" long; place in a deep pot with sugar on top. Let stand overnight at room temperature. In the meantime, cook peelings and cores with water for an hour. Strain liquid and reserve, discarding the pulp.

2. Begin cooking quince the next day on medium flame until tender, for an hour or so.

3. Stir in juice from peelings and continue cooking until quince is done. The color is translucent and deep, reddish brown; the liquid has turned to a thick sauce. Add lemon juice and *miski* and cook for 5 minutes. Place in sterilized jars and seal or refrigerate in clean jars for short term use.

Makes 2–3 pints of jam (depending upon size of quince).

ALICE'S KITCHEN
IF YOU MAKE IT WITH LOVE, IT WILL BE DELICIOUS!

Mishmosh

Apricot Jam

◆

Our apricot jam is distinctive because it is not overly sweet and has the fresh tartness of lemon. In addition, *Sitto's* recipe includes the almond-flavored, crunchy apricot kernels or nuts, which are found hidden in the center of the pit. This laetrile-laden, purportedly cancer-preventative nut, adds a delicious, slightly bitter, crunchy texture to the jam, and is well worth the time it takes to hammer each apricot pit open to uncover the nut from its hard shell. I like doing this outside, after rinsing and drying the pits, like *Sitto* did, sitting on the back step, with a hammer and a careful hand. Our thick jam is incomparable on toast without any butter and makes a great glaze for apple tarts, cakes or other confections.

> 6 cups fresh ripe, pitted apricots, rinsed and halved
> with pits reserved
> 2 cups sugar
> ⅛ cup lemon juice

1. Place apricots in deep pot with sugar on top. Let stand overnight.
2. Meanwhile, carefully crack open the apricot pits with a hammer and remove the nuts hidden within, without crushing them, if possible. Place nuts in a small pot of water and boil for about 10 minutes, which removes the bitterness and allows the skins to slip off. Drain the nuts and slip the skins off. Discard skins and set nuts aside.
3. Stir the jam and cook it over a low heat for a couple of hours.
4. Add nuts to the jam and continue cooking it down until jam thickens. This can take several hours, over several days. Be sure to stir and avoid burning the bottom as it thickens.
5. Five minutes before removing jam from heat, stir in lemon juice which enhances the flavor and is a natural preservative. Can in sterile jars or refrigerate for immediate use. Freezing the jam is an easy alternative to canning.

Makes 3 pints of jam.

Jlunt ou Jazar or Halawe Jazariyeh

PUMPKIN AND CARROT PRESERVE

◆

J*lunt* is a village term for pumpkin, which many Lebanese know as *laqteen*. Here's an interesting preserve using pumpkin and carrots along with the sweet fragrance of rose geranium leaves (*'utir*) or their fragrant water.

> 2 cups grated pumpkin
> 1 cup grated carrots
> 1 cup sugar
> 2 tablespoons lemon juice
> 1 fresh rose geranium leaf (*'utir*)
>   or 1 teaspoon rose geranium water (*may 'utir*)

1. Place grated pumpkin and carrots in a bowl with sugar on top and let stand overnight.

2. Strain off sugar syrup that has formed and squeeze all liquid from pulp into a 1 quart sauce pan. Set pulp aside.

3. Add lemon juice to syrup and bring to a hard boil. Stir in pulp and rose geranium leaf and continue cooking over low heat, stirring frequently, until pulp cooks and liquid thickens.

4. If you use a rose geranium leaf, remove it; if not, stir in the rose geranium water for flavoring in the last few minutes of cooking. Cool and refrigerate or can in sterile jars.

Makes approximately 2 pints of jam.

'Amariddine

DRIED APRICOT LEATHER

◆

The most basic way of preserving food is by naturally and simply drying it, as in this recipe for making apricot leather.

1 or 2 pounds fresh apricots, rinsed and pitted

1. Put rinsed, unpeeled, pitted apricots into a blender and blend until totally puréed. Spread purée evenly with a spatula about ⅛ to ¼-inch thick on an oiled wooden board, a food dryer tray, or a cookie sheet lined with baking parchment or plastic food wrap.

2. Cover with screen or cheese cloth and leave in the sun to dry if you live in a warm climate or use a commercial food dehydrator or gas oven that has a lit pilot light. When the top side has dried, turn over to dry other side. Leather must be thoroughly dry to avoid spoiling. Once it is totally dry, store in waxed paper in a dry place or in a plastic bag or a tin. It can also be stored in the refrigerator and it will keep even longer.

Makes approximately 4 sheets of fruit leather.

Teen ou Jouz Munashaf

DRIED FIG AND NUT LEATHER

◆

My latest healthy concoction for preserving the overwhelmingly and wonderfully abundant summer fig harvest, after having eaten my fill, shared mountains of fresh figs with friends, and canned and frozen jars of fig jam is a take off on apricot fruit leather (*amariddine*). A very simple-to-make mixture of fresh figs, nuts, and seeds becomes a nutritious, chewy energy bar. All you need is a food processor or blender, and a food dryer unless you live in a desert-like climate.

> 4 cups fresh ripe figs
> 1 cup almonds, walnuts, cashews, or other nuts (optional)
> 1 cup sunflower seeds (optional)
> ½ cup sesame seeds (optional)

1. Put rinsed, stemmed figs into food processor and pulse until puréed. Add nuts and seeds and pulse lightly to chop the nuts and mix with figs. Spread purée evenly with a spatula about ⅛ to ¼ inches thick on an oiled wooden board, a food dryer tray, or a cookie sheet lined with baking parchment or plastic food wrap.

2. If you live in a very warm and dry climate, cover with a screen or cheese cloth and leave in the sun to dry. Otherwise, use a food dehydrator or gas oven that has a lit pilot light.

3. When the top side has dried, turn over to dry other side. Fruit leather must be thoroughly dry to avoid spoiling. Once it is totally dry, store in waxed paper in a dry place or in a plastic bag or a tin. It can also be stored in the refrigerator and it will keep even longer.

Makes approximately 2 trays of fig-nut leather.

ALICE'S KITCHEN

IF YOU MAKE IT WITH LOVE, IT WILL BE DELICIOUS!

Mashroubat

◆

Beverages

An invitation to a Lebanese home includes at the least an offering of a beverage—fruit juices: pineapple, orange, grape, fresh mulberry (*shrab il tout*), lemonade; sweet, fragrant rose syrup with water (*shrab il warid*); *jallab,* a sweet cold beverage made with dates and tamarind served with pine nuts; *kharnoub* (carob) or hibiscus water. Depending upon the season and time of day, Arabic coffee or tea along with a sweet, *hilou,* are typically presented. Of course, a drink of Lebanese mountain spring water is incomparable. Shown above drinking Tannourine spring water from a traditional Lebanese water pitcher (*ibree'*) is my cousin Tony Ganamey!

Shaay

Tea

Wonderful winter warming teas can be made by boiling spices in water for 10 minutes—a few cinnamon sticks (*irfe*); a tablespoon of fennel seeds (*shumrah*) plus cinnamon sticks; or aniseeds (*yensoon*). Summer cooling teas are made by steeping ¼ cup herbs in hot water for 5 minutes: fresh or dried spearmint leaves (*na'na'*); camomile flowers (*babounaj*), which is good for digestion; or jasmine and hibiscus teas. Healing plants, herbs and flowers have long been used in Lebanon.

Ahwe Turkiye

ARABIC OR TURKISH COFFEE

Arabic coffee is easily made with the right grind of coffee: Arabic coffee (espresso grind), a little *rakwi* pot, and demitasse coffee cups to serve it in. A few cardamom pods impart extra fragrance and flavor to our strong, thick coffee. Made sweet (*hilweh*), medium sweet (*mazboutah*), or bitter (*murrah*), our recipe is for the middle path of *mazboutah*! Superb! Our word, coffee, is from the Arabic *qahwe*.

1. To make coffee for 6, fill *rakwi* with 6 demitasse cups of water and 3 teaspoons of sugar. Place on medium heat and bring to a boil, stirring the sugar.

2. Remove from heat; stir in 6 heaping teaspoons of Arabic coffee and 3 cardamom pods. Return to heat; bring to a full boil, lifting the pot from heat, stirring so it doesn't spill over. Return to heat, boil, and stir 2 more times.

3. Spoon a little froth from the pot into each demitasse cup; then fill each

cup with Arabic coffee. Serve with Lebanese pastries or alone, but be sure to read coffee grounds in each cup to entertain your guests when the cups are empty! Just swirl the cup with thick grounds at the bottom, cover with the saucer, and carefully turn upside down, letting it sit 5 minutes—and imagine you're in Lebanon!

During a trip to Douma, our mountain village, I remember walking from the round Hotel Douma that sits nestled among pine trees (*snobar*) at one end of town, towards the heart of town. As I passed this way every morning, one family greeted me daily and soon warmly welcomed me into their home to join them for coffee, not knowing me other than our few exchanges of "good morning"—generously befriending me with our age-old tradition of hospitality with Arabic coffee.

◆

Ahwe Bayda

WHITE COFFEE

My dear friend Josephine introduced *ahwe bayda* to me one night, as an alternative to drinking a strong Arabic coffee after dinner. Its intriguing name simply describes a lovely little glass cup of hot water with a few drops of orange blossom water (*may zaher*) or rose water (*may warid*) drizzled in. It tasted delightful and removed the fullness of the feast she'd lovingly prepared for us at her dinner party.

Limounada

LEMONADE

We drank gallons of lemonade in the warm southern California summers, just as they do in Lebanon, where the climate is so similar. Each glass is made with ½ cup lemon juice and water, sweetened with sugar, chilled with ice, and most importantly scented with a fresh sprig of spearmint. My sister Vivian and I set up a stand in front of our house and sold our lemonade to passers-by, who loved its flavor, just as we loved collecting those nickels!

♦

Asir il Burdan

ORANGE JUICE

Fresh-squeezed orange juice is the Lebanese way to start the day: healthy, pure, and simple, when oranges are in season. We were lucky to have an orange tree in our Los Angeles garden, and breakfasted on seasonal fresh juice. My first trip to Lebanon in 1971, my cousins and hosts, the Ganameys, sent fresh-squeezed orange juice to my room! How welcomed I felt, and comforted in the continuity of our culinary traditions across the oceans.

♦

Asir il Rimman

POMEGRANATE JUICE

In Damascus, I tasted fresh-squeezed pomegranate juice made by a street vendor who had a mountain of pomegranates on his cart. Using an old orange juicer with a lever, he put half a pomegranate where the orange normally goes, and smoosh!— a fabulous glass of gorgeous, sweet red juice made from a pomegranate and a half. With many varieties of pomegranate, the one used for juice was different than the deep, ruby-red fruit we eat here. Tart, bottled "pomegranate concentrate juice" (*dibis rimman*), which is really a molasses that is not sweet for beverages, but rather is used to add flavor and tartness to salads and savory dishes—an important distinction.

Arak

LEBANESE ANISE LIQUOR

In Douma, *arak*-making is a popular and annual tradition with the grape harvest. Made from grapes that are fermented and flavored with aniseeds, this highly prized liquor is served in tiny glasses with the main meal or special occasions. Sometimes diluted with water, it is transformed from a clear, water-like liquid to a milky, opaque one. Lebanon's national drink is the "best *arak* in the Middle East" and is similar to the Greek *ouzo*.

◆

Nbeed ou Birat

LEBANESE WINES AND BEERS

Lebanese wine is legendary; it was treasured by the ancient Greeks and was mentioned in the Bible. The word alcohol comes from an Arabic root—*al kohul*, indicating that Arab alchemists in the 13th century worked with distillation. Modern wines from Lebanon were developed with the help of French monks in the 19th century for sacramental use as well as pure enjoyment. Urban dwellers are more likely to drink wine, while villagers traditionally enjoy *arak*.

Beer has been made in the Middle East since ancient times and bottled in Lebanon since the 1930s. Lebanese beer is recently being imported, so taste it here, or in Lebanon, should you be so lucky as to visit!

HERBS
SPICES &
FRAGRANT WATERS
◆

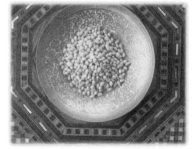

Along with the primary ingredient of Love, Lebanese herbs, spices, and fragrant waters are the essential secrets of Lebanese cuisine. Lebanon owes part of its rich and elegant culinary tradition to its location at the heart of the spice trade routes between the East and the West, and its perfect Mediterranean climate. Peppers, cumin, anise, cinnamon, allspice, oregano, cardamom, paprika, sumac, thyme, parsley, mint, *zaatar*, chamomile, cilantro, fennel, onion, garlic, sesame seeds, basil, bay leaves, purslane, scented geranium leaf, savory, cloves, caraway, rose water, and orange blossom water are essential elements in our cuisine.

Many of our most commonly used herbs are native to the eastern Mediterranean. *Yensoon* (aniseed) flavors our holiday cookies and a delicious tea, is the primary flavoring of the traditional Lebanese liquor (*arak*), and seasons a hearty winter breakfast (*'amah*).

Ancient mountain herbs, spices from the Silk Road, and fragrant waters extracted from the delights of Mediterranean plants, blossoms, and leaves give our cuisine complexity, earthiness, and an epicurean intricacy that were not known in northern climates. It is these qualities that distinguish our food and make Lebanese cuisine so loved all over the world. The migration of Lebanese transplanted their love of food to many continents, as they opened restaurants all over the world and introduced Lebanese food from Mexico to England, from Argentina and Brazil to Australia and Canada.

As immigrants to America, my family was typical of most Lebanese, Syrian, and Palestinian immigrants in having their own backyard mint and parsley patch, because the curly-leaved parsley found in America 50 years ago was used only for

garnish, and if you could find it in the stores, wilted it would be. The flat-leaved variety we grow, similar to Italian parsley, has much more flavor. Mother and *Sitto* would use the curly-leaved parsley along with spearmint (*na'na'*) for garnish. Mint, fresh or dried, refreshingly flavored our salads, spinach pies, mashed potatoes, lemonade, and our tasty Lebanese omelette (*'ijjeh*). Our backyard purslane (*baqle*), considered a weed by some Americans, is one of the natural wisdoms of our cuisine. We delighted in its crisp, succulent texture and lemony flavor in our salads. It is now finding favor for its health benefits as it is rich in omega-3 fatty acids.

The secret to our exquisite lamb dishes lies in the use of cinnamon, allspice, black pepper, cayenne pepper, and lemon juice, which enhance the meat's flavor. It is preferable to use organically grown spices and herbs that are as fresh as possible for the most potent flavor; for this reason, plus the joy of it, tending one's own herb patch brings much goodness. For spices, grind them just before using them to retain their vibrant aroma. Welcome to the world of Lebanese herbs, spices, and fragrant waters!

HERBS

◆

Whenever possible, use fresh and organically grown herbs. I remember spring, summer, fall, and even winter seasons, when my mother, Alice, and my grandmother, *Sitto* Dalal, pressed a pair of scissors into my small palm, gestured, and lightly nudged me out the back door toward our backyard mint and parsley patch in Los Angeles. *Jibbe na'na' wa ba'doonis! Rouje!* Bring mint and parsley! Hurry! they'd instruct. By the age of nine I knew how much they wanted me to pick for our big family *tabbouli* or *fattoush* dinner salads. And if it wasn't enough, surely I would be sent back out to pick some more. In the summer, *baqle* was added to the mix. Somehow it wasn't strange to me to go outside and pick "weeds", bring them in for Mother to rinse, and then eat them in our salads. The lemony tartness of the *baqle*, summer purslane, added an extra zing to my mother's already tasty and

ALICE'S KITCHEN
IF YOU MAKE IT WITH LOVE, IT WILL BE DELICIOUS!

224

colorful salads. Restaurant salads of the 1950s typically consisted of a wedge of head lettuce with pink thousand island dressing flowing lethargically down from the top. Our salads were from another world. Mint, parsley, celery, purslane, tomatoes, romaine lettuce, scallions, and cucumbers were drizzled with a dressing of garlic, lemon, and olive oil that perfectly accented the refreshing and varied flavors and textures of Mother's everyday salad. Following is a list of some of our more common herbs; for an extensive listing, please visit my website—www.lindasawaya.com.

•*babounaj*—camomile; used for tea, great for digestion

•*ba'dounis*—parsley; flat-leaved Italian parsley, rather than the curly variety more commonly used here; used in salads and as a garnish

•*baqle barriyeh, jewah*—purslane; wild or cultivated, used in salads: *fattoush, salata*, with olive oil, garlic and lemon; rich in healthy, beneficial omega-3 fatty acids

•*basal akhdar*—green onions; used in salads, stuffings, garnish, appetizers (*mezza*)

•*habaq*—basil

•*kizbra*—cilantro; used with okra

•*na'na'*—(Latin name: *Mentha viridis;* Latin name of Lebanese variety: *Mentha spicata longifolia*) mint, spearmint specifically; the Lebanese variety has narrow leaves (on left in photo), N. American varities have broader leaves (on right in photo); used fresh in salads, spinach pies, cabbage rolls or dried for use in yogurt and cucumber salad, cabbage rolls, etc. Fresh or dried leaves for tea; good for digestion. For Lebanese recipes, be sure to use spearmint rather than other mints like peppermint, which have very different flavors.

•*shoumra*—fresh fennel leaf; used in teas, also cooked with fava beans

•*'utir*—scented geranium leaf; used as flavoring in some desserts and preserves

•*waraq il ghar*—bay leaves; used in soups, broths

•*zaatar*—an herb and the name of an herbal mixture of thyme, savory, sumac, and sesame seeds mixed with olive oil eaten with or baked on bread

ZAATAR

One of the most cherished flavors of our cuisine is *zaatar*, the Arabic name of a mysterious herb native to the Middle East, with various names and varieties but difficult to translate precisely into

English. *Zaatar* refers to both Syrian oregano or Bible hyssop (*Origanum syriacum*), a member of the mint family, and other herbs, as well. Variously and uncertainly called thyme, oregano, marjoram, or savory in the U.S., *zaatar* is loved by Lebanese and Syrian immigrants because of its flavor and is cherished as an essential food that is not commonly available here.

Several varieties of *zaatar* grow in Lebanon, one being *Thymbra spicata*, according to *Rodale's Illustrated Encyclopedia of Herbs*. *Zaatar shahi'a* is a domesticated herb with the Latin name *Origanum vulgar*, while *zaatar barri* or *da'a* (Latin name: *Thymus serpyllum*), and Lebanese oregano, *Origanum libanoticum*, are other varieties grown in Lebanon (according to the *Encyclopedia of Medicinal Plants* by Michel Hayek, published by Librairie du Liban). Again, there is regional variation. In Lebanon, where these varieties are grown, fresh *zaatar* is the savory main ingredient of a salad and is added to early-season green olives.

Zaatar, in addition to being the name of the herb, has given its name to the savory blend of spices and dried herbs mixed in Lebanese villages in which it plays the dominant role as a topping for baked bread. *Zaatar* is gathered in the wild, dried, and then blended with other dried ingredients—sumac (the crushed fruits of Sicilian or elm-leaved sumac), sesame seeds, and salt—and stored for use all year. *Zaatar* mixtures vary from village to village and family to family, which contributes to the confusion in naming the herb or translating the name. Some *zaatar* blends are green and fresh, while others are darker and aged.

The blend is moistened with olive oil and pressed onto bread dough just before it is baked. This savory Lebanese favorite is served hot from the oven or at room temperature for breakfast, lunch, appetizers, or evening snack. It is the pizza or foccacia of Lebanon, made in individually-sized rounds at take-out bakeries. Townsfolk bring their own homemade *zaatar* blend to put on the bakery's dough to have custom baked, while others may buy the bakery's bread and its own blend of *zaatar* and *zeit* (olive oil).

I remember Mother baking Arabic bread for hours, and the aroma of *tilme bi zaatar*, bread with *zaatar*, and freshly baked bread from the basement way out back drew everyone around. The loaves disappeared almost as fast as she could bake them. We simply loved the *zaatar* baked onto bread dough, and it is a daily favorite and staple in Lebanon.

ALICE'S KITCHEN
IF YOU MAKE IT WITH LOVE, IT WILL BE DELICIOUS!

226

Mother says *zaatar* was called "the brain food" in Douma. An Arabic expression she grew up with, "Bread and thyme opens the mind," affirms that *tilme bi zaatar*, eaten for breakfast, is a healthy way to begin the day. In Lebanon, some families eat *tilme bi zaatar* or *manaqish,* as it's also called, filled with tomatoes, fresh spearmint leaves, green onions, or *labne* (yogurt cheese) and folded like a taco. When there's no time for baking, *zaatar* is mixed with olive oil and dipped with bread, accompanied by feta or homemade cheese and olives for breakfast. You must experience *zaatar* if you haven't and see how smart you become! *Zaatar* recipes are on pages 44 and 182.

SPICES

◆

Spices taste best when they are fresh and freshly ground. I remember the musical sound of Mother or *Sitto* pulverizing *mahlab* (pictured above) or allspice into a fragrant powder for use in one of their culinary creations. This is traditionally done in a sturdy and beautiful tool, a brass mortar and pestle (*hawin*). Porcelain or ceramic mortar and pestles can be used. Since wood absorbs flavors, our wooden mortar and pestle is reserved for garlic-mashing. An alternative to pounding is to use a coffee bean grinder. In many instances the spice is used whole, without grinding. See page 230 for sources and a more extensive listing on my website.

•*bhar*—allspice, whole or ground; used with lamb, chicken, string beans (*loubiyeh*)

•*craawee*—caraway seed, whole; used in baking bread (*kmaaj*)

•*fleyfle*—cayenne or black pepper; whole black peppers were ground; basic seasoning used in most savory dishes and salads; red cayenne available in mild, hot, and super hot; we use red cayenne in most of our dishes

•*hab il'hal*—cardamom pods; used in making Arabic coffee

•*irfe*—cinnamon, whole or ground in mortar and pestle, sifted; sticks are used in lamb, chicken, and vegetable dishes; enhances flavor of the meat; desserts; cinnamon sticks also boiled to make cinnamon tea (*shaay il irfe*)

•*krunful*—cloves, whole; used with stuffing, chicken, lamb shanks; lamb stock

•*mahlab*—Cornell cherry kernels; used whole or ground with sugar in various pastry doughs for flavoring: Holy bread (*qurban*), cookies such as *mamoul*

•*mileh*—salt; in Douma, it came in a cone and was ground; used as a preservative and for flavor; Lebanon on the Mediterranean Sea has natural salt flats for sea salt.

•*miski*—mastic resin from Lebanese pine trees; ground with sugar for preserves in figs, quince, Lebanese ice cream (*bouza*)

•*sahlab*—a powder extracted from an *orchis* plant root, salep; used in making ice cream (*bouza*); mixed with warm milk sprinkled with cinnamon as a beverage

•*shimrah*—dried fennel seeds; used for making tea, also seasoning in cooking

•*summaq*—sumac; crushed deep red berries from the sumac tree used as spice; tart in flavor from malic acid in the berries so it is used when lemon is unavailable as a substitute in salads such as *fattoush*, or grape leaves and cabbage rolls

•*yensoon*—aniseed; ground for pastry doughs; whole in wheat berry cereal (*'amah*); used in making anise liquor (*arak*) and tea (*shaay il yensoon*)

miski
summaq
sahlab

FRAGRANT WATERS
◆

Fragrant waters used in our cooking are one of the elements of alchemy or mystery that elevates our cuisine from the mundane to the sublime. Orange blossom and rose water keep for years in the bottle without spoiling, so a well-equipped Lebanese kitchen has a bottle of each of these on hand for when it is needed. They are not costly and yet they add a priceless element to the recipes they are used in. Of course, lemon juice is a more common fragrant liquid that is essential in our cuisine, providing an excellent source of Vitamin C, at the same time as the benefits of a preservative. Rose geranium leaf is common in Lebanon, and while its fragrant water was not a part of our California Lebanese kitchen, Mother grew some in a pot for those moments when it was called for; it is a beautiful plant.

- *'attar*—simple syrup flavored with rose water (*may warid*) or orange flower water (*may zahar*); used on pastries, such as the popular *baklawa*.

- *limoun*—lemon juice; even though it is simple, unaltered juice of the lemon, it is such an important ingredient in so many recipes, it begs to be listed here.

- *may warid* or *maward*—rose water; used to flavor pastries, tea, soft drinks, and lemonade; different from rose syrup, a sweet-rose flavored syrup used with water to make a beverage.

- *may zahar* or *mazahar*—orange and lemon flower water; used to flavor pastries and syrups for pastries, with nuts, in dough batter; stimulant, sprinkled in home on special occasions to eliminate odors; stored air tight in a bottle kept in the dark.

- *may 'utir*—rose geranium flower water or a rose geranium leaf; used in making desserts and fruit preserves.

FINDING INGREDIENTS & TOOLS

◆

Lebanese herbs, spices, fragrant waters, and the special ingredients called for in some of our recipes can be purchased in Middle Eastern food stores or online, where there are numerous sources for herbs and spices, as well as for special tools. Many of our recipes use herbs and spices that are common to American kitchens. For rennet tablets to make our homemade country-style cheese (*jibn baladi*) try a cheese-making supplier or your local supermarket; it is available online.

If you live in a major city, there is very likely a Middle Eastern food store in your area, which would carry the special Middle Eastern ingredients. If not, check online or check my website for resources, which will be updated from time to time, as things change. Listings include resources for special seeds, such as Lebanese squash (*kousa*), Middle Eastern cucumbers such as *miiti*, and other types. In addition, my website welcomes resource suggestions from my readers. *Ahlan wa sahlan!*

www.lindasawaya.com

See Glossary, Index, and About the Recipes for more ingredients and information.

GLOSSARY

◆

Abouna	Father; priest
akkidinne	loquat trees and the loquat fruit
burghul	bulgur; wheat that is parboiled, which allows for easier digestion, then cracked (cracked wheat is not boiled); sizes from fine to coarse depending on the dish; smaller sizes #0 #1 are used in salads, like *tabbouli,* and raw *kibbe* (*nayeh*) from Middle Eastern stores; coarser sizes #3 or #4) are used in cooked dishes, such as baked *kibbe,* and is generally what is available in health or natural food stores; store in refrigerator
citric acid	derived from citrus fruits, similar in appearance to salt, and used as a lemon substitute in our cooking; available from Middle Eastern stores, wine-making suppliers, health food stores, or online
Douma	town in northern Lebanon's Batroun region; our family village
fistuq	pistachio nuts
ghada	lunch; the main meal of the day
halaweh	sesame seed confection eaten with bread for dessert (halva)
hesroum	sour green grapes mashed and strained, the liquid used in *hommus* and *baba ghannouj* as a lemon substitute
khubz	Arabic flat or pita bread
Jiddo	grandfather
jibn	soft, unripened Neufchatel-type cheese; it also means "cheese"
jurn	stone mortar and pestle for mincing raw lamb *kibbe nayye*
jouz	walnuts
kishk	dried yogurt and bulgur ground into a coarse flour
kousa abyad	light-green Lebanese squash
laban	yogurt
labne	yogurt cheese; salted yogurt, drained in cheesecloth

limoun	lemon trees and lemons
mahrajan	a big outdoor Lebanese party with food, music, and dance
mezza	hors d'oeuvres; in our cuisine, a huge spread of appetizers
roube	yogurt culture/starter
samne	clarified butter
Sitto	grandmother
siyem(e)	Lent(en); vegetarian dishes created for Catholic Lenten meals
tahini	sesame seed butter; used extensively, providing good protein
tilme	Arabic flat bread that is thick, usually with an herb mix topping
teen	fig trees and figs
Um	mother
'unnab	jujube fruit; the size of an olive, the color of copper, the texture and flavor of an apple
warak 'inab	grape leaves
zibde	butter
zoum	sauce, usually tomato, from a stew

KITCHEN TOOLS

◆

'aalib	mold for making *mamoul* cookies
hawin	mortar and pestle, usually brass for grinding spices
ibree'	communal water pitcher used in Lebanon (pictured)
matahne	grinder for coffee, pepper, allspice, and other spices
manara	corer for *kousa* and eggplant
malqat	pincer for decorating cookies
qaalb	*falafel* ejecting tool
toule	cutting board
sikkine	knife
mabrad	sharpener
rakwi	Arabic coffee pot
shoubak	rolling pin

Arabic Expressions of hospitality & endearment

◆

Ahlan wa sahlan	Welcome to our home
A albit tnine!	Rhyming response to *sahtine!* meaning "to your hearts", (from my dear Aunt Adele)
Allah is sallmak	Peace to you, too (to a man) response to *Ma'issalemi* —*sallmik*—(to a woman); —*sallimkun*—(to a group)
Afwan	You're welcome
Al Hamdillah	Fine, thank you!
Bi khatirkun	By your leave or with your permission (upon leaving)
Bisma saleeb	Blessing in the name of the cross
Deimi	Forever (said upon finishing the meal to the host)
Dayetic	God bless your hands, too! (response to *sallem dayetic*)
Habibi or *habibti*	My love
Inshallah	God willing! (almost every other word in Lebanon)
Ma'issalemi	Go in peace (in response to *bi khatirkun*)
Mabrouk!	Congratulations!
Mahall 'amer	May your home be built up forever!
Ma'koul il hana!	Good eating!
Nishkourallah!	Thanks to God!
Ou intab khair	Response to *Tisbah akhair* (meaning to you, too!)
Ou aleikum sallam	And peace to you, too (in response to *Sallam aleikum*)
Sahteyn	Double health; bon appétite!
Sallem dayetkum	God bless your hands! (a compliment to the cooks)
Sallam aleikum	Peace to you!
Shimm il Hawa	Smell the air; sniff the wind! Get a breath of fresh air!
Shukran	Thank you
Sufra deimi	Good meals forever! (said at end of meal to the cook)
Tfaddalou	Welcome to the table; dinner is served
Tisbah akhair	May you morning into happiness! (Good night!)
Ya albi	My heart! (dear)
Ya 'ayne	My eyes!
Ya rouhi	My soul!
Yallah!	Hurry! or Let's go! (said enthusiastically!)
Yisslamou eydayki	God bless your hands! (a compliment to the cook)

Sample Menus

◆

In Lebanon, people commonly eat three meals a day with a very light breakfast, the main meal in the early afternoon, followed by a siesta and a very light dinner. Bread, cheese, olives, fresh vegetables, yogurt cheese (*labne*), and halva (*halawe*)are usually on the table, and could be a light breakfast or dinner.

◆ *Terwea*—Breakfast

Breakfast might be one or a combination of the following: fresh fruits, fruit juice, fresh-squeezed orange juice, eggs in a variety of styles such as hard-boiled with cumin or salt and pepper in bread, scrambled with *kibbe* or *labne*, or Lebanese om-elette (*'ijjeh*), yogurt cheese (*labne*), yogurt (*laban*), feta cheese or Arabic cheese (*jibn*), olives, honey, Arabic bread, *dibis* (grape molasses), fig and other jams, dates, halva (*halawe*) with bread, bread dipped in *zaatar* herb mixture with olive oil, Arabic bread with *zaatar* or *kishk* herb mixture baked on top (*tilme bi zaatar* or *tilme bi kishk*), *'amah* (winter wheat hot cereal), coffee, tea; special breakfasts of Lebanese nut or cheese-filled sweetened crepes (*'atayif bi jouz* or *jibn*).

◆ *Ghada*—Lunch

Lunch is the main meal of the day in Lebanon—usually several entreés and a salad served with bread, cheese, olives, and fresh vegetables. Seasonal cooking is typical of our cuisine—buying what is in season and fresh, for example: fresh bean dishes in spring and summer; dried beans in fall and winter. Chard and spinach in fall, winter, and spring; cucumbers, summer squash, tomato salads, and *tabbouli* and *fattoush* salad in summer. Here are a few combinations of what might be included in a well-balanced meal, scaled down from the huge spreads served in Lebanon. Lamb, chicken, fish, and vegetarian versions of these entreés are found in this book.

•lentils and rice with carmelized onions (*mjaddrah*), *hommus*, fried eggplant, Alice's salad (*salata*), *jibn baladi*, Arabic bread, olives, fruit

•lamb or chicken shish kebab (*lahm mishwi* or *shish taouk*), *hommus*, *tabbouli*, *fattoush*, or *salata*, Lebanese potato salad or mashed potatoes, Arabic bread, olives

•stuffed cabbage rolls or grape leaves (*malfouf mihshi* or *waraq 'inab*), *hommus*, fried eggplant, yogurt (*laban*), yogurt cheese (*labne*), olives, Arabic bread

•stuffed chicken with rice, *tabbouli* salad with romaine lettuce, *baba ghannouj*,

Alice's Kitchen
If you make it with Love, it will be Delicious!

hommus, fresh cut vegetables, olives, *jibn,* Arabic bread

•lentil soup, *fattoush* salad, fried eggplant or squash (*kousa*), *hommus,* Arabic bread

•stuffed summer squash (*kousa mihshi*), cut vegetables, *jibn,* Arabic bread, olives

•stuffed eggplant (*sheikh al mihshi*), meat or spinach pies (*sfeeha*), *tabbouli* salad, Arabic bread with *zaatar* (*tilme bi zaatar*), yogurt cheese (*labne*), olives

•chicken and rice with orzo (*djej ou sha'yriyeh*), yogurt, carrots, Arabic bread

•beans with lamb or vegetarian over rice (*riz ou fassoulia* or *loubiye*), fresh cut vegetables, *hommus,* Arabic bread, olives

•baked *kibbe* lamb and bulgur or pumpkin and bulgur (*kibbe bil sineyeh* or *kibbet jlunt*), yogurt cheese (*labne*), string beans with tomatoes (*loubiye bi zeit*), bread

◆ *MEZZA*—APPETIZERS (SEE *MEZZA* SECTION P. 25)

Lebanese appetizers are famous—a vast spread of tiny plates of amazing varieties of foods that can be a meal in itself or a few items served before dinner or as a snack. Cheeses such as feta and *jibn,* dips such as *hommus,* breads and savory pastries, fresh vegetables, vegetable patties, pickles, salted nuts like pistachios, almonds, cashews, peanuts, and seeds such as pumpkin and sunflower are commonly served.

◆ *ASHA*—DINNER

In Lebanon, a healthful custom is a very light dinner—usually a little bread, cheese, fresh cut vegetables or salads, and olives with some fruit; while in the United States, our largest meal is dinner. See *ghada,* above, for additional meal ideas.

•rice and squash (*riz ou kousa*), carrots, cucumbers, Arabic bread, cheese, olives

•stuffed grape leaves (*waraq 'inab*), yogurt and cucumber salad (*laban ou khyar*), Arabic bread, *jibn,* olives

•lentil soup (*shourbat adas*), *salata,* Arabic bread, *jibn,* olives

◆ DESSERTS

Fresh seasonal fruit is our traditional dessert served after meals. Grapes, figs, apples, pears, oranges, apricots, cherries, plums, peaches, persimmons, pomegranates, bananas, pineapples, watermelons, cantaloupes, honeydew melons, loquats, dates—basically whatever is available and in season. In winter: halva (*halawe*) with bread or dried fruits: dates, figs, apricots; nuts: walnuts, almonds, pistachio, cashews, and peanuts; jams: fig, apricot, or quince (*sfarjel*). Later in the evening, hot *'amah* for a winter treat or Lebanese fritters (*zlabye*). Rice pudding (*riz ib haleeb*) or Lebanese ice cream in summer. Cookies or pastries are served with coffee or tea to guests in the afternoon or evening, or during special holidays, not usually as dessert.

FOODS AND HOLIDAYS
◆

•*'amah*—sweetened, boiled wheat berries served with nuts and raisins; a less brothy version of *'amah* traditionally made when there was a death, served in little paper cups at the church memorial service; also served to celebrate births
•*Qurban*—Holy bread for Communion Host, offering for dead, Easter, Christmas
•Cookies—made at holiday times—*baklawa* at Christmas, *mamoul* at Easter
•Weddings—cookies: *mamoul, ghraybe, baklawa; sfeeha, kibbe bil sineyeh*
•New Year's Day—*'amah*, fritters (*zlabye*)
•Easter—hard-boiled eggs dyed with onion skin and cracked in a contest; *mamoul*
•St. Barbara, Halloween—*'amah* served with pine nuts, walnuts, pistachio nuts (*fistuq*), and raisins; Lebanese doughnuts (*'awamat*); lentil sprouts

A TYPICAL GARDEN IN OUR VILLAGE OF DOUMA
◆

◆ VEGETABLES (*KHUDRA*)
Romaine lettuce, bell pepper, tomato, green onion, okra, eggplant (*batinjan arabi*, which is similar to Japanese eggplants), cucumber, Armenian cucumber (*miiti*), summer squash (*kousa*), string beans, pumpkin, cabbage (*malfouf*), chard (*silq*).

◆ HERBS (*BHARAT*)
Lebanese parsley (*ba'dounis*)—a flat-leafed parsley; one plant was left to go to seed, to be collected and sown for a new patch. Spearmint (*na'na'*)—dies back in winter; perennial; propagated from root cuttings. Garlic (*toum*)—used raw, primarily; typically mashed into a paste for dressings and sauces; also used in cooked dishes.

◆ FLOWERS (*ZAHOUR*)
Cosmos, marigolds, tulips, daffodils, narcissus, roses, jasmine, gardenias, et cetera

◆ FRUITS AND NUTS (*FAWAKI OU JOUZ*)

Almond (*louz*), apricot, apple (*tuffaha*), quince, pear (*njoss*), plum, peach, orange (*burdan*), fig (*teen*), cherry (*caraz*), lemon (*limoun haamid*), sweet lemon (*limoun hilou*), olives, loquat (*akkidinne*), pomegranate (*rimman*), persimmon (*kaki*), walnut (*jouz*), filbert, grapes (*'inib*), jujube (*'unnab*, pictured at left)

ALICE'S KITCHEN

IF YOU MAKE IT WITH LOVE, IT WILL BE DELICIOUS!

INDEX

◆

A

About the recipes 21–24
'Ahwe bayda 220
'Ahwe turkiye 220
Alice's salad 65
Almond and farina pastry 198
Almond crescent moon cookies 197
'Amariddine 217
'Amah 207, 234, 236
Anise cookies 195
Anise liquor 222
Appetizers 25–32, 235
Apricot jam 215
Apricot leather 217
Arabic bread with olive oil 181
Arabic cheese, *jibn baladi* 34
Arabic coffee 220
Arabic expressions 23, 231–233
Arak 222
'Arishe, cheese 35, 189
'Arnabit miqli 176
Artichokes 41
Asabi bi ajwe 199
Asabi bil lahme mafroume 93
'Asha 235
Asir il burdon 221
Asir il rimman 221
Asparagus 41
'Atayif bi jouz 189
'Attar syrup 188, 203, 229
'Awamat 202

B

Baba ghannouj 161
Baklawa baklava 203
Balila 174
Bamye ou djej 124

Bamye ou lahm 100
Bamye ou riz 165
Baqle 63, 70, 223–225
Basic bread dough 177, 179
Bassel ou summaq 62
Batata madqou'a siyeme 168
Batata bil sineyeh 94
Batinjan (eggplant)
   baba ghannouj 161
   batinjan mihshi 104
   batinjan mihshi siyeme 145
   batinjan miqli 171
   batinjan mtabbal 162
   masbahit il darwish 150, 151
   sheikh il mihshi 102
Beans
   garbanzo (*see* garbanzo)
   lima or white, over rice 99, 152
   soup 54
   string (green) 101, 164, 170
Beef, substituting for lamb 23, 73, 75
Beer, Lebanese 222
Beet greens, spinach, chard, sautéed 169
Beet salad 71
Beverages 219–222
Bharat 223, 227, 236
Bouza 205
Bouillon, about 22, 75
Bread 177–186
   Arabic bread with olive oil 181
   basic bread dough 177, 179
   crackers 185
   Holy bread *qurban* 184
   Lebanese bread *zaatar, kishk* 182, 183
   pita chips 186
   pita or pocket 179, 186
   salad with crisped bread *fattoush* 61
Breakfast 234

ALICE'S KITCHEN

Bulgur, about 231
   and lentils 133
   and squash 136
   fish *kibbe* 127
   in salads 58–60
   lamb *kibbe* 83–86
   potato and walnut *kibbe* 155
   pumpkin *kibbe* 156
   with chicken 123
Burghul mfalfal 123
Burghul ou kousa 136
Butter, clarified 22, 39

C

Cabbage
   salad or coleslaw 69
   stuffed cabbage rolls 106, 146
Carrots 26, 166, 216
Cauliflower 166, 176
Chard 148, 169
Cheese, yogurt & butter 33–40
   'arishe 35
   feta 26, 141, 234
   jibn baladi 26, 34, 141
   yogurt cheese 36
Chicken 115–124
   about 23, 115
   barbequed chicken 119
   broiled chicken 120
   chicken and rice soup 51
   chicken vegetable soup 52
   cleansing 24
   grilled chicken kebabs 121
   stuffed with lamb and rice 116
   with bulgur 123
   with okra 124
   with orzo and rice 118
   with rice and garbanzo beans 122
Citric acid, lemon substitute 23, 24, 231
Clarified butter, *samne* 22, 33, 35, 39
Cleanliness, about 24
Coffee, Arabic/Turkish, white 220
Cookies
   almond crescent moons 197
   anise 195

   date fingers 199
   sesame 193
   shortbread 196
   walnut filled 191
Crackers, sesame 185
Crepes stuffed with cheese or nuts 189
Cucumber salads 66, 72

D

Date finger cookies 199
Dates 78, 187, 199, 212, 234
Desserts 187–210, 235
Dibis 212, 219
Djej 115–124
   burghul mfalfal 123
   ma bamye 124
   mhammar 120
   mihshi 116
   mishwi 119
   ou riz ma sha'yriyeh 118
   riz bi tfeen 122
   shish taouk 121
Doughnuts, Lebanese 202
Dried fruits 211, 217, 218

E

Eggplant
   and lamb stew 98
   and potato stew 150, 151
   fried 171
   stuffed with lamb 102, 104
   stuffed with rice and vegetables 145
   with garlic *mtabbal* 162
   with tahini *baba ghannouj* 161
Eggs 85, 141, 167, 173, 236

F

Falafel 153
Fat, about 22
   trimming on lamb 73–77
Fatayir 87
Fatayir bi sbanikh 138
Fatte bi hommus 40
Fattoush salad 61

IF YOU MAKE IT WITH LOVE, IT WILL BE DELICIOUS!

Fava/garbanzo bean patties, *falafel* 153
Fava beans with garlic 163
Fig and nut leather 218
Fig jam 213, 234, 235
Filo dough cheesecake 208
Filo dough filled with lamb 93
Finding ingredients & tools 230
Fish 125–130
  baked or broiled, tahini sauce 126, 130
  fried fish with *taratour* sauce 128
  kibbe 127
  patties, fried 129
  with bulgur and pine nut filling 127
Flour, about 23
Foods and holidays 236
Fragrant waters 223, 229
  may warid rose 229
  may zahar orange blossom 229
  'utir, scented geranium leaf 229
Fritters
  squash 167, 173
  sweet 201
  vegetable 173
Ful mdammas 163

G

Garbanzo beans
  with garlic, lemon 174
  purée with tahini *hommus* 159
  in *falafel* 153
  in entrées 122, 123, 146, 150, 151
  with *fatte* 40
Garlic lemon dressing 43
Garlic mayonnaise 44, 119, 120, 121
Ghada 234
Ghamme ma fatte 112
Ghraybe 196
Glossary 231
Grape leaves, stuffed 110, 148
Grilled ground lamb 80

H

Halawe halva 234, 235
Halawe jazariyeh 216

Haleeb 33–40
  'arishe 35
  jibn baladi 34
  laban 37
  labne 36
  samne 39
Harist il louz 198
Herbs 223–226, 236
Hilou 187–210
Hommus bi tahini 159
Hommus mtabbal or *mtoume* 174

I

Ice cream, Lebanese 205
'Ijjeh 141
Ijjet khudra 173

J

Jallab 219
Jibn baladi 26, 34, 141, 234, 235
Jlunt ou jazar halawe 216
Jouz 155, 189
Jujube 19, 236

K

Kaak 185, 193, 195
Kafta bil sineyeh ou bazella 81
Kafta mishwiye 80
Kharnoub 219
Khudra 157–176
Khudra mahkluta 166
Khubz mhammas 186
Khubz marqouq 177–178, 179
Kibbe, about 83, 156
  kibbe bil sineyeh 85
  kibbe nayye 83
  kibbet batata ou jouz 155
  kibbet jlunt 156
  kibbe 'raas 114
  kibbet samak 127
Kishk on *tilme* 178, 179, 183
Kishk soup 56
Kitchen tools 232
Kmaaj 179

Knafe bi jibn 208
Kousa
   burghul ou kousa 136
   kousa mihshi 108, 143
   kousa mishwi 172
   kousa miqli 171
   kousa ou riz 135
   kousa 'raas 167
   mfarket kousa 137
Khyar, salatat 66, 72

L

Laban 36, 37, 40, 42, 43, 96, 118
Laban ou khyar, salad 66
Laban ou toum, yogurt garlic sauce 43
Labne, yogurt cheese
   36, 85, 87, 111, 234
Lahm bi ajeen 90
Lahm mishwi 79
Lamb about 23, 73–114, cutting 73–77
   baked potato and lamb pie 94
   baked with bulgur, pine nuts 85, 114
   eggplant stew 98
   grilled ground 80
   ground with bulgur 83, 85
   meatloaf with peas 81
   meat pies 87, 90
   ravioli in yogurt sauce 96
   raw with bulgur 83
   rolled in cabbage 106
   rolled in filo dough 93
   rolled in grape leaves 110
   sautéed with pine nuts 78
   savory pastry 91
   shanks with bulgur 82
   shish kebab 79
   stuffing 78
   stuffed in eggplant 102, 104
   stuffed in squash 108
   tomato and rice soup 53
   tripe stuffed 112
   with lima beans and tomato 99
   with okra 100
   with string beans and tomato 101
Lemon juice 23, 229

citric acid and other substitutes 23
   dressing and marinade 43, 80
   lemonade 221
Lenten dishes (*see* vegetarian), 131–176
Lentils
   and bulgur 133
   and rice 132, 134
   noodle soup 48
   soup 46
   soup with potato *kibbe* 55
   soup with lemon and chard 47
Lifit 31
Lima beans with tomato 99, 152
Limounada 221
Loubiye 164, 170, 236

M

Mafroume 78
Mahlab 227, 228
Makhlouta 54
Makabis 32
Malfouf mihshi 106, 146
Malfouf, salatat 69
Mamoul 191
Manaqish 182
Masbahit il darwish 150, 151
Mashroubat 219–222
May warid 223, 229
May zahar 223, 229
Mdardarah 134
Measurements 21
Meatloaf 81
Meat pies stuffed, lamb 87–90
Mezza 25–32, 235
Mfarket kousa 137
Mfarkey 98
Mhallabiye 210
Mhammara 175
Mhamsa 78
Mihshi
   batinjan mihshi 104, 145
   djej mihshi 116
   kousa mihshi 108, 143
   malfouf mihshi 106
   malfouf mihshi siyeme 146

Mint (spearmint) 223, 225
Mishmosh 215, 217, 236
Miski 205, 213, 214, 228
Mixed bean and grain soup 54
Mjaddrah 132
Mjaddrah ma burghul 133
Molasses 212, 219
Monk's rosary 150, 151
Mshabbak 202
Mtabbal batinjan 162
Murabba 211–218

N

Nammoura 198
Nbeed ou Birat 222
Nus Qamar 197
Nuts (*see also mezza*, pine nuts)
  155, 189, 191, 198, 218, 236

O

Okra 100, 124, 165
Olive oil, about 22
Olives, cured, about 27–30
Omelette with parsley, mint, onion 141
Onions with sumac 62
Orange blossom water 229
Orange juice 221
Organic, fish, meats, vegetables, fruits 23
Orzo with rice and chicken 118
Ourma 73

P

Parsley, mint and bulgur salad 58
Pepper, grilled red and walnut dip 175
Pickled vegetables 31, 32
Pine nuts 78, 85, 87, 91, 93, 94, 102
  114, 126, 127, 156, 166
Pita or pocket bread 153, 177, 179, 186
Pita chips 178, 186
Pomegranate juice or syrup 24, 61, 221
Potato
  and lamb pie 94
  eggplant stew 150, 151
  mashed with garlic and lemon 168

salad with parsley 67
walnut and bulgur *kibbe* 155
Preserves 211–218
  apricot jam 215
  carrot and pumpkin 216
  dried apricot leather 217
  fig jam 213
  fig and nut leather 218
  quince jam 214
Pumpkin *kibbe* 156
Pumpkin preserves 216
Purslane (*baqle*) salad 70

Q

Quince jam 214
Qurban 184

R

'*Raas samak* 129
Ravioli in yogurt sauce 96
Raw minced lamb and bulgur (*kibbe*) 83
Rawayeh 223–229
Red pepper and walnut dip 26, 175
Rice, about 23
  and squash stew 135
  lima beans with lamb over 99
  pudding 209
  steamed with butter 158
  string beans with lamb over 101
  upside down rice 122
  with chicken or lamb 116, 118, 122
  with okra 165
Ricotta-type cheese, '*arishe* 35, 189, 208
Riz
  bamye ou riz 165
  riz bi tfeen 122
  riz ib haleeb 209
  riz mfalfal 158
  riz ou fassoulia 99, 152
  riz ou kousa 135
  riz ou loubiye 101
Rose geranium leaf, water 225, 229
Rose water 229
Rose water pudding 210
Roube 37

S

Safsouf salad 60
Salads 57–72
  Alice's salad 65
  beet salad 71
  cabbage salad/coleslaw 69
  cucumber salad 72
  My father Elias' tomato salad 64
  purslane salad 70
  Lebanese potato salad 67
  real Lebanese salad 63
  spinach salad 68
  tabbouli 58
  winter tabbouli, safsouf 60
  with crisped bread, fattoush 61
  yogurt and cucumber salad 66
Salatat 57–72
Salsaat 41–44
Salt, about 22–24
Samak 125–130
  kibbet samak 127
  'raas samak 129
  samak bil furn ma taratour 126
  samak miqli ma taratour 128
  samak mishwi 130
Sambousik savory pastries 91
Samne 39
Sample menus 234
Sauces 41–44
  garlic, lemon, and oil 43
  garlic mayonnaise (aioli) 44
  tartar (taratour) tahini 42
  yogurt garlic 43
  yogurt tahini 42
  zaatar 44
Savory pastry
  meat pies 87–90
  savory pastries (sambousik) 91
  spinach pies 138
Sesame cookies 193
Sesame crackers 185
Sfarjel ma'qoud 214
Sfeeha or Fatayir 87–89
Shaay 219

Sha'riyeh ou riz ma djej 118
Sheikh al mihshi 102
Shish barak 96
Shish kebab 79
Shish taouk 121
Shmandar, Sbanikh, or Siliq miqli 169
Shortbread cookies 196
Shourbat 45–56
  shourbat adas 46, 47, 48
  shourbat bazella 49, 50
  shourbat djej ou riz 51
  shourbat khoudra ma djej 52
  shourbat kibbet heeli 55
  shourbat kishk 56
  shourbat lahm ou riz 53
  shourbat makhlouta 54
Siyeme, Lenten or vegetarian 131–176
Snobar 78, 85, 87, 91, 93, 94, 102,
  114, 126, 127, 156, 166
Soups 45–56
  chicken and rice soup 51
  chicken vegetable 52
  kishk soup 56
  lamb, tomato, rice soup 53
  lentil soups 46, 47, 48
  mixed bean and grain soup 54
  split pea soup 49, 50
  vegetarian lentil kibbe soup 55
Spices 223, 227
Spinach, sautéed or steamed 169
Spinach pies 138
Spinach salad 68
Split pea soups 49, 50
Squash, Lebanese or zucchini
  fried 171
  fritters 167, 173
  stew with rice and tomato 135
  stuffed, vegetarian 143
  stuffed with lamb and rice 108
Steamed rice with butter 158
Stews
  bean 99, 101, 150, 152, 164
  eggplant and lamb 98
  eggplant and potato 150, 151
  squash 135, 137

String beans with lemon and garlic 170
String beans with lamb 101
String beans with tomato 164
Stuffed vegetables
    104, 106, 108, 143, 145, 146
Sumac, about 24, 228
Sumac with onion 62
Sweets/*Hilou* 187–210
    'amah, wheat berry porridge 207
    asabi bi ajwe, date finger cookies 199
    'attar, simple syrup 188
    'atayif bi jouz, Lebanese crepes 189
    'awamat, Lebanese doughnuts 202
    baklawa, baklava 203
    bouza, ice cream 205
    kaak bi haleeb, anise cookies 195
    kaak bi simsum, sesame cookies 193
    ghraybe, shortbread cookies 196
    harist il louz almond pastry 198
    knafe bi jibn, filo cheesecake 208
    mamoul, walnut-filled cookies 191
    mhallabiye, rose water pudding 210
    nus qamar, crescent moon cookies 197
    riz ib haleeb, rice pudding 209
    zlabye, Lebanese fritters 201
Syrup, orange blossom or rose water 188

T

Tabbouli salad 58
Taratour ma laban, with yogurt 42
Taratour sauce 42
Tartar tahini sauce 42
Tea 219
Teen ma'qoud 213, 234, 235
Teen ou jouz 218
Terwea 234
Tilme bi kishk 183
Tilme bi zaatar 182
Tilme bi zeit 181
Tomato garlic salad, my father Elias' 64
Toum ou haamid 43
Toum ou zeit 44
Tripe, stuffed 112
Turnips, pickled 31

U

'Unnab 19, 236
Upside down rice with chicken 122
'Utir 229

V

Vegetable patties 173
Vegetable stew 150, 151
Vegetables, beans and grains 157–176
    eggplant with garlic 161, 162
    fava beans with garlic and lemon 163
    fried summer squash or eggplant 171
    garbanzo beans & tahini *(hommus)* 159
    garbanzo beans with garlic, lemon 174
    grilled or baked summer squash 172
    mashed potatoes with garlic 168
    okra with rice 165
    red pepper and walnut dip 175
    sautéed cauliflower 166, 176
    sautéed greens with garlic, lemon 169
    sautéed vegetables with sauce 166
    steamed rice with butter 158
    squash fritters 167, 173
    string beans with tomato 164
    string beans with garlic and lemon 170
    vegetable patties 173
Vegetables with garlic, lemon sauce 170
Vegetarian entrées 131–156
    bulgur and summer squash 136
    cabbage rolls 146
    eggplant potato stew 150, 151
    eggplant, stuffed 145
    fava bean patties *(falafel)* 153
    grape leaves or chard, stuffed 148
    lentils and bulgar 133
    lentils and rice, carmelized onions 132
    lima beans with tomato and rice 152
    monk's rosary 151
    omelette with parsley, mint, onion 141
    potato, walnut, and bulgur *kibbe* 155
    pumpkin and bulgur *kibbe* 156
    rice and lentils 134
    rice and summer squash 135
    spinach pies 138

summer squash stew 137
summer squash, stuffed with rice 143
Vegetarian lentil *kibbe* soup 55

W

Walnut filled cookies 191
Walnut-potato *kibbe* 155
Waraq arish or *'inab* 110
Waraq 'inab, siyeme 148
Wheat berry porridge 207
White beans, tomato over rice 152
Winter bulgur (*tabbouli*) salad 60

Y

Yabra' 110
Yogurt and yogurt cheese 36, 37
Yogurt and cucumber salad 66

Yogurt garlic sauce 43
Yogurt, sauce in Lebanese ravioli 96
Yogurt tahini sauce 42

Z

Zaatar about 41, 225
    Zaatar on *tilme* 178, 182
    Zaatar sauce 44
Zeitoun, olives 27–30
    Black 30
    Green 28, 29
Zlabye 201

Our tradition is about living gently on the earth. Using resources of the earth respectfully. Sharing and preparing food with love. Eating what is in season. Growing our own food as much as possible. Living simply and richly. Honoring the earth. Honoring ourselves and each other. This is my gesture to honor and preserve that culture for myself, for my family, and for others who appreciate these traditions, values, and foods. My love for our food and culture continues to grow.

A portion of the proceeds of the sales of **Alice's Kitchen** will benefit the children of Lebanon. Thank you for joining us in **Alice's Kitchen**.

About the Author

♦

Linda **Dalal Sawaya** lives in Portland, Oregon, and is an artist and writer. As the youngest of five daughters of Lebanese immigrants, Alice and Elias, she was born and raised in Los Angeles, growing up in Alice's kitchen—where cooking became a great passion, along with baking bread and gardening. As a young child, she shared a bed with her grandmother, namesake, and inspiration—Dalal, who also graced and blessed Alice's kitchen with her skill and loving presence.

Sawaya studied photography, ceramics, and design at UCLA where she received a Bachelor of Arts degree. Having cooked both vegetarian and Lebanese cuisines in professional settings, she now prefers preparing meals and baking for family and friends in her own cozy kitchen. Writing and editing became a part of her life in 1977 when she moved to Oregon and worked in publication and graphic design.

In 1986 she started painting and fell in love with it. Integrating media—photography, painting, and ceramics—in her work, Sawaya has exhibited in galleries in Oregon, California, and New York. Her art has been published on the covers of numerous books that she has illustrated and designed including two children's books that she illustrated. *How to Get Famous in Brooklyn* was selected as one of the best children's books of the year for exhibition in New York by the New York Society of Illustrators and *The Little Ant/La Hormiga Chiquita*, a delightful bilingual Mexican folk tale, was one of Bank Street's Best Children's Books of the Year.

In 1996, Sawaya returned to Lebanon 25 years after her first visit there to research food, art, and family. A joyous and stimulating trip reunited her with family and provided an opportunity to gather photographs, recipes, and more inspiration for **Alice's Kitchen**. The love experienced was a blessing that carried forward in a "dream come true" trip in 1998—Linda had the joy of returning with Alice, visiting the home where she was born in 1910 and experiencing again the loving, expansive generosity of Lebanese family, culture, and tradition. This new edition of **Alice's Kitchen** has photographs and stories from that once-in-a-lifetime trip.

In the year 2000, Sawaya began study of Eastern Catholic iconography, an art form integral to her Lebanese spiritual tradition. Her art continues to develop, as she teaches adults and children Islamic tile painting, mandala painting, collage, and

other media. She also teaches Lebanese cooking classes and continues to work for peace and justice in the Middle East. These are the joyful and passionate essentials of her life. Linda's work can be viewed and purchased along with **Alice's Kitchen** at her website:

www.lindasawaya.com

About Alice

Alice **Ganamey Sawaya**, an epicurean Lebanese immigrant, is a mother of five, grandmother of seven, great-grandmother of nine, an artist celebrating her 95th year, and inspiration to all. Her story, and that of her mother, Dalal, are found in the introduction of **Alice's Kitchen**, which was written by her youngest daughter, Linda.

Praise for Alice's Kitchen

Al Jadid, A Review & Record of Arab Culture and Arts, Vol. 4 No. 25 (Fall 1998) review of **Alice's Kitchen,** 3rd ed. reprinted by permission (www.aljadid.com)

Art of the Cookbook *by Judith Gabriel*
This earthy, almost fragrant book is "self-published" in the same way that homemade bread is a "self-rising" mound of leavened flour. When you smell it baking, you can only be grateful someone did the kneading. (And the writing.) And then hope they give you a slice while it's still hot. Especially if it's *khoobz marouq* . . .

Linda Dalal Sawaya . . . is also a writer, and the pages of this very special cookbook contain not only recipes, but evocative descriptions of how her grandmother, Dalal, prepared the traditional dishes back in her Lebanese mountain village, and how her mother, Alice, followed the time-tested formulas in her American kitchen, making adjustments that Sawaya passes on . . . a highly useful reference . . . A truly literary picture emerges of such commonplace dishes as Lebanese pickles and *kibbeh*, which one would expect to find in such a setting. What makes the entries stand out is the context of descriptive nostalgia and culinary refinement that frames them.

"An exquisite, thorough cookbook . . . As a 22-year-old Lebanese American, I know that our food is not simply something thrown down your throat. It is love, it is nourishment to our souls as well as to our hearts. It is shared at every event, every home...sometimes when you are not even hungry! Sawaya starts the book with her family's history, which truly brought tears to my eyes. She explains all the ingredients, even their history. The book includes everything Lebanese I have ever eaten, and some I haven't. She covers all breads, preserves, herbs, sauces, hors d'oeuvres, salads, lamb, chicken, fish, sweets, beverages, grains, vegetables . . . It is many pages of hard work and lots of love. Family pictures of Sawaya's abound, and her hand-done illustrations grace the cover. I am moving away from home soon and will take this book with me, to share with all who come into my home, the pleasure and joy of Lebanese cooking. Thank you, Linda Sawaya, for this book."

Sally Farhat, Seattle, Washington

"I have never wept over a cookbook before, but I found myself tearing up reading **Alice's Kitchen**. I was holding love and family in my hands . . . *'Shukrun ktir'* for a lovely, lovely book."

Barbara Bedway, Hudson, New York

"Your stories about Douma and Lebanon are so interesting to me and I never tire of hearing them."

Philip Simon, Los Angeles

"Your artwork and recipes are superb efforts as well as the memories of your family life and the gems of cooking . . . I have tried two of the recipes already and they turned out delicious."

Frank Sumarah, Halifax, Canada

"**Alice's Kitchen** is a real treasure! . . . I absolutely love it and will cherish it forever. Linda, thank you for doing this for all of us out here—your mother and your grandmother: the best cooks ever!!"

Barbara Connor, Ventura, California

"The cookbook is an absolute gem—I love the new edition. You're wonderful to endow us with such lush history and tradition."

Joan Shipley, Portland, Oregon

"It's a rainy day here and your almond crescent moons are in the oven baking. Your family reaffirmed what we've always known, but forget. Time for family, food prepared with love, these things are our treasures."

Donna Stewman, Ben Lomond, California

Food is central to Arab culture in general and Lebanese culture in particular. It is also central to one of the most important factors in that culture which is **Hospitality**.

Food is served to family and guests in copious amounts and the variety of dishes on a well laid table is designed to delight the eye as well as to impress the appetite and the guest. Such a table is a proud work of art.

Artist Linda Sawaya's timely book, **Alice's Kitchen**, serves up such a work of art. In so doing, she passes on a cherished tradition to Arabic speaking immigrants' children and their well-assimilated descendants several generations deep. She beckons them to follow her lead and keep the wonderful tradition alive. She gives them, as well, mouthwatering recipes from which to create their own proud works of art.

Thank you, Linda

Alixa Naff, Ph.D, Middle East Social and Political History
Creator of the Naff Arab American Collection
National Museum of American History
Smithsonian Institution